Prologue

Decades and decades back in answer to somesueh incident Queen Victoria was reputed to have said, "We are not amused."

The "Royal we."

... *books that haunt us* ... can be said to be a variation of the *Royal We.*

... *books that haunt us.*

These are books that have haunted *me*—since I have been able to read. I read *McElligot's Pool,* by Dr. Seuss, when I was five. Dr. Seuss spoke to me then—

It was just like Dr. Seuss said!

... and you can read the Dr. Seuss essay in these pages to see what he spoke to a five-year-old Ohio boy about ...

And the rest, read over the years and decades since then and read again for this collection.

Books that I have never been able to get out of my memory—or perhaps never *wanted* to get out of my memory ...

Tortilla Flat, The Knights of the Round Table saga set in post-World War One California, among the paisanos ... published before John Steinbeck wrote *The Grapes of Wrath* ...

It Can't Happen Here, a warning by Sinclair Lewis that still resonates today. Maybe especially resonates today ...

Address Unknown, largely forgotten now ... a late 1930s warning about Hitler and Nazi Germany.

The Woman Who Could Not Die ... almost impossible to find now, but when it was first published it became part of the most world-famous dystopian novel of the twentieth century ... *1984.*

Darkness at Noon, perhaps the most horrific novel of the twentieth century ...

Hiroshima, the minutes and hours and days after the first atomic explosion, over Hiroshima, Japan, now a classic in nonfiction ...

If This Is a Man and *Night*, two timeless books about the Holocaust and the survivors ...

Black Like Me—includes, in this essay, the remarkable backstory of his ten years before John Howard Griffin became black in the pre-Civil Rights years of the late 1950s. The ten-year backstory was never mentioned in *Black Like Me*.

Eichmann in Jerusalem, Hannah Arendt's essay-study of the trial of Eichmann—flawed certainly, in style, her work ethic, her conclusions about Eichmann and her sources ...

Slaughterhouse-Five, Kurt Vonnegut's classic anti-war novel, but remarkably different from *If This Is a Man* and *Night* ...

A Desert Daughter's Odyssey ... in 1975, Primo Levi published *The Periodic Table*, a collection of 21 short stories, each a vignette from his life; each has a name of one of the chemical elements: Argon; Hydrogen; Zinc; Iron; Potassium; Nickel; Lead; Mercury and others—and each story is connected to the element in some way.

In 2000, Sharon Wanslee's memoir, *A Desert Daughter's Odyssey* was published, after her death—and each of her 37 chapters, each a brief episode of her life, leads to a Survival Rule—how to conquer cancer. She was brilliant and courageous—and her own Survival Rules gave her 20-plus years her cancer doctors never thought possible, after cancer struck her in the early 1970s.

Years apart and a half world away, Mr. Levi and Ms. Wanslee would probably have enjoyed meeting and enjoyed discussing each other's work, strikingly similar in design.

The Plot Against America—just as much a warning as *It Can't Happen Here* ...

I Heard You Paint Houses—a true crime memoir/expose of the man who reputedly killed Jimmy Hoffa and was responsible, over the year for 25 "mob hits." Since publication in book form, it has been made into a major film, under the title *The Irishman*.

Frank Sheeran, who was Irish, died peacefully years past major mob figures; he was one of the few non-Italians in organized crime during the years of Jimmy Hoffa and the mobs …

A Book of Great Worth—charming fictionalized nostalgia by Dave Margoshes of his father's life—and his family—in. New York in the 1930s. Read the beginning paragraphs of A *Desert Daughter's Odyssey* and *A Book Of Great Worth* to "hear" how exceptional writers "talk" to their readers on the page.

The Tattooist of Auschwitz, a true love story of two Holocaust death camp inmates who fell in love in Auschwitz and survived the war and got married after the war. A world-wide best seller, but flawed by major, major errors about Auschwitz, *even including spelling the male protagonist's name wrong throughout the book.* The love story was true—all other errors of fact about Auschwitz make the book historically worthless.

All these, with the possible exception of *The Woman Who Could Not Die*, are available on Amazon and elsewhere.

The Epilogue lists other titles and other authors—you may well find the books that have haunted you, in the past.

Tortilla Flat
John Steinbeck / 1935

The Knights of the Round Table in California

genre: novel

If we can match a novelist with a locale, John Steinbeck will forever be linked with Monterey, California and Monterey Bay, the site of three of his most famous novels: *Tortilla Flat*, *Cannery Row* and its sequel *Sweet Thursday*; and his subsequent portrait of his friend Ed Ricketts, in *The Log from the Sea of Cortez*.

Although Steinbeck was born in Salinas, his family owned a home in Pacific Grove, in the Monterey area, and Steinbeck was often there, captivated by the mix of humanity in Cannery Row, fascinated by the sea and captured by marine biology.

Steinbeck attended Stanford University intermittently from 1919 through 1925, and although he never did receive a degree, he benefitted from courses in English and marine biology. He worked at various times as winter caretaker for an estate in the Lake Tahoe area, as a lab technician in a Spreckle sugar plant, and as a laborer building the original Madison Square Garden in Newb York and as a dally newspaper reporter in New York.

The story of his first three books are now part of the Steinbeck legend: *Cup of Gold* (1929); *The Pastures of Heaven* (1932) and *To a God Unknown* (1933) were published by three different publishers. Each went bankrupt during the Great Depression. *Cup of Gold* sold only 1,533 copies, because few critics bothered to review it when it was first published, two months after the beginning of the Depression. *The Pastures of Heaven* earned Steinbeck an advance of $400. Neither *Cup of Gold* nor *To a God Unknown* earned Steinbeck more than the publisher's advance of $250 each.

Before the publication of *The Pastures of Heaven*, Steinbeck met and married his first wife, Carol Henning. Between 1930 and 1933, they lived in Pacific Grove, moved to the Los Angeles area, then moved back again to the Monterey area, site of *The Long Valley*; *Tortilla Flat*, *Cannery Row* and *Sweet Thursday*. The Watsonville area was the location of an apple strike, which Steinbeck fictionalized in *In Dubious Battle*, and the Salinas area was the locale of *East of Eden*.

For many of Steinbeck's major works, he figuratively never left the California coast and the images of people and places in Del Monte, Pacific Grove, Pebble Beach, Monterey, Carmel, the Corral de Terra (which became the fictional *The Pastures of Heaven*) and Salinas.

With the film scripts for *The Forgotten Village* and *Viva Zapata!* And in *The Pearl, Sea of Cortez* and *The Log from the Sea of Cortez*, he ventured across the border into Mexico, but still stayed close to the land of his childhood.

While Steinbeck's first three books were languishing on bookstore shelves in mid-Depression America, he was already at work on his fourth book *Tortilla Flat*. As he was working on that manuscript, a chance meeting in Chicago between two friends helped change Steinbeck's career forever. The meeting was between Ben Abramson, a bookstore owner, and Pascal Covici, who had previously owned his own bookstore in Chicago and had begun his own publishing company.

Abramson urged Covici to read *The Pastures of Heaven*; Covici did so and decided that Steinbeck was worth publishing. He contacted Steinbeck's literary agent at the firm of McIntosh and Otis. Covici published *Tortilla Flat* in 1935, a year and one half after Steinbeck had sen it to McIntosh and Otis.

And who, during the years of the Great Depression, couldn't be enchanted by reading *Tortilla Flat*? For many during the Great Depression, reading and the movies were escape, pure and simple.

Escape from grinding poverty, escape from worrying about how to pay the rent, escape from worrying about how to find a job (or keep a menial one), even escape from worrying about where money for the next week's groceries would come from.

For many who read *Tortilla Flat* during the Depression, the novel was pure escapism and entertainment. Steinbeck wrote of Danny and his band of brothers, the *paisanos* who lived above Monterey:

> *What is a paisano? He is a mixture of Spanish, Indian, Mexican and assorted Caucasian bloods. His ancestors have lived in California for hundred or two years. He speaks English with a paisano accent and Spanish with a paisano accent. When questioned concerning his race, he indignantly claims pure Spanish blood and rolls up his sleeve to show the soft inside of his arm is nearly white. His color, like that of a well-browned meerschaum pipe, he ascribes to sunburn. He is a paisano, and he lives in that uphill district above the town of Monterey called Tortilla Flats, although it isn't a flat at all.*

Indeed, Tortilla Fast wasn't flat, but for many it was intensely real and altogether charming. In the second chapter of the book, when Danny comes back from World War One, he discovers that he has inherited two houses. Even before he inspects his property, he buys a gallon of cheap wine, gets outrageously drunk in Monterey and spends thirty days in the Monterey jail. During the Depression, for some, a thirty-day stay in a county jail meant that you had "three squares" (meals) a day and a warm place to sleep.

Many readers discovered that Danny and the rest of the *paisanos* live by their own rules: they have little to do with the respectable "downtown" Monterey culture. Their chief purpose seems to be simply earn enough to buy wine. Property, as Danny discovers, is an inconvenience, as property means responsibility.

When rent money was a real problem during the Depression, readers were amused that Danny rents his second home to his friends, who sublet it and none of the parties involved ever expects that the rent can, or will, be paid.

Property—such as watches—is only valuable to the extent that it can be traded for wine; for the paisanos, Steinbeck wrote, the best timepiece is "the great golden watch of the sun."

For some of Steinbeck's readers, Monterey's Tortilla Flat was idyllic; money is seldom needed when items can be traded for wine. All the paisanos really want is enough food, a warm place to sleep, wine and—occasionally—women and parties.

Were the paisanos real? Like many other novelists, Steinbeck built upon stories he knew or had heard from others and composites he invented. He heard many of the stories from Monterey native Susan Gregory. (He eventually dedicated the book to her.) He heard others from the Monterey police and from coworkers in the Speckles sugar factory and elsewhere.

In *A History of Steinbeck's Cannery Row*, Tom Mangelsdorf writes:

> *Gregory's real love, however, centered on a group of fascinating people known as the paisanos, who inhabited shanties and shacks on a forested hillside overlooking Monterey. These olive-skinned men and women were the descendants of the original Spanish settlers who had come to Monterey in 1770. Through the years of haphazard intermarriage between the Spanish, Indians, Mexicans and various other groups, the paisanos had evolved. As a group, they went without formal education and were either unemployable or given the most menial labor to perform. A good paisano, however, cared little for work. Their cultural values remained almost unfathomable to nearly everyone except another paisano and a few outsiders such as Gregory who had taken the time to understand. It was Gregory who introduced Steinbeck to the vagaries of*

the paisanos and the section of Monterey where they lived, which was commonly called Tortilla Plat.

The basis for the character Pilar in Steinbeck's novel was a paisano named Eddie Romero, according to Mangelsdorf. Romero was born south of Monterey and was never sure of his own age. In the summer of 1891, Romero and another ranch hand engaged in a brief horse race. Romero lost and attempted to settle the matter of his injured manhood by drawing a pistol and wounding his opponent in his shoulder. The rider had his wound treated, but the doctor accused Romero of assault with a deadly weapon.

At his trial Romero could not fully explain that the shot was a matter of paisano interpretation of justice; he was sentenced to two years in San Quentin. According to Mangelsdorf, after Romero was released, he returned to Monterey. Through the years he was arrested again and again, usually for drunkenness but in 1932, he met a construction worker, and the two began drinking—then arguing—a pistol appeared and Romero's opponent was shot. Romero later claimed that's opponent, named Olaf Olson, had made rude comments about Romero's heritage, a terrible affront to a paisano.

He was tried and the jury was hung on a manslaughter charge. A second jury voted guilty. Because of the prior sentence, Romero served a sentence of two to ten years in Folsom prison. He entered Folsom just as Steinbeck was working on *Tortilla Flat*.

Longtime Monterey resident Bruce Arlis has also speculated on the origins of *Tortilla Flat*. In his book *Inside Cannery Row: Sketches from the Steinbeck Era*, he writes:

> *The actual place name of Tortilla Flat was derived from another part of the (Monterey) Peninsula entirely. It came from the Carmel side of the hill, and dated back to the early days of the 1906 earthquake.*
>
> *At the time a number of well-known bohemian artists and writers from San Francisco took up residence in*

Carmel, some one hundred miles to the south, and they hoped, outside of the zone of another earthquake like the one that destroyed the City (San Francisco).

Arlis also believes he knows the origin of Steinbeck's character "the Pirate":

> Shakey Tom, the old character after whom John had patterned the Pirate, lived in the last little shack at the top of our particular Huckleberry Hill (in Monterey), beside an old wooden water tank …
>
> "I soon discovered that Shakey Tom or Old Shakey, as the kids called him because of his palsy, wasn't the Pirate's real name either. It was an English name—Lloyd Lytton. He wasn't a paisano, but an eccentric Britisher, not quite right in the head, who kept a dozen mongrel dogs for his closest companions. He called himself "The Poet of the Pines" and wrote doggerel that was occasionally published in the little Pacific Grove weekly newspaper.
>
> Unlike Steinbeck's Pirate (large, black-bearded, slovenly), Shakey Tom was small, clean-shaven and neatly dressed. His white hair was carefully combed. He usually wore a white shirt and pale blue trousers, held up by black suspenders. Like the Pirate, he was followed wherever he walked by his pack of mongrel dogs. Steinbeck said there were six. I counted over ten, more than enough to pull up a dog or two, if he got cold at night, as John described it in one scene in his book.

Arliss writes that Steinbeck visited other paisano locations near Monterey and eventually they became part of Steinbeck's novel.

Tortilla Flat was an immediate hit for Steinbeck's publisher, Pascal Covici. It allowed the firm Covici-Priede some welcome financial breathing room. The book won the annual Gold Medal awarded by the Commonwealth Club of California for the best work by a native Californian. The film rights were sold and eventually resold before the film version was ever made. (MGM released the film version of *Tortilla Flat* in 1942. In the book *Steinbeck and Film*, Joseph Millicamp called the film "an unreasonable sepia-toned sham that could have only been made in Hollywood.") But Steinbeck discovered that readers didn't completely accept the palsanos with the generosity of spirit that he did. Readers didn't fully appreciate their convoluted logic and morality. They were judged by many to be bums—colorful perhaps, eccentric yes, but bums nonetheless. And that stung Steinbeck. In a foreword to a 1937 Modern Library (Random House) edition of the book, he wrote:

> *When this book was written, it did not occur to me that palsanos were curious or quaint, dispossessed or underdoggish. They are people whom I know and like, people who merge successfully with their habitat. In men this is called philosophy and it is a fine thing.*
>
> *Had I know that these stories and these people would be considered quaint, I think I never should have written about them.*
>
> *I remember a little boy, a school friend. We called him the piojo (a louse, a troublesome hanger-on—TF). And he was a nice, kind, brown little boy. He had no mother or father—only an elder sister whom we loved and respected. We called her, with a great deal of respect, a hoor-lady. She had the reddest cheeks in town and she made tomato sandwiches for us sometimes. Now in the little house where the piojo and his sister, the hoor-lady lived, the faucet at the sink was broken off. A wooden plug had been pounded into the pipe to keep it from leaking. The water for cooking and drinking was drawn from the toilet. There was a tin dipper on the floor to get it out. When the water supply was low, you simply flushed the toilet and there was new*

> *supply. No one was allowed to use this toilet as a toilet. Once when we sequestered a colony of pollywogs in the bowl, the hoor-lady gave us hell and then flushed them down the sewer.*
>
> *Perhaps this is shocking. It doesn't seem so to me. Perhaps it is quaint—God help it, I have been subjected to decency for a long time and stilll can't think of the hoor-lady as (that nastiest of words) a prostitute, nor of piojo's many uncles, those jolly men who sometimes gave us nickels, as her clients.*
>
> *All of this gets around to the point that this is not an introduction, but a conclusion. I wrote these stories because they were true stories and because I liked them. But literary slummers have taken these people up with the vulgarity of duchesses who are amused and sorry for a peasantry. These stories are out, and I cannot recall them. But I shall never again subject to the vulgar touch of the decent these good people of laughter and kindness, of honest lusts and direct eyes, of courtesy beyond politeness. If I have done them harm by telling a few of their stories, I am sorry. It will never happen again.*

His anger satiated, this foreword was never reprinted; the 1937 Random House edition is now rather rare.

Over the years, Steinbeck critics, scholars and educators have become increasingly uneasy (and even embarrassed) with Steinbeck's portrayal of the paisanos in *Tortilla Flat*.

In his essay, "Steinbeck's Mexican-Americans" (in the 1971 book *Steinbeck: The Man and His Work*, edited by Richard astro and Tetsumaro Hayashi) Charles R. Metzger largely defends Steinbeck's view of the paisanos, but offers the caveat, "It is necessary now ... to point out that Steinbeck's portrayal of paisanos in *Tortilla Flat* does not purport to do more than represent one kind of Mexican-American, the paisano errant, in one place, Monterey, and at one time, just after World War 1."

Two years later, in the essay "Fables of Identity: Stereotype and Caricature of Chicanos in Steinbeck's *Tortilla Flat*" (in *Journal of Ethic Studies*, volume 1, 1973). Philip D. Ortego writes that Philip Roth may view American Jewish life in a particular light as an "insider," while F. Scott Fitzgerald's portrait of Meyer Wolfsheim in *The Great Gatsby* comes across as stereotype and caricature. Likewise, William Styron, a white Southern novelist, could never portray Nat Turner as a black novelist could.

Ortega writes that in *Tortilla Flat*, "while Steinbeck struggles through an 'alien' milieu as the voice of the narrator, the question of ethnic identification became important and crucial in determining the reliability of the representation."

In his brief essay, Ortega charges that "few Mexican Americans of Monterey today see themselves in *Tortilla Flat* any more than their predecessors saw themselves in it thirty-four years ago." Steinbeck's language is also wrong, Ortego charges. Mexican Americans don't speak as Steinbeck's characters do, either in Spanish or in English.

Ultimately, he says, "to believe Steinbeck's descriptive diagnosis of the Chicano ethos in *Tortilla Flat* is to reinforce the most prevalent stereotypes and caricatures about Chicanos" and "the portrait of Mexican Americans ... is an injustice to the people whose ancestors—both Hispanic and Indian—have been on this continent for centuries."

Tortilla Flat "is a sad book in more ways that John Steinbeck may have ever imaged," Ortego writes.

In *Images of the Mexican American in Fiction and Film*, (1980) Arthur C. Pettit is just as frank (and damning): "Tortilla Flat stands as the clearest example in American literature of the Mexican as jolly savage. For better or worse, this is the book that is most often cited as the prototypical Anglo novel about the Mexican American. That it has spawned relatively few imitators enhances its isolated position while highlighting the fact that the novel contains characters varying little from the most negative Mexican stereotypes."

As examples, Pettit writes, "If the Mexicans of *Tortilla Flat* drink enough to kill most people ... they suffer neither physical ill effects nor psychological traumas. These children of nature also share their women with a degree of generosity that simply is not a part of Mexican nor Mexican American culture."

Ultimately, Pettit concludes, "Steinbeck's treatment of the paisanos arouses suspicion of ethnically based distortions. Steinbeck's Anglo misfits are usually genuine freaks—idiots, cripples and outcasts, teetering on the edge of their own race. Danny and his companions, on the other hand, *are* their own race, as Steinbeck permits us to see it."

In her essay, "Steinbeck and Ethnicity" (in *After the Grapes of Wrath: Essays on John Steinbeck*) Susan Shillingshaw quotes Steinbeck critic Louis Owens as saying "Steinbeck doesn't offer a greta deal of multiculturalism. His treatment of women and what today would be called people of color leaves a lot to be desired. He was a white, middle class male from Salinas. He was a product of his times."

Steinbeck's interest in the paisanos, she writes "is in part psychological—the study of group men—and in part realistic—the 'history of a subculture'—and finally in part aesthetic—wrestling with the contours of artistic expression."

It seems likely in the future there will be additional criticism like that made by Ortego, Pettit and Owens.

Steinbeck often used ancient myths and themes or biblical stories in his novels. *Cup of Gold* is a retelling of the myth of Henry Morgan, the pirate; *To a God Unknown* uses the ancient myth of the fisher-king; *Tortilla Flat* and *Cannery Row* employ King Arthur fables; *In Dubious Battle* evokes—it seems to me—the biblical story of the loss of innocence and the fall from grace in the Garden of Eden. *Of Mice and Men* and *East of Eden* are clearly retellings of the Cain and Abel story (Am I my brothers keeper?); and *The Grapes of Wrath*, which contains many, many biblical references, is a retelling of the story of the tribe of Israel and its journey from Egypt, the land of bondage, through the desert, to its own land—except the journey of the Okies to California is a stark reversal of the biblical story: the Okies find no freedom in California, only additional prejudice and suffering in the land of sun and oranges.

The chapter titles of Tortilla Flat help tell the story. Apparently they were not in the first version of the manuscript. Some critics believe that Steinbeck's first wife, Carol, suggested the King Arthur motif. But is is well known that the first book that captured Steinbeck's youthful imagination was a juvenile version of the King Arthur stories.

As Jay Parini writes in John Steinbeck: a Biography:

> *He was introduced to Malory's version of the Arthurian legend by Aunt Molly, his mother's bookish sister, when he visited her in the summer of 1912. He later recalled sitting under a tree "dazzled and swept up" by those powerful tales, which made a permanent impression on the young boy. The structure of these heroic stories would explicitly undergird many of his best novels, such as Tortilla Flat and Cannery Row, while aspects of the Camelot myth implicitly influences almost everything he ever produced. (The Malorian quest for the "good man," was crucial to his fiction, for instance. One also finds versions of Malory's idealized woman cropping up regularly. Sir Lancelot's betrayal of his king was pivotal image in Steinbeck's mind, and it informed a good deal of his work and, perhaps, his life.) The extent to which Malory overwhelmed him is registered in the fact that he spent the last decade of his life obsessed by the work, even renting a cottage for a year in Somerset, England—just to be be near the supposed site of Camelot.*

(In fact, be rewrote some the Thomas Malory manuscript stories into his own version of the King Arthur myths: *The Acts of King Arthur and His Noble Knights* was published posthumously, in 1976, not by Steinbeck's decades-long publisher, The Viking Press, but by the firm of Farrar, Straus and Giroux.)

And Steinbeck probably knew enough paisano Spanish to know that Monterey is translated as "King's Mountain."

In 1934, Steinbeck wrote to his literary agent, Mavis McIntosh (cited in *Steinbeck: A Life in Letters*):

> I want to write something about Tortilla Flat and about some ideas I have about it. The book has a very definite theme. I thought it was clear enough. I have expected that the plan of the Arthurian cycle would be recognized, that my Gawaine and my Lancelot, my Arthur and Galahad would be recognized. Even the incident of the Sangreal in the search of the forests is not clear enough I guess. The form is that of the Malory version, the coming of Arthur and the mystic quality of owning a house, the forming of the roundtable, the adventures of the knights and finally, the mystic translation of Danny.

Steinbeck critic Joseph Fontenrose shows how closely *Tortilla Flat* parallels the Arthurian saga (in "*Tortilla Flat* and the Creation of a Legend" in Jackson Benson's *The Short Novels of John Steinbeck*). He sees these parallels: After an obscure boyhood Arthur inherits a kingdom and is transformed from ordinary manhood to lord of the land (Danny inherits two houses); the new king has trouble with subject kings and barons who refuse to pay homage (Pilon and Pablo refuse to pay rent on Danny's second house), but are finally defeated (the house burns down) and reconciled. Arthur (Danny) gathers knights (friends) to his Round Table and give them lands (shelter and place to sleep). The knights swear an oath of devotion (Danny's friends promise to see that he will never go hungry). Arthur and his knights give their attention to Pelles, the Maimed King, and the Grail that he kept (the Pirate and his treasure). Percival, unappreciated by the knights, is placed along the knights (the Pirate is given a corner of Danny's house, where he sleeps among his dogs).

These are fewer than half of the parallels Fontenrose finds. In fact, he traces such parallels throughout the entire book. (Service and symbols of the Catholic Church are also keys to both the King Arthur legends and *Tortilla Flat*).

Steinbeck's reworking of the Malory legends is ingenious indeed. God sent a boat to Galahad, who discovers on it a silk crown and a marvelous sword. On another occasion, another empty boat floats to Arthur as he stands on a riverbank; it carries him to a castle where he is served wine and meats. Steinbeck offers a drifting boat to Jesus Maria near Seaside, California—he rows it to Monterey, sells it for seven dollars and buys wine for himself and a gift for Arabella.

In the most famous (and the most obvious) twist on the Malory legends, the knights (paisanos) go searching for the Holy Grail; instead of finding the Grail, they find a U.S. Geodetic Survey marker, which they recognize they can't dig up and sell for wine because no one would dare buy it.

Mark Twain's *A Connecticut Yankee in King Arthur's Court* is surely the same type of book as *Tortilla Flat*. Samuai Clemens may have read the King Arthur tales as child, as Steinbeck did, then come back to them as an adult, also as Steinbeck did.

But Steinbeck has signaled—publicly and privately—that we are not to take *Tortilla Flat* as a hundred-percent perfect retelling of the King Arthur story.

In his book *John Steinbeck's Re-Vision of America*, Steinbeck critic Louis Owens observes that "Steinbeck's very careful use of the litotes in his preface should also alert us to his method in *Tortilla Flat*. ("Litotes" are understatements in which an affirmative is expressed by the negative of the contrary, such as she is "not a bad singer.")

The preface begins quite simply with the statement "This is the story of Danny and Danny's friends and of his house. It is a story of how these three became one thing." And Steinbeck continues, "For Danny's house was not unlike the Round Table and Danny's friends were not unlike the knights of it."

With the use of the litotes, Steinbeck suggests we are not to take the parallel of the Round Table too closely.

Later, in *Tortilla Flat*, Steinbeck asks, "Where is Arthur Morales?" His answer: "Dead ... in France ... Dead for his country. Dead in a foreign land." In his grave in Europe, killed in the war (World War 1). In Steinbeck's version of the Round Table, there is no King Arthur.

In the same 1934 letter to Mavis McIntosh, Steinbeck wrote:

> I don't intend to make the parallel of the round table more clear, but to simply show that a cycle is there. You will remember that the association forms, flowers and dies. Far from having a hard theme running through the book, one of the intends is to show that rarely does any theme into lives of these people survive the night.

Elaine Steinbeck and Robert Wallsten, in *Steinbeck: A Life in Letters*, note that the problem of the theme was solved, at least in part, with the use of the Arthurian-like chapter titles, (which were apparently added to the manuscript sometime after Steinbeck had completed his first manuscript version).

In *Tortilla Flat*, Steinbeck begins discussing the poor and the downtrodden. They are seen again and again: in *In Dubious Battle*; as Lennie and George in *Of Mice and Men*; as the Joads and the other Okie families in *The Grapes of Wrath*; in *Cannery Row* and its sequel *Sweet Thursday*. Indeed, it could be said that Steinbeck is at his best when he writes of Danny and the paisanos, of George and Lenny, of Tom and Ma Joad and of the boys along Cannery Row, rather than when he (later) turns to other locales and other more successful (and more commonplace) heroes, such as Ethan Allen Hawley in *The Winter of Our Discontent*.

In *Tortilla Flat*, Steinbeck also had a convenient vehicle for his philosophy of group-man. During the Depression, it was difficult for a family to stay together, financially, spiritually, psychologically. In *Tortilla Flat,* Steinbeck shows us that the individuals (the knights) became Danny's house (the round table) and that Danny's house is part of Tortilla Flat and that Tortilla Flat is part of greater Monterey and Monterey is part of the greater world.

Steinbeck was interested in the birth, survival and ultimate death of the group, a "phalanx"—the "I" which becomes "we." In his paisano round table in Tortilla Flat, he imagined the ideal birth, life and deaths of the phalanx.

The phalanx was a biological /philosophic idea that Steinbeck and his marine biologist friend Ed Ricketts discussed throughout their relationship.

In "Tortilla Flat: and the Creation of a Legend," (in *The Short Novels of John Steinbeck,* edited by Jackson Benson), Fontenrose also writes:

> *The house was the body of an organism. In Tortilla Flat Steinbeck's biological point of view becomes explicit, and, for the first time he make deliberate, if humorous, use of the conception of the group as organism. The first words are: "This is the story Danny and of Danny's friends and of Danny's house. It is a story of how these three became one thing, so in Tortilla Flat if you speak of Danny's house, you do not mean a structure of wood flaked with old whitewash ... No, when you speak of Danny's house you are to understand to mean a unit of which the parts are men, for which comes sweetness and joy, philanthropy and, in the end, a mystic sorrow." The group organism is more than just the sum of its parts, and the emotions of its unit parts coalesce into a single group emotion.*

In his foreword to the 1937 Modern Library edition of *Tortilla Flat,* Steinbeck suggests the ecological principle that an organism will adapt to its environment: the paisanos are, he writes, "people will merge successfully with their habitat. In men this is called philosophy, and it is a fine thing."

Steinbeck and Ricketts also shared the philosophy of non-teleological thinking, that is, emphasizing the *now* or *is* rather than the *why* of a situation. The paisanos of Tortilla Flat are perfect vehicles for Steinbeck's non-teleological thinking. (Later, Steinbeck's belief in non-teleological philosophy was revealed in the working title for *Of Mice and Men*: "Something That Happened." *Tortilla Flat* examines what *is*, rather then *what should be*. Non-teleological also involves the following principles: a love of freedom, surely a key to the life of the paisanos; an acceptance of things as they are, also a key element in the life of those in Tortilla Flat; an acceptance of a God and a church and religious matters; the lack of concern with material things (possessions, yours or those belonging to others, can be traded for wine) and the value of friendship above that of money.

In the paisanos, Steinbeck creates perhaps the ideal expression of his non-teleological thinking, although he returns to this philosophy in *Of Mice and Men* and elsewhere.

Charles Metzger, in his essay "Steinbeck's Mexican-Americans," writes:

> *Steinbeck's paisanos have refused to subscribe to those views of the world and for right conduct in it which would render them respectable and/or understandable to such neighbors or readers as have bought the white Anglo-Saxon Protestant ethic. They have refused essentially by way of defending their own positive, more liberal, more newly aristocratic, ... romantic, in the old sense, image of an appropriate lifestyle. It was not at all by accident or in the interest of irony that Steinbeck chose to describe his paisanos in Arthurian terms—after the manner of that great and wistful romantic Thomas Malory, who celebrated the ancient, embattled, and romantic Britons, the knights of the round table, in his own prose.*

To the charge, often made, that Steinbeck's treatment of his paisanos is romantic and sentimental, I can only answer that: (a) it most certainly is romantic, and (b) that such romanticism is not sentimental but rather appropriate—that actually fits the facts of life as life was conducted by the kinds of real persons who provided Steinbeck with models for his fictional characters. Steinbeck of course makes these two assertions himself practically outright by pointedly directing his readers' attention to the Arthurian analogues by means of which he develops his narrative.

That such analogues puzzle some readers is due in part to the fact that they, not Steinbeck, are perhaps excessively literal minded. But it may be due in part also to the fact that Steinbeck does not specifically tell his Anglo readers what he knows, and what most Mexican-Americans know, about the very real and actively operating conceptions of the "dignidad de la persona," of being "muy hombre," of being "macho." These conceptions describe in Mexican terms some of the very real things Steinbeck is talking about when he refers to the paisanos "different philosophic moral system," when indeed, he describes his paisanos, as seen through their own eyes, in aristocratic terms.

In short, Steinbeck values the Arthurian legends and the paisanos too highly to demean either. By adding the language of the paisanos and their convoluted moral code to his novel, he elevates them toward Arthurian status, without demeaning them or the tales of the knights that he was so captivated by throughout much of his life.

Critics have suggested that the tone changes throughout the novel; it does indeed. Steinbeck mixes a serious regard for his paisanos with mock heroism; respect with jests; rollicking good fun with seriousness. Some have charged that the ending of the novel is far blacker than much of the text, but Steinbeck foreshadows the collapse of the house of Danny and his death with the outrageous drunken destruction Danny wreaks at the beginning of the narrative.

Tortilla Flat was the first novel in which Steinbeck matched structure and subject throughout; in it he combined his love of the Arthurian legends with his knowledge and love of the paisanos of Monterey; he was able to perfectly add elements of his phalanx theory and the non-teleological thinking that he developed with "friend Ed," Ed Ricketts.

The sardines are all long gone from Monterey Bay and the factories of Cannery Row are gone too. Left is Steinbeck's marvelous beginning to Cannery Row:

> *Cannery Row in Monterey in California is a poem, a stink, a grating noise, a quality of, light, a tone, a habit, a nostalgia, a dream. Cannery Row is the gathered and scattered, tin and iron and rust and splintered wood, chipped pavement and weedy lots and junk heaps, sardine canneries of corrugated iron, honky tonks, restaurants and whorehouses, and the little crowded groceries, and laboratories and flophouses. Its inhabitants are, as the man once said "whores, pimps, gamblers and sons of bitches," by which he meant everybody. Had the man looked through another peephole he might have said "Saints and angels and martyrs and holy men" and he would have meant the same thing.*

Above the Bay, and in Carmel and elsewhere, the shacks and shanties of the paisanos are gone now too, bulldozed for tract houses, shopping centers and roads. But through Steinbeck's eyes, we see them still, talking and laughing under the golden warmth of the sun, in those idyllic days of the Great Depression, when friendship and wine meant more than money.

from Tortilla Flat

This is the story of Danny and of Danny's friends and of Danny's house. It is a story of how these three became one thing, so that in Tortilla Flat if you speak of Danny's house you do not mean a structure of wood flaked with old whitewash, overgrown with an ancient untrimmed Rose of Castile. No, when you speak of Danny's house you are understood to mean a unit of which the parts are men, from which comes sweetness and joy, philanthropy and, in the end, a mystic sorrow. For Danny's house was not unlike the Round Table, and Danny's friends were not unlike the knights of it. And this is the story of how that group came into being, of how it flourished and grew to be an organization beautiful and wise. This story deals with the adventuring of Danny's friends, with the good they did, with their thoughts and their endeavors. In the end, this story tells how the talisman was lost and how the group disintegrated.

It Can't Happen Here
Sinclair Lewis / 1935

Fascism in America

genre: alternative American history

Sinclair Lewis was the first American to win the Nobel Prize for literature, in 1930.

Subsequent American winners were: Eugene O'Neill, 1936; Pearl S., Buck, 1938; William Faulkner, 1949; Ernest Hemingway, 1954; John Steinbeck, 1962; Saul Bellow, 1976; Isaac Bashevis Singer, 1978; Joseph Brodsky, 1987, Toni Morrison, 1993 and Bob Dylan, 2016.

Lewis—born Feb. 7, 1885, died Jan. 10, 1951—became widely known for his novels, which were indictments of a variety of areas of American life: *Main Street*, published in 1920, was an astonishing success. It was projected to sell perhaps 25,000 copies, but in the first six months had sold 180,000 copies and within few years, two millions copies, earning Lewis as much as three million in 2005 dollars. It mocked small-town America.

He followed *Main Street* with *Babbitt*, 1922, an indictment of middle-class business culture and ethics. The term *babbittry* was fashionable for a while, out-of-date now, to define his view of boosterism in American life and business.

Arrowsmith, 1925, concerned the challenges faced by an idealistic doctor. It won the Pulitzer Prize, which Lewis declined.

Elmer Gantry, 1927, was his view of a religious leader deeply hypocritical. It was banned in some cities and denounced by religious leaders. It was the basis of the 1960 film of the same name starring Burt Lancaster.

Subsequently, he published: *The Man Who Knew Coolidge*, 1927 (later prompting novelist Vance Bourjaily to publish *The Man Who Knew Kennedy*, in 1967); *Dodsworth*, 1928; *Ann Vickers*, 1933, *Work of Art*, 1934 and, in 1935, *It Can't Happen Here*.

In later years he published *Kingsblood Royal*, 1947, based on the Sweet trials in Detroit in which a black doctor was denied the chance to buy a house in an all-white section of the city. It was an early contribution the civil rights movement.

Lewis eventually published 24 novels; the last *World So Wide*, was published posthumously.

Richard Lingeman's massive, 624-page biography, *Sinclair Lewis: Rebel from Main Street* (2002), summarized Lewis perfectly in four paragraphs:

> *The critic Edmund Wilson called Sinclair Lewis "one of the national poets." In the 1920s, Lewis fired off a fusillade of sensational novels, exploding American shibboleths with a volatile miniature of caricature and photographic realism. With an unerring eye for the American scene and an omnivorous ear for American talk, he mocked such sacrosanct institutions as the small town {Main Street), business {Babbitt), medicine {Arrowsmith) and religion {Elmer Gantry). His shrewdly observed characters became part of the American gallery, and his tales part of the language.*
>
> *Despite his books' innate subversiveness, they were best sellers and widely discussed—and almost as widely damned. They had small-towners worried about being called "Main Streeters," preachers fearful of being branded "Elmer Gantrys," and Babbitts defiant of being labelled "Babbitts." Lewis touched a nerve among Americans who secretly yearned for something more from life than hustling, making money and buying new cars.*
>
> *Lewis danced along the fault line between the old, small-town, frugal, conservative, fundamentalist America*

and the modern, big-business-dominated, youth-obsessed, advertising-powered consumer society that was reshaping the American character in the iconoclastic 1920s.

For all his use of humor and satire, Lewis probed serious themes: feminism {The Job, Main Street, Ann Vickers), commercial pressure on science {Arrowsmith), racial prejudice {Kingsblood Royal) and native fascism {It Can't Happen Here). In 1930, he became the first American to win the Nobel Prize for literature, but he feared he could never live up to it. In his heart, he was a scold with a conscience, a harsh truth-teller who laughed out loud. His novels, born out of passionate conviction that America could be better, are as alive today as when they were written.

And, Lingemen writes:

He was a literary sociologist who believed in seeing America first and knew his country better than most writers of his generation. His politics were a blend of old-fashioned populism and urban reformers' idealism; his literary mentors were Dickens and Wells. He measured American life by high standards and found it was not good enough. Yet who else depicted his own country's faults with such coruscatingly funny, ambivalently loving satire?

His fiction functioned at it highest pitch when galvanized by a anger at some banality or stupidity or injustice. His iconoclasm chimed with America's coming of age after World War 1, but he wrote with a real moral passion. He really cared.

Lewis married political reporter Dorthy Thompson May 14, 1928. Beverly Gage summaries the genesis of *It Can't Happen Here,* in her article "Reading the Classic Novel that Predicted Trump":

Lewis's second wife the journalist Dorothy Thompson, provided much of the inspiration for "It Can't Happen Here." In 1931, she interviewed Hitler, scoffing at his "startling insignificance" when encountered face-to-face, back in the United States. Thompson interviewed Huey Long who had vowed to challenge Franklin Roosevelt for the presidency in 1936. She noted that Long's populist message and swaggering style reminded her of Hitler and according to Lewis's biographer Richard Lingemen, Lewis took the message to heart. A recent Nobel Prize winner, known for his superhuman productivity, Lewis churned out the entire manuscript of "It Can't Happen Here" between May and August of 1935. The novel was in bookstores that October.

It's a surprise that his productivity didn't harm his health. It happens.

During the Dust Bowl years, John Steinbeck knew of the migration of the Okies from the mid-west—Oklahoma and many other farm-belt states—to California. He met some, interviewed them and traveled with some from the Nevada-California border into California. He later stated that he had traveled with some from Oklahoma to California, which wasn't true.

Steinbeck's biographer Jackson Benson writes (Elizabeth Otis was Steinbeck's literary agent):

In March 1938 he still had confidence that he could combine art and propaganda. In response to Elizabeth Otis's inquiry (he had said little about the book in progress during recent months), he wrote:
"Yes, I've been writing on the novel but I've had to destroy it several times. I don't seem to know more about writing a novel than I did ten years ago. You'd think I would learn. I suppose I could dash it off but I want this

one to be a pretty good one. There's one other difficult too. I'm trying to write history while it's happening and I don't want to be wrong.

Steinbeck called his novel *L'Affair Lettuceberg*. It didn't work. He scrapped it. He began again.

Benson also writes:

> There was something in his makeup that seemed to make it impossible for him to slowly plan, develop and then deliberately write a long work of fiction. The pressure of material and emotion built up in his mind so that once his direction had finally been determined, he took off like a sprinter rather than a long distance runner. When at last he did get into the writing of the final draft of The Grapes of Wrath he made it a long sprint, rather than a marathon and the strain very nearly destroyed him.

That was not hyperbole; Steinbeck wrote the final draft of *The Grapes of Wrath* in 100 days and very nearly had a nervous breakdown. George Orwell also ruined his health writing *1984* (cited later).

In his Introduction to the Signet edition of *It Can't Happen Here*, Michael Meyer writes:

> In March of 1935, two months before Sinclair Lewis began writing It Can't Happen Here, Walter Lippmann lamented in a popular magazine that the United States had "come to a period of discouragement ... Pollyanna is silenced and Cassandra is doing all the talking." There was much for Cassandra to talk about: the administration of the New Deal seemed hopelessly bogged down and the force strident policies of popular leaders such as Huey Long and Father Coughlin seemed to speak more directly to the poor, the dispossessed, the frustrated, and

the angry. Neither the Louisiana Kingfish nor the populist radio priest freighted their remedies for the country's ills with feasible ideas or coherent programs. Immediate solutions were too important to be burdened with details and troublesome facts; it was enough for Long to simply announce the justice of a $5,000 "homestead allowance" coupled with an annual income of at least $2,000 for every American family. The Kingfish was long on proposals but short on perceiving potential problems.

"Who cares," he said, "what consequences may come following the mandates of the Lord, the Pilgrims, of Jefferson, Webster and Lincoln? He who fails in this flight fails in the radiance of the future."

The liberals who worried about the possible consequences that attended this future brave new world were particularly wary because the Old World had already produced Hitler and Mussolini. Fascism was becoming fashionable, a fact manifested by the Brown Shirts, Black Shirts, Khaki Shirts, White Shirts and Silver Shirts—complete with matching boots—that came out of the closet all over Europe and the United States. In October of 1935, the month It Can't Happen Here was published, William Randolph Hearst encapsulated the problem with a statement that delighted shirt makers but terrified liberals. He counseled his fellow citizens: "Whenever you hear a prominent American called a 'Fascist,' you usually make up your mind that the man is simply a LOYAL CITIZEN WHO STANDS FOR AMERICANISM."

Lewis transforms this advice into a warning in his novel by showing how Americans elect as their president Berzelius Windrip, a folksy New England version of the dictatorial Kingfish, who ushers in a fascistic regime of suppression, terror, and totalitarianism—all draped in red, white and blue bunting. Invoking the highest patriotic principles, Windrip disguises his fascism in the historical

> *trappings of the Republic; his Gestapo, for example, is called the Minute Men. Lewis projects a dire version of the immediate future—the story begins in 1935 and ends in 1939—by creating fictional equivalents of the trepidations liberals experienced in the mid thirties. Although Lewis looks to the future for the actualization of what liberals feared might happen, he turns to the past for the antidote to a poisoned America. To combat Windrip's deceptive use of a past that is employed to corrupt the present, Lewis draws upon a national heritage of individualistic and democratic values in order to redeem the country from the fascism masquerading in a patriotic costume.*

The plot of *It Can't Happen Here*, as Lewis conceived it, chronicled the rise of Senator Berzelius "Buzz" Windrip, a politician in the Huey Long mode; Windrip runs on a Populist platform, promising every citizen $5,000 a year and promotes himself as the champion of "traditional American values."

But how to guarantee revelry citizen $5,000 a year?

Buzz Windrip is vague about details—

In the Afterword to the Signet edition of *It Can't Happen Here*, scholar Gary Scharnhorst writes, about Huey Long:

> *The slogan of Long's "Share Our Wealth" movement was "Every man a King (But No One Wears a Crown)." Lewis revised the slogan in It Can't Happen Here: "Every man a king so long as he has someone to look down on." Like Senator Berzelius ("Buzz") Windrip in It Can't Happen Here, Long proposed to limit individual fortunes and inheritances through taxation, to double the amount of money in circulation to facilitate credit, and to provide each family with guaranteed income upwards of four thousand dollars. In February, 1935, according to Axel Knoenagel, "there was supposedly more than 27,000 (Share the Wealth) clubs with a total of more than 7 million*

members." In the U.S. when he died, The "Kingfish," as he was nicknamed, was building a political machine to supplant the Democrats and election him President in 1940. In none of these plans, however, do the figures make sense. All of them depended upon smoke and mirrors to disguise their impracticality.

Windrip defeats Senator Walter Trowbridge and Franklin Roosevelt and assumes the presidency.

Windrip abolishes Congress, jails political opponents and establishes a military force—the Minute Men—which quickly outnumber the U.S. Army. He establishes a "corporatist" policy, which is quickly abbreviated *Corpo*.

Faculty members in such universities as Harvard, Dartmouth and Brown, are thrown out or jailed and the buildings and grounds are turned into concentration camps.

The rights of women and minorities are abolished.

The "liberal press" is stifled. Editors and reporters are thrown out of their newspapers—some are brought before military courts staffed by Minute Men members with no legal training and no thought of anything except revenge—revenge from being maltreated, ignored and marginalized earlier.

In the article "Getting Closer to Fascism With Sinclair Lewis's "It Can't Happen Here," in *The New Yorker* October 19, 2016, Alexander Nazaryan writes:

"It Can't Happen Here" is an argument for journalism as a basic pillar of democracy. And civic education, too, which many of Windrip's supporters appear to lack. So do many Americans today, regardless of their convictions. That makes people easily exploitable by modern-day Windrips who know that they will not be made to account for their promises—or for their flagrant violations of democratic principle. The curious pronoun in Lewis's title, lacking an antecedent, may well refer to rise of fascism in the United States. But a less liberal reading of the title suggests that "it" is something more subtle; a collective apathy, born of ignorance, and a populace that can no longer make the kind of judgment that participatory democracy requires.

Windrip loves huge political rallies; spectators are mesmerized by him, but an hour later many can't remember any significant thing he said—all platitudes—just all smoke and mirrors ...

In his article, "It really can happen here: the novel that foreshadowed Donald Trump's authoritarian appeal," in the website *Salon*, September 29, 2015, Malcom Harris writes:

> *With his careful mix of plainspoken honesty and reactionary delusion, Trump is following an old rhetorical playbook, one defined and employed successfully in the 1936 presidential campaign of senator Berzelius "Buzz" Windrip. In his campaign's promotional book, "Zero Hour," Windrip laid out the classic nativist call to action that Trump would pick up nearly word-for-word:*
>
>> *My one ambition is to get all Americans to realize that they are, and must continue to be, the greatest Race on the face of this old Earth, and second, to realize that whatever apparent differences there may be among us in wealth, knowledge, skill, ancestry or strength—though of course all this does not apply to people who are racially different from us—we are all brothers, bound together in the great and wonderful body of National Unity, of which we all should be very glad.*
>
> *After Windrip's coup at the Democratic convention, he won a three-way race when the other two candidates split the reasonable vote. Once elected, President Windrip appealed directly to his core constituency of unprosperous and resentful white men to help him repress dissent and*

bring fascism to America. It is a chilling historical lesson even though it didn't actually happen.

… President Windrip abolished individual states, replacing them with multi-state areas "administrative sections."

Many citizens saw these authoritarian measures and lawless changes necessary to maintain law and order.

Dissenters—such as the novel's protagonist Doremus Jessup—a Vermont newspaper editor—are appalled; Jessup is brought before a Minute Man kangaroo court run by Shad Ladue, Jessup's former handyman. He is imprisoned.

Windrip is forced into exile by his colleagues in the Corpo state, when his promises of $5,000 for each citizen can not be achieved or are not achieved. In turn, a coup replaces those who replaced Windrip.

Jessup and others plan escapes to Canada, by way of an Underground Railroad, trekking through the woods and avoiding roads, in attempts to evade the Minute Men; being caught meant long years in concentration camps or being shot on the spot.

Those who replaced Windrip order all-out conscription—to build the Minute Men army to invade Mexico.

Dissent grows as many understand they had been monumentally duped by Windrip and his successors in the Corpo state. Their only chance is to escape one-by-one across the border into Canada and establish a government-in-exile.

The entire country falls into chaos.

Lewis's novel is relentlessly bleak;.

Ultimately, Jessup is shown, a solitary figure, slowly marching north through the forests to safety in Canada. There is no shimmering rainbow of hope in the sky ahead of him.

from It Can't Happen Here

Doremus had never heard Windrip during one of his orgasms of oratory, but he had been told by political reporters that under the spell you thought Windrip was Plato, but that on the way home you could not remember anything he had said.

There were two things, they told Doremus, that distinguished this prairie Demosthenes. He was an actor of genius. There was no more overwhelming actor on the stage, in the motion pictures, nor even in the pulpit. He would whirl arms, bang tables, glare from mad eyes, vomiting Biblical wrath from gaping mouth, but he would also coo like a nursing mother, beseech like an aching lover, and between tricks would coldly and almost contemptuously jab his crowds with figures and facts—figures and facts that were inescapable even then, as often happened, they were entirely incorrect.

But below this surface stagecraft, his uncommon natural ability to be authentically excited by and with his audience, and they by, and with him. He could dramatize his assertion that he was neither a Nazi nor a Fascist but a Democrat—a homespun Jeffersonian-Lincolnian-Clevelandian-Wilsonian Democrat—and (sans scenery and costume) make you see him veritably defending the capital against barbarian hordes, the while he innocently presented as his own warm-hearted Democratic inventions, every anti-libertarian, anti-Semitic madness of Europe.

Aside from his dramatic glory, Buzz Windrip was a Professional Common Man.

Oh, he was common enough. He had every prejudice and aspiration of every American Common Man. He believed in the desirability and therefore the sanctity of thick buckwheat cakes with adulterated maple syrup, in rubber trays for the ice cubes in his electric refrigerator, in the special nobility of dogs, all dogs, in the oracles of S. Parkes Cadman, in being chummy with all waitresses in all junction lunch rooms, and in Henry Ford (when he became President, he exulted, maybe he could get Mr. Ford to come to supper at the White House), and the superiority of anyone who possessed a million dollars. He regarded spats, walking sticks, caviar, titles, tea-drinking, poetry not daily syndicated in newspapers, and all foreigners, possibly exempting the British, as degenerate.

But he was the Common Man twenty-times magnified by his oratory, so that while the other Commoners could understand his every purpose, which was exactly the same as their own, they saw him towering among them and they raised hands to him in worship.

Address Unknown
Kressmann Taylor / 1938

Adressat unbekannt ...

genre : epistolary novel

It is, at once, one of the shortest books published in the twentieth century and one of the most powerful, poignant and unforgettable.

The premise is simple—a series of letters exchanged between a German-American Jewish art dealer in San Francisco and his long-time friend and former business partner, a German in Munich. The timeline is brief—from November, 1932 into early March, 1934.

Katherine Kressmann was born in 1903; she graduated from the University of Oregon and moved to San Francisco, where she took a job in advertising copywriting. There she met Elliott Taylor, who had his own advertising agency; they married after a very brief courtship, in 1928.

In 1939, they moved to New York where he had a job as an editor. She finished *Address Unknown* there and showed it to Whit Burnett, editor of *Story* magazine. He immediately wanted to publish it but thought that it was far to powerful to be published under a woman's name. Her husband and Burnett decided on Kressmann Taylor, which she used for the rest of her life.

Within ten days the issue of *Story* magazine was sold out; columnist Walter Winchell called it "the best piece of the month, something you shouldn't miss." *Reader's Digest* reprinted it and reached three million readers.

Simon and Schuster printed it in book form and sold 50,000 copies; a huge sale for those years. The British publisher Hamish Hamilton also issued the book for the United Kingdom.

In 1939, *The New York Times Book Review* wrote, "This modem story is perfection itself. It is the most effective indictment of Nazism to appear in fiction."

There was a Dutch edition which disappeared in 1939, when Europe was dominated by Hitler; the only other mention of the book was on the *Reichkommisar's* list of banned books. (During the same time, to own John Steinbeck's *The Moon Is Down* in Scandinavia meant a Nazi death sentence.)

Later Kressmann Taylor said, about the origins of the book:

> *A short time before the war, some cultivated, intellectual warmhearted German friends of mine returned to Germany after living in the United States. In a very short time they turned into sworn Nazis. They refused to listen to the slightest criticism about Hitler. During a return visit to California, they met an old, dear friend of theirs on the street who had been very close to them and who was a Jew. They did not speak to him. They turned their backs on him when he held his hands out to embrace them. How can such a thing happen? I wondered. What changed their hearts so? What steps brought them to such cruelty?*
>
> *These questions haunted me very much and I could not forget them. It was hard to believe that these people whom I love and respected had fallen victim to the Nazi poison.*
>
> *I began researching Hitler and reading his speeches and the writings of his advisors. What I discovered was terrifying.*
>
> *What worried me most was that no one in America was aware of what was happening in Germany and they also did not care. In 1938, the isolationist movement in*

> *America was strong; the politicians said that affairs in Europe were none of our business and that Germany was fine. Even Charles Lindbergh came back from Germany saying how wonderful the people were. But some students who had returned from studying in Germany told the truth about the Nazi atrocities. When their fraternity brothers thought it would be fun to send them letters making fun of Hitler. They wrote back and said "Stop it. We're in danger. These people don't fool around. You could murder one of those Nazis by writing letters to him."*

Kressmann Taylor's husband read that and took the idea home. It became the key to the narrative she wanted to write; in the form of letters. And she also said:

> *I wanted to write about what the Nazis were doing and show the American people what happens to real, living people swept up in a warped ideology.*

(The "stop it" reference appears in slightly different form in *Address Unknown.*)

* * *

The most comprehensive, accurate, recent summary/analysis of *Address Unknown* is Jonathan Freedland's article, "Address Unknown: the great forgotten anti-Nazi book everyone must read."

Sub-titled "First published in 1938, US author Katherine Kressmann Taylor's forgotten classic is a devastating work of political fiction that still resonates today."

This appeared in the British publication *The Guardian,* August 23, 2019 (and in its U.S. website). It is worth reprinting in its entirety:

Some the largest themes have been addressed in the shortest books. That is especially true in the realm of what might be called political fiction. The single best evocation of communism—and especially the distance between the ideal and the Soviet reality—remains George Orwell's brief allegory, Animal Farm. In the same way, few works have conveyed the brutal nature of imperialism more effectively than Joseph Conrad managed in fewer than a hundred pages in Heart of Darkness.

Address Unknown was first published in Story *magazine in September, 1938, and then in book form a year later, becoming an instant bestseller. It has been translated across the world, adopted into a 1944 film and into multiple productions for the stage and radio—all under the name of Kressmann Taylor, after Story's editor, along with Katherine Kressmann Taylor's husband, Elliott, decided it was "too strong to appear under the name of a woman." The impact was immediate, the story credited with having "jolted America," alerting to the horror unfolding in Germany.*

It consists of nothing more than an intermittent correspondence between two friends. Yet the epistolary form is deceptively efficient, supply backstory, plot, character, dialogue and more than one narrative voice before a conventional novel might have cleared its throat. Within page of two, we are in the world of Martin and Max, both German, the latter a Jew now living in San Francisco, the former back in Munich—two men who have been business partners, friends and whose families have, as we shall discover, been intimately connected.

Their exchange, spanning just 16 months between 1932 and 1934, illuminated not just the specific texture of the early Nazi period, but something more timeless. It serves as a guide to the way politics of identity—specially one that involves "the people," rooting that idea in blood and soil—eventually, and often very rapidly, divided and polarizes. Max and Martin have shared "the fireside," there finding "warmth and understanding, where small selfishnesses are impossible and where wine and books and talk give a different meaning to existence." But even the best of friends can be rent apart. Once a dividing line is drawn, it's astonishing how swiftly people can break from those who stand one the other side of it. In that sense, Address Unknown is a warning. We tell ourselves, as these characters do, that friendship is eternal, that some bonds will never be broken. This short story warns us that ideology, once it has turned to fever, is stronger than friendship.

That's because any total, all-consuming creed will first separate "us" from "them," and then separate "them" from the rest of the human family. Dehumanization has been the overture to every genocidal opera (though it's worth stressing that Taylor was writing in 1938, before the Nazis' "final solution to the Jewish problem" was under way). It happened that way in Rwanda in the 1990s, when the pro-government radio station started telling Hutus to see the Tutsi minority now as people but as inyenzi, or cockroaches, or as inzoka or snakes. And it happens in the correspondence that forms Address Unknown, as steadily Martin come store see Max not as a friend, not even Max but as a representative of "the Jews." The antisemitism that comes out of Martin's mouth—the Jewish race—is a sore spot to any nation that harbors it"—thus shocks, not because we don't expect a German in 1933 to be expressing anti-Jewish racism, but because it is expressed by one man towards another who used to be his friend.

If that shift from seeing the individual, Max, to seeing only a collective, "the Jewish race," resonates today, it might be because the political rhetoric of our time keeps making a similar move, one visible beyond the resurgence, on left and right, of antisemitism. On the United States border, to take just one example, there are not individual mothers and fathers and children trying to come to the America, but rather—at least in the language of the current US president and his cable TV amplifiers—a "caravan," and "invasion." If there is a Texan Martin writing to a Mexican Max today, perhaps he too can no longer quite see his old friend as a person.

Taylor is perceptive too about how racism sneaks up on the individual who lets it in. Martin tells Max it wasn't that, in the past, he didn't notice the fact that Max was a Jew, but rather that he made an exception for him. "I have never hated the individual Jew," Martin writes, "yourself have always cherished as a friend, but ... you will know I speak in all honesty when I say that I have loved you not because of your race but in spite of it." The exempting of the occasional good Jew from a merited disdain for the Jewish people as a whole has long been a feature of antisemitism, and it's a device that remains in use to this day.

Nor are self-described liberals or progressives immune from the virus of bigotry. Max tells Martin he has faith in his old friend's "liberal mind and warm heart." And, sure enough, Martin is not seduced by Adolf Hitler immediately. "Is he quite sane?" He asks himself. "I do not know." But it does not take long for him to succumb. Soon he is adoring "the Gentle Leader," ready to assent to whatever surgery may be required to cut out "the cancer" that ails the Fatherland.

In this way, the story traces the universal contours of fascism—the leader-worship, the compulsory group-think, the surveillance, the summons to men to act as men—as well as the particular topography of the Nazi landscape. In Address Unknown, Jews are associated with art forms that Hitler would have despised—modern painting and theater—as well as with commerce. On this point, Taylor shows good moral sense—she makes clear that, however *much Nazi propaganda might have insisted otherwise, Ayran Germans were as implicated in using and selling, profit and loss, as the Jews they loathed for those very activities. Max makes money selling art, but so does Martin.*

All of this is achieved with concision even as it leaves room for some memorable writing. 'The old wound has healed, but the scar throbs at times, my friend," writes Martin. Later, speaking of the change of mood in his country, he says: "The old despair has been thrown aside like a forgotten coat." As if that were not enough, Address Unknown comes with a killer twist.

That this short, fleeting story has lasted so long its not only because of its artistic achievement, and not only because, written in 1938, it astonishingly anticipated the horror that was yet to come.

It is because its prescience is not confined to its time. It saw into our own future too.

Katherine Kressmann Taylor died in July, 1996; she was almost 94 years old.

from Address Unknown

Schloss Rantzenburg
Munich, Germany

February 12, 1934

Mr. Max Eisenstein
Eisenstein Galleries
San Francisco, California, U.S.A.

Max, My Old Friend:

My God, Max, do you know what you do? I shall have to try to smuggle this letter out with an American I have met here. I write an appeal from a despair you cannot imagine. This crazy cable! These letters you have sent. I am called in to account for them. The letters are not delivered, but they bring me in and show me letters from you and demand I gave them the code. A code? And how can you, a friend of long years, do this to me?

The Woman Who Could Not Die
Julia de Beausobre / 1938

... lost in the Soviet prison system ...

genre: memoir/autobiography

It is, at once, one of the most memorable memoirs of the twentieth century and one which has become completely lost in time; as this is written, late October, 2019, four copies exist for sale back and forth, here and there, throughout the internet; none any better than thrift-shop resale quality, if that. Four copies, perhaps fewer (and none have the Rebecca West Preface, cited below).

But it became, when first published, a major influence on the writer of the most famous dystopian novel ever written, then or now.

Julia Michaelovna Kazarina (born 1893) was brought up in St. Petersburg, Russia. She married Nicolai de Beausobre, a Russian diplomat, subsequently arrested for anti-Soviet activities. She too, was arrested, separately. She spent about 10 months in prison, most of the time in solitary confinement, before learning her fate; she was forced to sign a document (without a trial of any sort) agreeing that she was arrested February 4, 1932, because she was supposed to have "connived to commit crimes of high treason plotted by Nicolai de Beausobre and other citizens of the U.S.S.R." She had been arrested by the G.P.U., the Soviet secret police.

She writes:

The warder takes me into the middle of the Promenade. We are alone. He has a typed form in one hand, an ink pot with a pen sticking out of it in the other.

> "I shall now read your sentence to you."
>
> Then words, words. The dead, official kind of that convey no meaning until it culminates in:
>
> "... sentenced to five years' hard labor in the G.P.U. Penal Camps, according to article 58, 8 of the Soviet Code. Sign here."

She became *a 58*, a political prisoner, usually housed with thieves, pickpockets, prostitutes. With women whose language or dialects she couldn't understand.

Shunted from camp to camp. Nearly starving. Her diet? "A half pound of milk and a half pound of grey bread a day," all the while wondering where her husband was (spelled Nicolay in the book) or if she would ever see him again. (She did not discover until much later that he had been shot by the G.P.U. shortly after being arrested .)

Medical treatment also almost non-existent. At one point it was feared she would lose both arms and both legs from frostbite; luckily she did not. She was eventually deemed medically unfit for physical labor, based on heart trouble and other ailments.

Her experiences? harrowing, unimaginable. Fighting somehow not to starve, to stay warm, simply to ... *survive, day after day, week after week, month after month, toward an unfathomable future in the penal camps.*

Eventually she did survive, and in a way she perhaps did not expect. She was ransomed by her former governess, a British woman, and immigrated to England. She left Russia in 1934, after signing a paper stating that she would not attempt to return (the irony of that document was probably not lost on her).

* * *

In a 1976 edition of *If This Is a Man*, for academic readers, Primo Levi explained the differences between the Nazi concentration camps / death camps (Lagers) which he survived and the Soviet prison system which Julia de Beausobre survived. He wrote:

> *The main difference consists in the purpose. The German Lagers constitute something unique in the admittedly bloody history of humanity: to the old goal of eliminating or terrifying political adversaries they added a modern and monstrous goal, that of annihilating from the world entire peoples and cultures. Starting around 1941, they became gigantic machines of death; gas chambers and crematoriums were planned deliberately to destroy live and human bodies on a scale of millions; the horrific record belongs to Auschwitz, with 24,000 dead in a single day in August, 1944. The soviet camps certainly were not and are not places for a pleasant stay, but not even in the darkest years of Stalinism was the death of the prisoners explicitly sought. Death was frequent, and tolerated with brutal indifference, but not in essence deliberate; it was, in other words, a by-product of hunger, cold, disease, exhaustion. In this grim comparison between two models of hell it should be also added that in the German Lagers, in general, one entered not to come out: no end other than death was expected. In the Soviet camps, on the contrary, there was always an end; In Stalin's time, the "guilty" were sometimes given very long sentences (even fifteen or twenty years), with frightening carelessness, but a hope of freedom, however slight, existed.*

24,000 dead in one day. Auschwitz, August, 1944, according to Primo Levi.

She published *The Woman Who Could Not Die* in 1938; sales were mediocre. (The book was also published, by The Viking Press in New York the same year.)

Ten years later, the publisher, Victor Gollancz, convinced

noted novelist, essayist and reviewer Rebecca West to contribute a Preface, to improve sales of the book.

She wrote:

> *To write of Russia today is dangerous. I do not allude to the obvious material danger that, as has occurred more than once in the United States and on the continent of Europe, one may afterwards be found dead in a hotel bedroom, having, apparently, committed suicide. That is a danger which the courageous must face as part of this very disagreeable day's work.*
>
> *I allude to the danger that what one says, if it is not condonation of all Russian practices, may be taken as propaganda for the idea of declaring war on Russia. But one may regard the Government of Russia as given to trafficking with evil without wishing to kill Russians or devastate Russian land. There are, as this book suggests, other ways of contending with evil.*
>
> *This books tell a true story. Those of us who knew Julia de Beausobre know that if one imprisoned her, this is how she would behave and how she would elude one. She is a woman who is always working. She works with her clever hands, or with her clever mind, or with her clever heart. She had received from the past the great Russian tradition and she knows that it is her duty to transmit it, with that added to it which the best in her had been able to give it, to the future. Of course, she continued with this task in prison as she would have in her home had she been allowed to stay there.*
>
> *Of course she took with her into her cell the Orthodox Church, Aksakov, Dostoevsky, Trurgeniev, Tchekov. Her jailers found themselves proving a workshop for their enemies; and the work they did was as you may see in these pages. They annulled circumstances; they would suffer no interruption in the story they told of the obligation laid on*

the human being to achieve a state of beauty even when destiny seems to have imposed ugliness on it by an ineluctable degree.

What does the story mean? It has many meanings. One meaning is that the Tsardom was vile. Slippety-slop, it shuffled along, down at heel and mindless. The great souls, like Julia de Beausobre, refused to keep step with it, and when it fell by the wayside they scattered across the road, and hurried on, eager to make their way to national and individual salvation. But the little souls which the Tsardom had maimed also scattered across the road, surrounding the great souls and treading them down. If there had been freedom in Russia when the twentieth century dawned, if there had not been merely isolated attempts on the parts of humane aristocrats and the intelligentsia to try to give freedom to all, there would not have been these multitudes who, when the Tsardom fell, could not think, "Who now will be free?" But who thought "Who now will be slaves and can be knouted?" Tyranny begets tyranny. Tyrant cells multiple like cancer cells. Many men and women were responsible for the suffering of Julia de Beausobre in her prison. One of them most to blame was Lenin, whom, though a great man, was not courageous in demanding justice for his opponents from his followers. But as much to blame was Pobiedonostsev, who at the right hand of the last Tsars, urged always, on the highest grounds, repression and repression, and therefore taught generation after generation the dark delights which are incidental to the repressing trade. Anyone, anywhere, who consents to the restriction of any other human being's civil rights may find themselves as guilty as the jailers of Julia de Beausobre.

Another meaning of this story lies in its buffoonery. If the jailers of Julia de Beausobre had jumped up and down on a stage, wearing funny striped and spotted clothes and smearing their faces with flour, they would not have been going anything any more irrelevant to the betterment of the Russian people than what they were doing to Julia de Beausobre and her husband. The Beausobres were not doing anything hostile to the interests of soviet Russia.

They were among those who had decided that they were Russians and that Russia was their country which they must serve whether it was Tsarist or Bolshevik. They were people who were happy when they were working, and assuredly there was work to do in building a home for the Russian people out of the ruins left by the Tsardom. It was a foolish thing to do, to shoot the man, to persecute the woman for years, to make her breathe prison air and kill the lice on her body, and run temperatures in a labour camp. It protected the State? What protection did it ensure compared with the work those two might have done to repair Russia now, at this moment, when she needs the work of every hand and brain that can be pressed into her service, to repair the damage done by the Nazis? This book is a record of waste.

But obviously the argument is that Julia de Beausobre was imprisoned and her husband shot for the sake of the State is a pretence. Cruelty is one of the most dominant appetites of man.

We were all brought up to believe that human beings were perpetually in danger of losing their dignity and power and value because of their incapacity to resist the temptation of drink and sex. This appears not to have been true. Most people do not like more than a certain amount of drink, and are limited in their enjoyment of the companionship of the opposite sex by their physiological and economic capacities. But many people find an irresistible delight, which can never be sated once they give it an indulgence, in hurting other people. That was the strength of the Fascist and the Nazi movements. It is the strength of the Soviet system, which gives its executives powers to shoot and deport and imprison their fellow human beings. That alone explains the story told in these pages, and in these pages, with their unconscious revelation of the woman who wrote them, the reader can see what guilt a society surrenders when it give cruelty its head.

It is not known now how the Rebecca West Preface may have improved sales of the second edition of the book, re-issued ten years after the first publication.

* * *

Once ensconced in England, de Beausobre published *The Woman Who Could Not Die*, then *Creative Suffering*, 1940, a translation of *Russian Letters of Direction by Macarius the Elder of Optino*, 1944 and *Flame in the Snow*, a life of St. Seraphim, in 1945.

She married the historian Lewis Bernstein Namier in 1947 and, after his death in 1960, she wrote *Lewis Namier: A Biography*, published in 1971.

* * *

What other writer read *The Woman Who Could Not Die*—and remembered it?

George Orwell.

Like Rebecca West, Orwell was a prolific (in the best sense of that word) essayist and reviewer for British publications. He owned a copy of *The Woman Who …* but apparently did not review it.

The mention of rats on her prison bed—may have triggered his memory of rats in his quarters during the Spanish Civil War ("as big as house cats, or nearly …") mentioned in his *Homage to Catalonia*.

His memory of rats and her experiences may easily have led him to the most horrific torture scene in modern writing: hungry rats in a wire cage placed over a victims' head, in Room 101, toward the end of *1984*.

George Orwell died in 1950—Julia de Beausobre outlived him by *27* years and died in 1977; *The Woman Who Could Not Die* is long gone and her memory perhaps now, too (although her fable *Flame in the Snow* is still actively in print).

But Julia de Beausobre will live on forever, as the character *Julia* in George Orwell's timeless masterpiece *1984*, surely named for her.

from The Woman Who Could Not Die

The sun sets late, all are quiet. I lie down and doze off. Presently a marvelous something begins to move over my blanket, up my body. Four small legs, beautifully muscular, strong. Delightful, the muscular tension of those small strong legs ... Rat! I realize jumping to my feet and hurting them so that I sit down quickly on the bed next to mine. The woman in it, a rowdy who will bear her child any time, cannot understand my strange behaviour. The others who happen to be awake think me foolish. I suppose I am, why should I mind a rat after all? I must learn not to.

Darkness at Noon
Arthur Koestler / 1940

... admitted guilt, was convicted and executed ...

genre: fictionalized history

It is, perhaps, the most harrowing book published in the twentieth-century—the most *haunting*.

Arthur Koestler was born September 5, 1905, of a Jewish family in Prague, in the later days of the old Austro-Hungarian Empire. His family lost much of their livelihood when World War One began; they moved briefly to Vienna than returned to Budapest. By 1922, he had enrolled in the Vienna Polytechnic University to study engineering, but when his father's business failed, he was expelled for not paying fees. In March 1926, he told his family in a letter he was traveling to Palestine for year to find work. He left Vienna April 1,1926.

His early months in Palestine were unproductive; but by late 1927 he became Middle East correspondent for the Berlin-based Ullstein-Verlag group of newspapers; he wrote political essays interviewed various heads of state, kings, ministers and others. He eventually understood he would never have a future as a political writer in Palestine; he applied for a transfer and was appointed science editor for the *Vossiche Zeitung* and science editor for all the Ullstein newspapers.

He became the only journalist on the week-long first voyage of the *Graf Zeppelin* to the arctic; his live broadcasts, and subsequent follow-up articles brought him additional fame (that alone would have been a fascinating movie). He was then appointed foreign editor and assistant editor-in-chief of the *Berliner Zeitung am Mittag.*

In 1931, he became a supporter of Marxism-Leninism and on the last day of 1931, applied for membership in the Communist Party of Germany.

He then believed that the liberal polities of the *Vossiche-Zeitung,* politics of firing Jewish writers and abandoning a long-standing policy against capital punishment could not work. A second step in his thinking was that liberals and moderate Democrats would not—could not—stand against the rise of Nazism; the only real counter-force—in his thinking—to Nazism was Communism.

He spent two years—1934-1935—working in anti-Fascist movements. In 1936, during the Spanish Civil War, he traveled to General Francisco Franco's headquarters in Seville, pretending to be a Franco sympathizer, pretending to work for the London *News Chronicle,* as a correspondent. He found evidence that Franco's forces were being aided by Fascist Italy and Nazi Germany; he was outed and denounced as a Communist by a German former colleague. His work in Spain was included in his subsequent book, *Spanish Treatment*, published in 1937. He escaped to Paris.

Koestler returned to Spain in 1937, as a correspondent for the *News Chronicle* and was in Malaga when it fell to Mussolini's troops. He found refuge in the home of a retired professor, Sir Peter Chambers Mitchell; both were arrested by Franco's chief propagandist, Luis Bolin, who had earlier vowed he would shoot. Koestler "like a dog" if he was ever captured.

From February until June he was imprisoned in Seville—under a death sentence. He was later exchanged as a "high value" prisoner, *thus becoming one of the very few authors—anywhere in the world-sentenced to death and who lived to tell about it,* he wrote, in *Dialogue with Death* (1942).

He subsequently credited his wife Dorothy Ascher, (whom he married in 1935, but was was separated from, at the time) who worked tirelessly behind the scenes in London, to secure his release. They later tried to reconcile their relationship, but their daily life together was a failure, as was, subsequently, their marriage.

In July, 1938, Koestler finished his novel,The *Gladiators*, to be part of a trilogy; later that same year he resigned from the Communist Party and began a new novel. In 1939 he met Daphne Hardy; they lived together in Paris and she translated *Darkness at Noon* from German into English; she smuggled it out of France to England, where it was published. Both escaped together, but he subsequently returned to Paris and was arrested October 2, 1939. The French government considered him an "undesirable alien" and he was moved to the Le Vernet Internment camp.

Koestler was released in early 1940, thanks to the work of Milicent Bagot, an intelligence officer at the British spy service MI5; she recommended his release from Le Vernet, but suggested he not be granted a British visa. (She was later the model for the character Connie Sachs in the George Smiley spy novels of John le Carré and was the first to warn MI5 that Kim Philby was probably spying for the USSR.)

Koestler wrote about this period in *Scum of the Earth*, published in 1941.

Shortly before the Nazi invasion of France, Koestler joined the French Foreign Legion to get out of the country. He deserted in North Africa to get back to England, While waiting for a ship passage out of Lisbon, he heard a rumor that a ship that Daphne Hardy was on had been sunk and with it, the manuscript of *Darkness at Noon* was lost. He attempted suicide, but recovered. The rumor was not true.

When he got to England he was (again) imprisoned; he was still in prison when the English language version of *Darkness at Noon* was published.

* * *

Koestler had been imprisoned three times: in Franco's Spain; in Nazi France and in England. Surely it is worth considering how others—for instance—Ernest Hemingway—would have survived and reacted to those imprisonments. Hemingway spent a considerable amount of time during World War Two playing soldier, with a crew on board his motor yacht the Pilar, hunting for Nazi submarines off the waters of Cuba, near Havana. Playing at beating the Nazi U-boats. He had the improbable idea—*improbable at best*—he could capture a Nazi submarine by tossing a hand grenade down the (open) conning tower while it was on the surface. The U.S. Ambassador to Cuba funded his sub-hunting missions, much to the fury of J. Edgar Hoover and the American FBI, who had an FBI agent (the "Legal Attache") stationed in the U.S. Embassy in Havana.

So how would Hemingway—the very essence of masculinity—as individual and as writer—have reacted to the three different imprisonments—that Koestler endured?

* * *

Koestler's imprisonment in Franco's Spain was incorporated into *Darkness at Noon*.

When Koestler was released from a British prison, he volunteered for military service and was accepted into the Pioneer Corps; while in the service *Scum of the Earth* was published, which included the period of 1939-1940 and his imprisonment. In March, 1942, he was assigned to the Ministry of Information, where he worked as a scriptwriter for propaganda broadcasts and films, essentially the same work George Orwell was doing.

During this period he wrote *Arrival and Departure*, the third of a trilogy, which included *The Gladiators* and *Darkness at Noon*.

Daphne Hardy joined Koestler in London in 1943, but they left each other; they remained friends until Koestler's death.

He traveled to Palestine in December, 1944 and remained there until August 1945; he met Menachem Begin and urged

Begin to accept a two-state solution to Palestine, which Begin refused. Koestler later ruefully admitted his solution was naive and impossible.

He returned to England and joined Mamaine Paget, whom he hah met earlier. In August 1945, they moved to the cottage of Bwlch Ocyn, in the vale of Ffestiniog. There he met George Orwell—and they became close friends, two cut from the same cloth, to coin a cliche'. Bertrand Russell lived nearby.

Koestler was nothing if not peripatetic; he lived, at various times, in Israel, in Europe, in England and the United States.

He and Paget traveled to Israel in June, 1948 in June and stayed until October. They decided to leave England and move to France, but he learned that his long-delayed application for British citizenship has been granted and they returned London. In June, 1957 he gave a lecture in Alpbach, Austria, loved the village and had a house built there; he used it as a vacation retreat for 12 years.

Koestler and his first wife Dorothy Ascher agreed to a divorce and he married Mamaine Paget April 15, 1950 in the British Consulate in Paris.

He had also hired Cynthia Jefferies, as a secretary and manuscript typist; she would later become his third wife.

A dramatic version of *Darkness at Noon* opened in New York January, 1951 and won the New York Drama Critics award. Koestler donated all his royalties from the play to a fund he had set up to help struggling writers, the Fund for Intellectual Freedom (FIF).

In June, 1951, a bill was introduced in the U.S. Senate to grant him permanent residence in the United States. It was sponsored in the Senate by Owen Brewster and in the House of Representatives by Richard Nixon; the bill became law August 23, 1951.

His marriage to Mamaine Paget failed in August 1952; they remained friends until her sudden death in June, 1954.

On April 13, 1945, Janine Graetz who had known Koestler off-and-on for a period of years, gave birth to his daughter,

Cristina. Despite her entreaties, he never had any interest at all in the daughter, throughout his life.

Koestler eventually published *five* autobiographies: *Spanish Testament,* published in 1937; *Scum of the Earth,* 1941; *Arrow in the Blue; The First Volume of an Autobiography, 1905-1931,* published in 1952; *The Invisible Writing: The Second Volume of an Autobiography, 1932-1940,* published in 1964 and *Stranger on the Square,* the third volume of the Autobiography, written with his wife Cynthia Jefferies, published in 1984.

His income from *Darkness at Noon* was considerable and allowed him the freedom to devote his time and energies to a wide varsity of topics.

He led, shall we say, a varied life; his three imprisonments, political causes ranging from Zionism to Communism to anti-Communism; to voluntary euthanasia (suicide), campaigns against hanging, early scientific use of hallucinogens. He also wrote about creativity, the paranormal, the origins of the Ashkenazi Jews (like himself) and his disagreement with Darwinism.

His journalism, articles and essays, were written a variety of languages:, including German, Hebrew, French and English.

His novels had a variety of origins: *The Gladiators,* originally written in Hungarian; *Darkness at Noon,* originally in German, and *Arrival and Departure* in English.

Much of the last 30 years of his life were projects devoted to science and scientific methods.

* * *

Darkness at Noon is a horrific book; the origins of that book can said to be 1,200,000 times more horrific.

1,200,000. The upper estimates of those killed in the Stalin-era Great Purge or Great Terror of 1936-1938.

The Great Purge was the large scale elimination of Communist Party and governmental bureaucrats, repression of the Kulaks (affluent peasants), repression of the Red Army leadership and ... widespread police surveillance, suspicion of saboteurs, counter-revolutionaries, imprisonment and sudden executions.

Robert Conquest's 1968 book *The Great Terror*, helped popularize that phase regarding the Stalin years—but *the great terror* itself originally referred to the Reign of Terror during the French Revolution.

How did this Soviet Great Purge originate? Stalin's paranoia, coupled with his desire to consolidate all his authority are reasons enough.

> *The Timeline of the Great Purge is as follows:*
> *October 1936–February, 1937*
>> *Reforming the security organizations, adopting official plans on purging the elites;*
>
> *March 1937–June, 1937*
>> *Purging the elites; adopting plans for the mass repressions against the "social base" of the potential aggressors, starting of purging the "elites" from opposition.*
>
> *July 1937–October 1938*
>> *Mass repressions against "kulaks," dangerous: ethnic minorities, family members of oppositionists, military officers, saboteurs in agriculture and industry.*
>
> *November 1938*
>> *Stopping of mass operations, abolishing of many organs for extrajudicial executions, repressions against some organizers of mass repressions.*

The program begin with purges within the Red Army, then spread; to the leadership of the Communist Party, government bureaucrats—lower and upper-echelon—no one was seemingly spared.

Conquest's book, and a 1956 speech by Nikita Khrushchev both claimed that a great number of accusations, (the exact number surely unknown), were obtained through torture. And vague references to Article 58 of the RSFSR (Russian Soviet Federated Socialist Republic) Penal Code, with dealt with counterrevolutionaries. The phrase a *58 inmate*, or variations, became common. (Julia de Beauspore refers to herself as a 58, in *The Woman Who Could Not Die*).

Hundreds of thousands of victims were accused of a wide variety of political crimes, including sabotage, anti-Soviet agitation, conspiracies and attempt to stage uprisings agains the Stalin-led government.

These victims were sent to Gulag prison camps (like Julia de Beausobre), where they were worked to death, staved, often died of disease or of exposure.

Victims were often simply shot.

The term *purge* early on meant simply expulsion from the Party—in 1933, the party expelled some 400,000 citizens. Bur between 1936 to 1938 that phrase meant almost certain arrest, imprisonment, a guilty verdict often without a trial and execution.

Leon Trotsky's death—and the earlier death of his family—resulted from the Stalin-era purges. Most of Lenin's Politburo were shot.

Moscow Show Trials began in 1936, including:

> *The first trial was of 16 members of the so-called "Trotskyite-Kamenevite-Zinovievite-Leftist-Counter-Revolutionary Bloc." Held in August, 1936, at which the chief defendants were Gregory Zinoviev and Lev Kemenev, two of the most prominent former party leaders. Among other accusations, they were incriminated with the assassination of Kirov and plotting to kill Stalin. After confessing to the charges, all were sentenced to death and executed.*
>
> *The second trial in January, 1937 involved 17 lessor figures known the "Anti-Soviet Trotskyite-centre"*

which included Karl Radek, Yuri Piatakov, and Girgory Sokolnikov, and were accused to plotting with Trotsky, who as said to be conspiring with Germany. Thirteen of the defendants were eventually executed by shooting. The rest received sentences in labor camps where they soon died.

There was also a secret trial before military tribunal of a group of Red Army commanders, including Mikhail Tukhachevsky, in June, 1837.

Western trial observers at the time were convinced the trials were fair and unbiased and that the guilt of the accused had been established fairly. They observed that confessions in open court appeared to be given freely, without coercion, and not by torture, beatings or other sadistic methods. A member of the British Parliament, D. N. Pritt, observed "Once again the more faint-hearted socialists are beset with doubts and anxieties" but "once again we can feel confident that when the smoke has rolled away from that battlefield of controversy it will be realized that the charge was true, the confessions correct and the prosecution fairly concluded."

"... when the smoke has rolled away from that battlefield of controversy ..."

Later—much later—it became known that confessions were given only after great psychological pressure and torture. Former OGPU ("Joint State Political Directorate" or Soviet secret police, 1923-1934, when it was re-named) officer Alexander Orlov and others, said such confessions were obtained by repeated beatings, simulated drownings ("waterboarding," in our parlance), making prisoners stand or go without sleep for days on end, and/or threaten to arrest and or execute family members. After months of such interrogations, defendants/victims, were driven to despair and exhaustion and would agree to any charge, sign any document.

Zinoviev and Kamenev demanded as a condition for

"confessing," a direct guarantee from the Politburo that their lives and that of their families and followers would be spared. This offer was accepted, but when they were taken to the alleged Politburo meeting, only Stalin, Kliment Voroshilov and Yezhiov were present. Stalin claimed that they were the "commission" authorized by the Poltiboro and gave assurances that death sentences would not be carried out. After the trial, Stalin not only broke his promise to spare the defendants, he had most of their relatives arrested and shot.

In America, in May, 1937, the Commission of Inquiry into the Charges Made against Leon Trotsky in the Moscow Trial, commonly known as the Dewey Commission, was set up in the United States by supporters of Trotsky, to establish the truth about the trials. The commission was headed by the noted American philosopher and educator John Dewey. Although the hearings were obviously conducted with a view to proving Trotsky's innocence, they brought enough evidence which established that some of the the specific charges made at the trials could not be true.

For example, Georgy Pyataknov testified that he had flown to Oslo in December, 1935 to "receive terrorist instructions" from Trotsky. The Dewey Commission established that no such flight had taken plane. Another defendant, Ivan Smirnov, confessed to taking part in the assassination of Sergei Kirov, in December, 1934, at a. time when he had already been in prison for a year.

The Dewey Commission later published its findings in a 422-page book titled *Not Guilty*. Its conclusions asserted the innocence of all those condemned in the Moscow Trials. In its summary, the commission wrote:

Independent of extrinsic evidence, the Commission finds:

- *That the Conduct of the Moscow Trials was such as to convince any unprejudiced person that no attempt was made to ascertain the truth.*
- *That while confessions are not necessarily entitled to the most serious consideration, the confessions themselves*

> *contain such inherent improbabilities as to convince the Commission that they do not represent the truth, irrespective of any means used to obtain them.*
> - *That Trotsky never instructed any of the accused or witnesses in the Moscow trials to enter unto agreements with foreign powers against the Soviet Union (and) that Trotsky never recommended, plotted, or attempted the restoration of capitalism in the USSR.*

The commission concluded: "We therefore find the Moscow Trials to be frame-ups."

The Purge of the Red Army and Navy (Military Maritime Fleet) included removal of three of the five marshals (then equivalent to four-star generals), 13 of 15 army commanders (then equivalent to three-star generals) and eight of nine admirals. The purge fell heavily on Navy personnel who were suspect in exploiting their opportunities for foreign contacts.

50 of 57 army corps commanders were purged, along with 154 out of 186 division commanders, all 16 army commissars and 25 of 28 army corps commissars.

Mass executions were carried out by the NKVD (The People's Commissariat for Internal Affairs); it was left entirely to NKVD agents whether a prisoner was to be shot or set to the prison camps. Those to be executed were often shot at night, either in prisons, in NKVD cellars or in a secure area or forest, usually with pistols.

In the 1920s and 1930s, 2,000 writers, intellectuals and artists were imprisoned and 1,500 died in prisons and concentration camps. 27 weather forecasters disappeared between 1936 and 1938; the Meteorological Office was violently purged as early as 1933 for failing to predict weather harmful to crops !

Writers were especially suspect by the NKVD; poet Osip Mandelstam was arrested, exiled for three years, arrested again and eventually died in a prison camp December 27, 1938. Boris Pasternak was on purge lists but was reportedly "saved" by Stalin, who said, "Don't touch this cloud dweller."

In November, 1938 the purges ended; in fact, the head of the NKVD was himself executed. Most of the NKVD orders regarding executions were cancelled; but for some, the end date was not then. It is said that smaller acts continued into the 1940s and later.

On the night of August 12, 1952, 13 Yiddish poets were all executed. Aleksandr Solzhenitsyn argues in his *The Gulag Archipelago* that the purges extended in both directions in the timeline—in his view—from 1918 to 1956; the 1936-1938 Purge the most infamous.

The statistics: in the years 1937-1938: 681,692 executions and 136,520 deaths in the Gulag; the higher totals said to be 1,200,000, although exact figures will never be known.

Did Arthur Koestler know all this? Surely not all—probably not the numbers of NKVD executions; the names, the exact details of the major 1936-1938 Purge, but he did know enough; and he surely could not forget his own imprisonments—two in Europe, before his last in England.

He knew enough that—after months of savage interrogations—he knew that victims would be driven to despair and would agree to sign anything, any document, any confession.

He knew enough to make *Darkness at Noon* a *haunting*, timeless classic.

* * *

Darkness at Noon was first published in English in 1940. It was then—and now—widely assumed to be about the Soviet Union under Stalin. In fact, Stalin is represented only as "Number One," and described as being "in a widely distributed photo which hung over every bed or sideboard in the country snd stared at people with its frozen eyes."

Hitler and Nazi Germany are also not specifically described. The novel was, and is, intended to be a universal testament to one individual caught in the grasp of any totalitarian ideology.

Koestler's companion at the time, Daphne Hardy, changed

the title from the original *The Vicious Circle* to *Darkness at Noon*, a biblical reference to Job 5:14: "They meet with darkness in the daytime and grope in the noonday as in the night," which can describe not only the protagonist's struggles with Stalinist ideology but also the Koestler's imprisonment just earlier; he described imprisonment by Nazi France, for four months, in late 1939 and into early 1940 as "Kafkaesque events" in his life.

Darkness at Noon is, in fact, an allegory; based on Koeslter's imprisonment by Franco's Spanish forces—earlier—in which he was kept in solitary confinement and expected to be executed at any moment.

His protagonist, Nikolai Salmanovich Rubashov, is a composite character, based on a number of men Koestler had known, old Bolsheviks who became victims in the Moscow Show Trials. He is a minor functionary in the Party.

In the first section of the book, "The First Hearing," Rubashov is arrested—he is kept in solitary confinement and expects to be shot. He is interrogated by two members of the Soviet secret police, one old, Ivanov, one younger, Gletkin. The older, more courteous, the younger more brutal, thus the difference between the old regime and the newer.

Despite membership in the Party for 20 years, Rubashov is now torn between loyalty and his awareness of the Party's widespread brutality. Koestler contrasts the brutality of Soviet-style communism and the tranquility of Christianity.

In the earliest translation of the book, from Koestler'e German, the term "Hearing," was used, for the first three sections of the book: "The First Hearing," "The Second Hearing," and "The Third Hearing." To modern readers this made the techniques of the Soviet inquisitors seem more humane than they were; later, in a 2019 edition, the term was translated "Interrogation" or "Interrogations," rather than "Hearings."

Rubashov had been interrogated again and again, over and over, by Ivanov and Gletkin. Eventually Ivanov disappears; Rubashov asks, "where is he?"

He was identified as an enemy of the people and was executed, Gletkin says.

Eventually, in the last section "The Grammatical Fiction,"—it would come as no surprise to *any* reader—that Rubashov, worn down by endless psychological and physical torture, "confesses" to his "crimes," knowing all too well the consequences to come—

"The Grammatical Fiction," meaning of the last part? We can suggest the *fiction* is—were—the "confessions" made at the Moscow Show Trials and the individual Rubashov-style confessions made throughout the Soviet Union during those days. The "crimes," the victims all confessed to were fiction, all of them.

In an Introduction to a 1980 Folio Society edition of the book, Vladimir Bukovsky writes:

> *Arthur Koestler's book is strikingly up-to-date and topical. It is hard to believe that it was written almost forty years ago, and it is quite clear that this book will always remain forbidden reading in Communist countries.*

Koestler had long advocated for legal suicide; early in 1976 he was diagnosed with Parkinson's disease. His trembling hand made writing increasingly difficult. By 1980 he was also diagnosed with chronic lymphocytic leukemia. His final book, *Kaleidoscope*, was published in 1981.

He wrote a suicide note that read, in part:

> *To whom it may concern,*
> *The purpose of this note is to make it unmistakably clear that I intend to commit suicide by taking an overdose of drugs without the knowledge or aid of any other person. The drugs have been legally obtained and hoarded over a considerable period.*

He also wrote:

Since the above was written in June, 1982, my wife decided that after thirty-four years of working together she could not face life after my death.

She also added her own farewell note:

I fear both death and the act of dying that lies ahead of us. I should have liked to finish my account of working for Arthur—a story which began when our paths happened to cross in 1949. However, I cannot live without Arthur, despite certain inner resources.

Double suicide has never appealed to me, but now Arthur's incurable diseases have reached a stage where there is nothing else to do.

Arthur Koestler and his wife Cynthia killed themselves with overdoses of the drug Tuinel, taken with alcohol, on the evening of March 1, 1983; their bodies were found the morning of March 3, when they had been dead for 36 hours.

from Darkness at Noon

It seemed to him that they had been walking along this corridor for several minutes already. Still nothing happened. Probably he would hear when the man in uniform took the revolver out of its case. So until then there was a time, he was still in safety, Or did the man behind him proceed like the dentist, who hid his instruments in his sleeve while bending over his patient? Rubashov tried to think of something else, but had to concentrate his whole attention to prevent himself from turning his head.

Strange that his toothache had ceased in the minute when that blessed silence had closed around him, during the trial. Perhaps the abscess had opened in just that minute. What had he said them?

"I bow my knees before the country, before the masses, before the whole people ..." And what then? What happened to these masses, to this people? For forty years it had been driven through the desert, with threats and promises, with imaginary terrors and imaginary rewards. But was this the Promised Land?

Did there really exist any such goal for this wandering mankind? That as a question to which he would have liked an answer before it was too late. Moses had not been allowed to enter the land of promise either. But he had been allowed to see it, from the tops of the mountain, spread at his feet. Thus, it was easy to die, with the visible certainty of one's goal before one's eyes. He, Nicolai Salmanovitch Rubashov, had not been taken to the top of a mountain; and wherever his eye looked, he saw nothing but desert and the darkness of night.

A dull blow struck the back of his head. He had long expected it and yet it took him unawares. He felt, wondering, his knees give away, and his body whirl round in a half-turn. How theatrical, he though as he fell, and yet I feel nothing. He lay crumpled up on the ground, with his cheek on the cool flagstones. It got dark, the sea carried him rocking on its nocturnal surface. Memories passed through him, likes streaks of mist over the water.

Outside, someone was knocking on the front door, he dreamed that they were coming to arrest him, but in what country was he?

He made an effort to slip his arm into his dressing gown sleeve. But whose colour-print portrait was hanging over his bed and looking at him?

Was it no. 1 or was it the other—he with the ironic smile or he with the glassy gaze?

A shapeless figure bent over him, he smelt the fresh leather of the revolver belt; but what insignia did the figure wear on the sleeves and shoulder-straps of its uniform—and in whose name did it raise the dark pistol barrel?

A second, smashing blow hit him on the ear. Then all became quiet. There was the sea again with its sounds. A wave slowly lifted him up. It came from afar and traveled sedately on, a shrug of eternity.

This is the denouement ...

Koestler's narrative ends here. Did Rubashov die of the second blow as described? Or was he killed a moment later, by a pistol shot to the head? Was he dragged off, half dead and executed elsewhere? Was he dragged off, half-dead, thrown into a railroad car, sent into the Gulag where he died later of exposure, overwork, starvation, disease or randomly executed by a NKVD agent?

As dramatic as this is, Koestler understates the ending, but the meaning is clear; 1,200,000 Rubashovs were executed, before, during and after The Great Purge.

Hiroshima
John Hersey / 1946

... a noiseless flash ...

genre: journalism/ reportage (New Journalism)

Since it was first published, it has been, perhaps, the most memorable and most acclaimed book ever written about our atomic age.

John Hersey was born in Tientsin, China, June 17, 1914; he knew Chinese before he learned English. His parents were missionaries working for the Y.M.C.A. They returned to American when he was ten; he attended school in Briarcliff, New York, then the preppy school Hotchkiss, then Yale.

After Yale, he got a job as private secretary and driver for Sinclair Lewis, but was bored and began working for *Time* magazine, after writing an essay complaining about *Time's* dismal editorial quality.

During World War Two, Hersey covered the fighting in Europe as well as Asia, writing for *Time* and *Life*. He witnessed the allied invasion of Sicily, survived four airplane crashes and was commended by the Secretary of the Navy for his role in helping evacuate wounded troops from Guadalcanal.

After World War Two ended, during the winter of 1945-1946, Hersey was in Japan, reporting for *The New Yorker* magazine on the reconstruction of the country, when he found a document written by a Jesuit missionary who had survived the atomic bomb. Hersey visited the missionary, who introduced him to other survivors.

Hersey then began negotiations with William Shawn, editor at *The New Yorker*, about the possibility of a long *New Yorker* article, a long, major narrative about some who survived the first bombing of the atomic age.

Colonel Paul Tibbets and his crew in the B-29, the Enola Gay (named after his mother) dropped the first atomic bomb, on Hiroshima, August 6,1945.

The destruction of the city was nearly one hundred percent.

Earlier, after watching the first atomic test In the New Mexico desert, J. Robert Oppenheimer, scientific director of the Manhattan (atomic bomb) Project said:

> *We knew the world would not be the same. A few people laughed, a few people cried, most people were silent. I remembered the line from the Hindu scripture, the Bhagavad-Gita: Vishnu is trying to persuade the Prince that he should do his duty and, to impress him, takes on his multi-armed form and says "Now I am become Death, the destroyer of worlds." I suppose we all thought that, one way or the other.*
>
> *Destroyer of worlds.*

Did Hersey encounter any survivors of the bomb in Hiroshima *unable* to articulate what they had seen, *unable* to express what they had experienced? Or, in the title of the 1967 memoir by Vladimir Nabokov, *Speak Memory* ... Hersey needed to find survivors who *could* speak, who *could* articulate what they had seen, who they helped, what they encountered, how they survived ...

* * *

On November 10, 1975, a massive ore carrier, the Edmund Fitzgerald then in Lake Superior, which was bound for the Detroit area to unload and then on to Cleveland, its home port, encountered a massive winter storm. The captain radioed that water was coming in; the 29-member crew worked desperately to save the ship. It apparently broke in half and sank. All on board were lost.

Canadian singer/songwriter Gordon Lightfoot, wrote and recorded an haunting song about the disaster, "The Wreck of the Edmund Fitzgerald" barely a year later. (You can find the song and play it free on YouTube, on the internet.) It was released November 20, 1976 and became a number one hit in Canada and also a number one in the United States. He considers it his best work. In his song, a key line could *almost* be applied to the wounded, the maimed, the dying in Hiroshima, years earlier, moments after the cataclysmic bomb blast:

Does anyone know, where the love of God goes, when the waves turn the minutes to hours ...

Change Lightfoot's line just a bit:

Does anyone know, where the love of God goes, when the blast turns the minutes to hours ...

One listener to the Lightfoot song on the internet wrote that "the Edmund Fitzgerald was the Titanic of the Great Lakes ..."

* * *

How many residents of Hiroshima who survived, who *witnessed*, but *who could not speak* about the devastation, about those killed in their homes, in the streets, in the parks, along the rivers that flow through Hiroshima; those maimed, others whose memories could not dredge up that day, unable to recount those minutes, that hour ...?

Hersey traveled to Hiroshima in May, 1946, and spent three weeks doing research. He returned to America and began the project, writing about six Hiroshima survivors: a German Jesuit priest; a widowed seamstress; two doctors; a minister and a young woman who worked in a factory. All *could* remember and articulate the experiences they had been through. Experiences that they survived.

So he recounted those minutes, those hours, that first day, through the lives of the six survivors; six who *could* tell their stories.

Other journalists, newspaper reporters or magazine writers might have asked a question, thus: "what happened to you when the bomb exploded?" The answer might have been "everything fell on me; I was buried when my roof collapsed, and it took friends hours to dig me out. I thought my legs were broken; I could not move."

A solid quotation; most reporters would have used that.

Hersey did not substantially use such material.

In the book "*Hiroshima:* a new edition with a final chapter written forty years after the explosion" (Alfred Knopf, 2001) the first chapter begins on page 3 and runs through page 23. There are *no significant direct quotations* from anyone Hersey describes.

There are very few direct quotations elsewhere; those that he has are scattered throughout the rest of the book, 196 pages in that edition.

What Hersey did do was marry journalism—nonfiction—with the techniques of novelists; in that book he was one of the first practitioners of the techniques of New Journalism, later enthusiastically practiced by Tom Wolfe and others.

He essentially used a symbolic camera to scan, to survey the damage, viewing large-scale destruction, then focusing narrowly on small items; individual victims; debris, wreckage, carnage.

When statistics are needed, he inserts them seamlessly into longer paragraphs:

> *The lot of Drs. Fuji, Kanda and Machii right after the explosion—and, as those three were typical of the majority of the physicians and surgeons of Hiroshima—with*

their offices and hospitals destroyed, their equipment scattered, their own bodies incapacitated in varying degrees, explained why so many citizens who were hurt went untended and why so many who might have lived died. Of a hundred and fifty doctors in the city, sixty-five were already dead and most of the rest were wounded. Of 1,780 nurses, 1,654 were dead or so badly hurt to work, In the biggest hospital, that of the Red Cross, only six doctors out of thirty were able to function, and only ten nurses out of more than two hundred. The sole uninjured doctor in the Red Cross Hospital staff was Dr. Sasaki.

... and ...

Wounded people supported maimed people; disfigured families leaned together. Many people were vomiting. A tremendous number of schoolgirls—some of them who had been taken from their classrooms to work outdoors, clearing fire lanes—crept into the hospital. In a city of two hundred and forty-five thousand, nearly a hundred thousand people had been killed or doomed at one blow; a hundred thousand more were hurt. At least ten thousand of the wounded made their way to the best hospital in town which was altogether unequal to such a trampling, since it only had six hundred beds and they all had been occupied.The people in the suffocating crowd inside the hospital wept and cried.

Some of the sights were *beyond horrific*—as the example in the section: *from* Hiroshima, in the following pages.

Hersey also chronicles the mysterious illness, somewhat later diagnosed as radiation sickness, which devastated survivors with a variety of ailments, most particularly low white cell counts. Radiation sickness was a wholly new problem, never encountered before; surviving doctors in Hiroshima had no real basis of understanding, or techniques to be used, for treating these cases. Radiation sickness included:

- *Initial stage—the first 1-9 weeks, which included the most deaths from thermal injury; i.e, exposure to radiation from the bomb;*
- *Intermediate stages—10-12 weeks. Death in this period are also from radiation;*
- *Late period—13-20 weeks later. Survivors may show improvement over this period;*
- *Delayed period—from 20 plus weeks after theexplosion. Survivors may show a wide variety of complications: blood disorders, an increased probability of dying from cancer.*

These stages were all examined in Japan and in the United States and elsewhere at length—eventually—eventually, including:

- *Bone marrow death;*
- *Gastrointestinal death;*
- *Central nervous system death (the main cause of death in 24-48 hours after exposure to significant radiation);*
- *Long-term genetic damage;*
- *Infectious disease resulting from nuclear attack, including: dysentery; typhoid; infectious hepatitis; salmonellosis; cholera; meningococcal meningitis; tuberculosis; diphtheria; whooping cough; polio; pneumonia.*

Months later, some bomb survivors would suddenly fall ill with malaise, weariness, feverishness—and worse: radiation poisoning.

All of this, of course, was unknown to doctors in Hiroshima and surrounding areas after the catastrophic bomb, and indeed, discovered only much later.

Initially, Hiroshima residents called the bomb a *Molotoffano hanakago*—a "Molotov flower basket," the delicate Japanese name for a "bread basket," or self-scattering cluster of bombs. Some soon realized that the extent of damage throughout Hiroshima, clearly, certainly, could not possibly have been done by a simple cluster bomb; this was a new weapon no one could easily understand.

The New Yorker published the entire 31,000 word article "Hiroshima" in the issue of August 31, 1946. It occupied almost the entire issue, something the magazine had never done before. The issue sold-out, and was something of a sensation, like the publication of Kressmann Taylor's *Address Unknown* in *Story* magazine.

Some skeptics or critics thought there was something unseemly about the columns and columns of Hersey's prose, about the thousands of deaths, the wounded, the maimed, the dying—side-by-side with *New Yorker* advertisements of high dollar jewelry, hotels, vacations, investment programs and the like.

The book version was published soon after by the Alfred Knopf firm and is still in print.

John Hersey became known in three areas: his nonfiction reportage, culminating with *Hiroshima*, which many believe to be his masterwork; his novels and his teaching.

Just before the publication of *Hiroshima*, Hersey published his novel, *Of Men and War*, an account of war through the eyes of soldiers rather than war correspondents. One of the stories was inspired by John Kennedy and his PT-109.

(Ernest Hemingway did largely the same thing with the book *Men at War: The Best War Stories of All Time,* with selections by Stephen Crane, Theodore Roosevelt, T.E. Lawrence, C.S. Foster, William Faulkner, Leo Tolstoy, Winston Churchill and a wide variety of other contributors. He edited the selections and wrote the Introduction. It was published by Crown Publishers, in 1942, the only book by Hemingway not published by his life-long publishers, Scribners.)

Hersey's 1950 novel, *The Wall* was supposedly a rediscovered journal recording the beginning and end of the Warsaw ghetto.

It won the National Jewish Book Club award and the Sidney Hillman Foundation Journalism award.

His article "Why Do Students Bog Down on First R? A Local Committee Sheds Light on a National Problem: Reading," published in *Life* magazine in 1954, led to a result he surely could not have anticipated: the publication of one of the best-selling children's books of all-time. Theodor Geisel recognized the problem; children needed to be able to read for themselves. After very considerable work, taking months, he published *The Cat in the Hat*, (under his pseudonym Dr. Seuss), which children *could* read for themselves, and did, and still do.

Sales for *The Cat ...* are now in the range of 16 million copies, and still selling—in fact, sales from *The Cat in the Hat* alone could fund a publishing company.

Hersey's novel *A Bell for Adano,* about the Allied occupation of a Sicilian village, won the Pulitzer Prize in 1945; his 1965 novel *White Lotus was* an alternative history exploration of white Americans being enslaved by the Chinese after losing "the great war."

From 1965 to 1970, he was "master" of Pierson College, one of the 12 residential colleges at Yale University, a role largely equivalent to a university Dean; he taught non-fiction and fiction courses there for 18 years; he taught his last class in 1984. During the Vietnam war, his opposition to the war made him controversial with some Yale alumni.

He returned to Hiroshima in 1985 and wrote a follow-up article to his original *New Yorker* article. His follow-up appeared in *The New Yorker* issue of July 15, 1985 and was published in a 40-year re-issue of the original book, by Knopf in 1985 and reprinted again in 2001.

John Hersey maintained a winter home in Key West, Florida and died there March 24, 1993, at 78. He apparently wanted his reputation to rest on his novels—in total he wrote 25 books—but for many, his masterwork was, and will remain, *Hiroshima*.

from Hiroshima

Father Kleinsorge found a faucet that still worked—part of the plumbing of a vanished house—and he filled his vessels and returned. When he had given the wounded the water, he made a second trip. This time the woman by the bridge was dead. On his way back with the water, he got lost on a detour around a fallen tree and as he looked for his way through the woods, he heard a voice ask from the underbrush, "Have you anything to drink?" He saw a uniform. Thinking there was just one soldier, he approached with the water. When he had penetrated the bushes, he saw there were about twenty men and they were all in exactly the same nightmarish state: their faces were wholly burned, their eye sockets were hollow, the fluid from their melted eyes had run down their cheeks. (They must have had their faces upturned when the bomb went off; perhaps they were anti-aircraft personnel.) Their mouths were mere swollen, puss-covered wounds, which they could not bear to stretch enough to admit the spout of the teapot.

If This Is a Man
Primo Levi / 1947

Häftling. I have learned I am a Häftling.
My name is 174517 ...

genre: memoir/autobiography

*H**äftling*: trans: prisoner.

Show me your number: you are 174517. This numbering began eighteen months ago and applies at Auschwitz and the subcamps. There are now ten thousand of us here at Buna-Monowitz; perhaps thirty thousand between Auschwitz and Birkenau. Wie Sind die Andere? Where are the others?

Häftling. Prisoner.
Elie Weisel was only a young boy when he and his family were swept up by the Nazi juggernaut, shunted into railroad cars enroute to the concentration camps. He later said "I lost my adolescence in the cattle cars." He was 15 or perhaps 16 when he entered Auschwitz.

Primo Levi was born in 1919, of a Jewish family in Turin, Italy. When he was 14 he joined the *Avanguardisti* movement for young Fascists, expected of all Italian boys. He avoided rifle drill by joining the ski division and spent Saturdays during the ski season on the slopes above Turin. At that time in his life he decided he wanted to become a chemist. Much later, in 1975, his book

The Periodic Table, was judged by the Royal Institution of Great Britain as one of the best science books ever written. *The Periodic Table* was a series of short stories, based on episodes from his life, including two short stories he wrote before Auschwitz. Each is related in some way to one of the chemical elements.

In 1929, Mussolini signed an agreement with the Catholic Church which established Catholicism as the state religion and relegated other religions to the status of "tolerated cults."

In 1937, Levi was summoned before the Italian War Ministry and accused of ignoring a draft notice from the Italian Navy. His father was able to keep him out of the Navy by enrolling him in the Fascist militia, the *Milizia Volontaria per la Sicurezza Nazionale*. The Italian Racial Laws of 1938 forced his expulsion.

Italy enacted the Italian Racial Laws in 1938; Jews lost their basic civil rights, lost their positions in public offices, and their assets. Books by Jewish writers were prohibited; Jewish writers could no longer publish material in magazines owned by Ayrans; Jewish students who had begun their studies were allowed to continue, but new Jewish students were barred from university work. Levi has enrolled a year earlier which allowed him to continue.

By 1940, the situation of Jews in Italy changed dramatically with Italy's alliance with Nazi Germany.

He graduated in mid-1941, but his degree certification bore the notation "of Jewish race," which barred him from finding a permanent job after graduation. He did find work in an asbestos mine in San Vittore; a job working to extract nickel from the spoilage from the mine. He was told his work would aid the Nazi war effort. The job required him to work under a false name with false identity documents. He subsequently took a job with a Swiss firm, working to extract an anti-diabetic substance from vegetable matter; this job allowed him to escape the Italian race prohibitions; the project had no chance to succeed, but it was in no one's interest to admit that.

In July 1943, King Victor Emmanuel deposed Mussolini and appointed a new government, which signed an armistice with the

Allies, but when the armistice was made public, Nazi Germany occupied northern and central Italy, liberated Mussolini from imprisonment and appointed him head of the Italian Social Republic, a puppet government in northern Italy.

Levi joined the increasingly active Italian resistance movement, journeyed to the foothills of the Alps and established a partisan group, hoping to be affiliated with the liberal *Giustizia e Liberia*.

Levi and his companions were arrested by the Fascist militia December 13, 1945. When he was told he would be shot, Levi admitted to being Jewish, which saved his life. He was taken to an internment camp at Fossoli, which was very nearly idyllic—for an interment camp. They were allowed to keep their money and even received money from the outside. They worked in the camp kitchen and even had a sparse dining room.

But Fossoli was taken over by the Nazis and deportations to the death camps began. In February, 1944, Levi was among inmates transported in cattle trucks, to Monowitz, one of the satellite camps of Auschwitz.

It was there he received the tattoo: 174517 and became a *häftling*.

Levi spent eleven month as a prisoner—until the Nazis abandoned the camps as the Russian Army approached. The camp was liberated January 18,1945.

Of 650 Italian Jews in that camp, Levi was one of 20 who survived.

The life expectancy of a new prisoner in that camp was three to four months.

Levi had survived—like countless others, he did what he had to do. With his prior experience in chemistry he got a "job" as assistant in the IG Farben's Buna works, which was tasked to produce a synthetic rubber for the Nazi war machine. His job kept him inside out of the freezing cold and that alone, probably saved his life. He stole materials from the laboratory and traded them for extra food.

Just prior to the Red Army's arrival, Levi got scarlet fever and was transferred to the camp's hospital. The SS forced all other inmates into a prolonged death march—Levi stayed behind and that also saved his life.

With the war over, Levi began a lengthy odyssey that took him, belatedly, to Italy, via Romania, Russia, Poland, Hungary, Austria. He wrote about this in *The Truce*, eventually published in 1963, almost 16 years after *If This Is a Man*.

When he returned to Italy, he was a shadow of his former self; he arrived in Turin wearing an old Red Army uniform. He moved to Milan, but was unable to find work there and returned to Turin and got a job with DUCO, a DuPont paint factory outside Turin. He stayed in a factory dormitory during the week which gave him opportunities for countless hours to write about his experiences; writing the manuscript took ten months.

He had met Lucia Morpurgo, in January, 1946; his manuscript, *If This Is a Man*, was completed in January, 1947 and she helped edit it, to make the narrative smoother, more cohesive.

He and she found a publisher, Franco Antonicelli; they were married September, 1947 and a month later *If This Is a Man* was published with a print run of 2,500 copies. Antonicelli was an amateur publisher and a anti-Fascist but then the publishing house closed. The book became neglected until 1958.

Eventually, 1,500 copies of the first edition were sold (the first edition suffered the same fate as John Steinbeck's first three books. They were published by three different publishing firms, all went bankrupt during the Depression. Pascal Covici found them, read them and thereafter published Steinbeck, successfully.)

In 1958, Einaudi, a major publishing firm released *If This Is a Man* in a revised form, and promoted it.

The first American edition, published in 1959, carried the title *Survival in Auschwitz*.

In November, 1976, in an Appendix to a school edition, Levi wrote:

> *If I hadn't had the experience of Auschwitz, I probably would not have written anything. I would have had no motivation, no incentive to write. I had been a mediocre student in Italian and poor in history; physics and chemistry interested me more, and then I chose a profession, chemist. It was the experience of the Lager that forced me to write. I didn't have to fight laziness, problems of style seemed to me ridiculous, I miraculously found time to write without ever missing an hour of my daily work. It seems to me I had this book ready in my head, that I only had to let it out, let it fall onto the paper.*

It was a long-belated epiphany:

> *It seems to me that I had this book ready in my head, that I had only to let it out, let it fall onto the paper.*

Regarding the style of the book, he also wrote, in the Appendix to the school edition of the book:

> *I thought that my word would be more credible and useful the more objective it appeared and the less impassioned it sounded; only in that way does the witness in court fulfill his function, which is to prepare the ground for the judge. It is you who are the judges.*

And, in the same Appendix, he attributed his writing style to his life-long career as a chemist-scientist:

> *My model was that of the weekly reports, a normal practice in factories; they must be concise, precise and written in a language accessible to all levels of the firm's hierarchy.*

Levi had become Technical Director at a paint firm named SIVA; he was able to travel and made several trips to Germany. He deliberately wore short-sleeved shirts which revealed his Lager tattoo. When he wrote *If This Is a Man*, he wanted Germans to face at least partial responsibility for what they had done.

"A thousand years will pass and the guilt of Germany will not be erased ..."

Who said that? Weisel? Levi?

It was Hans Frank, Nazi Governor-General of Poland, found guilty of crimes against humanity at the Nuremberg war crimes trials and executed by hanging, Oct 16, 1946, at 46. (Did he hope that statement would somehow mitigate his death sentence at Nuremberg?)

It could easily be said that Elie Weisel's *Night* and Primo Levi's *If This Is a Man* could be bookends on the same shelf; all the other titles about the Holocaust lie somewhere in between these two memoirs, now judged to be classics.

At 58, he retired from the part-time job he had held at the paint company, to devote full-time to his writing. He became a major literary figure in Italy—and elsewhere—and his books were widely translated. *The Truce* became a standard text in Italian schools; he made a 20-day speaking tour of the United States in 1985, but the trip was a major strain on him.

He suffered a major bout of depression in 1963; he had married, had children, had traveled widely, previously had a major position in his factory and the year as an inmate in Auschwitz was now nearly 20 years behind him ... *but ... but ...*

He could not blot out the trauma nor the experiences, the deaths of his acquaintances (no one could—or should—make friends in the deaths camps, as a friend one day would be gone the next day, usually without any warning, or any chance to say goodbye).

The sheer, unrelenting barbarity of the Nazis—the starvation, hangings, the deaths, the corpses ...

Levi was treated for depression at a time when the connection between trauma and depression was not well known.

* * *

It is now recognized as P.T.S.D.: Post Traumatic Stress Disorder, and it became acknowledged during and after the Vietnam war, as returning U.S. soldiers encountered it and were often mystified at what they were experiencing months or years after their own horrors in Vietnam.

P.T.S.D. has been characterized as having three main components:

- *By experiencing the trauma through intrusive recollections of the event, flashbacks and or nightmares;*
- *Emotional numbness and avoidance of places, people and activities that are reminders of the trauma;*
- *Difficulty sleeping, concentrating, feeling jumpy and / or being easily irritated or angered.*

And the event itself? P.T.S.D. can be triggered, initially, by:

- *Directly experiencing the traumatic event or events;*
- *Witnessing in person the dramatic events;*
- *Learning that the event occurred to a close family member or to a close friend. Causes of actual or threatened death must have been violent or accidental;*
- *Distorted blame of the self or others about the cause or consequences of the traumatic events;*
- *Experiencing repeated or extreme exposure to adverse details of the traumatic event. (These days this does not seem to generally apply to exposure through electronic media, television, movies or pictures.)*

Specialists may recognize these symptoms (and other symptoms) in those experiencing P.T.S.D.:

- *Feelings of detachment or estrangement from others.*
- *Persistent inability to experience positive emotions.*

* * *

As a most recent example, this essay by Adam Linehan appeared in the series "At War," in *The New York Times*, Nov. 15, 2019:

Dear Reader:

My friend Paul Critchlow fought in Vietnam, earning a Purple Heart and a Bronze Star with valor. Then he returned to Omaha, Neb., and nobody wanted to talk about it. So he did what many combat veterans did after the war. He kept his head down and drove on, built a career, raised a family, avoided anything that reminded him about Vietnam, compartmentalized the trauma, drank heavily and abused drugs. He did as his old coach once advised him after he broke his leg playing college football: "You've got to play above the pain, Critchlow." It was a productive approach.

He eventually landed on Wall Street and rose to become head of communications for Merrill Lynch. But then one morning in 1994, he woke up and couldn't get out of bed. As hard as he tried, he couldn't find the will to move. The doctors told him he had clinical depression. In Critchlow's mind, however, it was much more specific than that; a hill in the Central Highlands of Vietnam that the Army numbered 102. Many of his close comrades died there during the battle in which he was wounded. He blamed himself.

> There were fewer than 200 American soldiers on Hill 102 when it came under siege by the entire Second North Vietnamese Army Division on the afternoon of Aug. 19, 1969. Critchlow was a 23-year-old forward observer for Charlie Company, responsible for calling in airstrikes and artillery barrages. As the Vietnamese troops advanced farther up the hill, the grunts dug in along the perimeter, shouted over the radio to Critchlow for more and more bombs. The battle raged through the evening, and once it got dark, Critchlow lay on his back in a roofless French plantation house and used a strobe light to guide an AC-47 Spooky gunship to its targets. Just before midnight, a lone figure appeared in Critchlow's periphery. He was armed with a rocket-propelled grenade launcher, and Critchlow knew he was an NVA soldier by the shape of his helmet. The explosion lifted Critchlow off the ground, and suddenly he was immersed in brilliant white light, spinning slowly through the air, certain he was dead. Five hours later, he was tossed onto a helicopter packed with bodies, and bullets pierced the fuselage as the bird lifted of the ground. Critchlow begged God not to let him die after all he had just survived. He prayed to go home. But as soon as he got there, he wanted to turn back around. He felt as if he had abandoned his men. "By putting myself in harm's way, I left them behind," he recalled thinking after waking up in a hospital in Danang.

Critchlow met with a therapist but did not talk about Vietnam; he thought his problem was work-related. But he eventually visited the Vietnam Wall Memorial in Washington, D.C. and also eventually returned to Hill 102 in Vietnam. He ultimately regained his stability in life, but it must be said that he was surely never the same.

In part of the conclusion to his essay, Adam Linehan writes:

How does a person survive trauma and not be miserable?

Prime Levi died April 11,1987, in a fall from the interior landing of his third floor apartment to the ground below. His death *was* ruled a suicide. Three biographers: Carole Anger, *The Double Bond: Primo Levi, A Biography,* 2002; Ian Thompson, *Primo Levi,* 2002 and Myriam Anissimov, *Primo Levi: The Tragedy of an Optimist,* 1999, all agreed.

Others remained skeptical. He had left no suicide note, and had short-term and long-term plans for his future. Diego Gambetta, a sociologist at Oxford suggested that he may have simply lost his balance and fell, as he had complained to his doctor of dizziness shortly before his death. Rita Levi-Montalcini, a Nobel Prize winner suggested that, as an engineer, Levi could have chosen a better way to commit suicide, rather than plunging down to the floor and risking paralysis, but not death.

But he is gone.

Suggested readings:

In 2015, Liveright, a division of the W.W. Norton firm, published a handsome three-volume boxed set, *The Complete Works of Primo Levi.*

The first volume contains *If This Is a Man, The Truce; Natural Histories* and *Flaw of Form.*

The second volume contains *The Periodic Table, The Wrench, Uncollected Stories and Essays, 1949-1980, Lilith and Other Stories* and *If Not Now, When?*

The third volume contains *Collected Poems, Other People's Trades, Stories and Essays, The Drowned and The Saved* and *Uncollected Stories and Essays, 1981-1987.*

from If This is a Man

In less than ten minutes all the able-bodied men had been gathered in a group. What happened to the others, to the women, to the children, to the old people, we could not establish neither then nor later: the night swallowed them up, purely and simply. Today we know that in that rapid and summary choice each one of us had been judged capable or not of working usefully for the Reich; we know that of our company only ninety-six men and twenty-nine women entered the camps, respectively, in Monowitz-Buna and Birkenau, and that all the others, more than five hundred in number, not one was alive two days later. We also know that not even this tenuous principle of discrimination between fit and unfit was always followed, and that later the simpler method was often adopted of merely opening both doors of the car without warning or instructions to the new arrivals. Those who by chance got out on one side off the train entered the camps; the others went to the gas chamber.

This is the reason that three-year-old Emilia died: the historical necessity of killing the children of Jews was self-evident to the Germans. Emilia, the daughter of the engineer Aldo Levi of Milan, was a curious, ambitious, cheerful, intelligent child; during the journey in the packed car, her parents had succeeded in bathing her in a zinc tub with tepid water that the degenerate German engineer had allowed them to draw from the engine dragging us all to death.

Thus, suddenly, in an instant, our women, our parents, our children disappeared. Almost nobody was able to say goodbye. We saw them for a short while as a dark mass at the other end of the platform; then we saw nothing more.

McElligot's Pool
Theodor "Dr. Seuss" Geisel / 1947

and other Seussian delights ...

He spoke to me ... !

genre: children's literature

He is one of the four writers known world-wide for their pen-names:

- *Charles Lutwidge Dodgson—Lewis Carroll;*
- *Samuel Langhorne Clemens—Mark Twain;*
- *Eric Blair—George Orwell ... and ...*
- *Theodor Geisel—Dr. Seuss.*

His success in witting children's books was as improbable—and yet as inevitable—as anything in publishing.

He published over 60 children's books through the course of his. career. Many—almost all but a dozen—were published under the Dr. Seuss pseudonym; the others were published under the name Theo. LeSeig (LeSeig = Geisel spelled backwards) and one under the name Rosetta Stone.

His books have sold 222 million copies and have been translated into at least 15 languages.

In 2000, when *Publisher's Weekly* magazine compiled its list of the best selling children's books all-time, 16 of the top 100 hardcover books were Ted Geisel's Dr. Seuss books:

Green Eggs and Ham, # 4;
The Cat in the Hat, # 9;
One Fish Two Fish Red Fish Blue Fish #13.

The Cat in the Hat alone has sold 16,000,000 copies; profits from that title alone could financially fund (and financially sustain) a small—or medium sized—publishing company.

Oh! The Places You'll Go (1960), instantly became a high school and college-university graduation gift; it was based on a cynical phrase from his own college days decades before at Dartmouth.

Also late in his career he was dumbfounded and flabbergasted, gobsmacked, as the Brits say, when female children's literature experts informed him that there had never been a Dr. Seuss book featuring a little girl. He hadn't realized. *Daisy-Head Mayzie* was published—posthumously—in 1995, based on his notes.

> "He was ..." Time magazine wrote in a feature obituary after his death, "one of the best doctors to make house calls—some 200 million of them in 20 languages. By the time of his death last week at 87, Dr. Seuss had journeyed on beyond Dr. Spock to a unique and hallowed place in the nurseries of the world."

* * *

Theodor "Ted" Geisel (March 2,. 1904—September 24, 1991) was born in Springfield, Massachusetts which, at that time, seems idyllic—even quaint. There were family names like Wickersham, Terwilliger and McElliott, which he would later use in his books.

The Geisels (pronounced GUY-sell) were of German background and there was a large German community of about 1,000-1,200—in Springfield. There were three events in Ted Geisel's early life that would be memorable:

- *In 1907, when Ted was three, a sister, Marnie, named after his mother, died of pneumonia in their home. Geisel was haunted hearing the "terrible sounds of her cough." Her little coffin was displayed in their home. Later the family owned a "Pooley Cabinet"; a narrow New England-made cabinet in which his father kept Caruso records. Ted Geisel was haunted by the similarity of the Pooley cabinet to the small coffin which held his sister. His only action to her death: a stoic silence.*
- *In 1914, America entered the Great War—World War One—as German-Americans, the Geisel family faced considerable hostility. Sauerkraut was renamed "victory cabbage," frankfurters became hot dogs. The Geisels were suspect in their own community They spoke German at home, ate bratwurst and drank beer. Ted Geisel often wondered why they were suddenly the other ... (the same happened to the family of Kurt Vonnegut.)*
- *Worse, Geisel's grandfather—also know as Theodor Geisel—along with a partner, Christian Kalmbach, had begun a brewery, Kalmbach and Geisel, which everyone called Come back and guzzle. Eventually it became one of the largest breweries in New England. It grew and merged and became Liberty Breweries—with, at one time, 25 matching horses to pull black and gold brewery wagons through the streets, but Prohibition began in 1920 (and ended in 1933) and that put Come back and guzzle out of business. (The same also happened to the relatives of Kurt Vonnegut.)*

Geisel's father, who had been with the brewery, joined the Springfield Park Board, which included the Springfield Zoo.

Ted Geisel ...

> *... took a pencil and pad to the Zoo and began to draw the animals that he saw. But his animals were awkward, misshapen and, well, tended toward the bizarre. Any normal parent inspecting the drawings of a precocious child might reasonably expect that the drawings would become more accurate and realistic over time and the experiences and the age of the child. Ted Geisel's animals remained awkward, misshapen and bizarre. Over the years, he sharpened his skills at making them awkward, misshapen and bizarre.*

This became an accident of great fortune, although Ted Geisel may have been too young to clearly understand it at the time. (Much like Dave Margoshes' discovery of the art and craft of writing at 13.)

One of Geisel's first and sustaining memories was playing with lion cubs ... and he could hear, from his bedroom window, the night sounds of the animals at the Zoo.

Years later he could remember the rainbow colors of the Victorian homes in Springfield, and the sounds and the smells of the Zoo animals.

He was also fascinated by the comics—his father brought a newspaper home every night. And Ted was influenced by "Crazy Kat," and other comic strips of the time.

He had taken an art class in Springfield's Central High School in the fall of 1917. He later explained what happened:

> *Our model that day was a milk bottle containing a few scraggly late autumn daisies. I was having a had time trying to capture the beauty of this setup and immortalize it with a hunk of charcoal and a sheet of paper. To add to my frustration, my teacher kept fluttering about and giving me hell for turning my drawing board around and working on my picture upside down. "No Theodor," she*

said, "Not upside down. There are rules that every artist must abide by. You will never succeed if you break them."

Geisel transferred out of that class.
We can almost hear it later in a typical Dr. Seuss rhyme:

*No Theodor, No Theodor,
Not upside down, not upside down.
Not even once, not evermore ...
This I implore, not evermore ...*

Geisel was doing as other youngsters always do—he was creating a world with no rules. Why shouldn't you, *why shouldn't you draw upside down?* He was also drawing from the right side of his brain (the creative side) and making perfect sense while doing so. And when his acknowledged to himself that he would take no more art-by-the-books classes, he permanently freed himself from any more *not upside down* rules. (The same incident also happened to James Thurber, later much known for his dog drawings.)

After graduating from high school, Geisel decided to attend Dartmouth, because a favorite teacher had gone there. The tuition in the fall of 1921: $250. annually. He had no special interest in fraternities, but was surprised when no fraternity pledged him. He discovered why: with a sharp nose and black hair, the fraternities thought him Jewish. He turned to the campus humor magazine, the *Jack-o-Lantern*, which staffers called the *Jacko*. He was a natural.

And, in the words of a college friend, Frederick "Pete" Blodgett:

He never had any money but he never spent much. He was always raising hell and laughing a lot and didn't study worth a damn.

It was popular—and cynical—for the Dartmouth students to exclaim: "Oh! The places you'll go. The people you'll meet!"

Over six decades later, in 1990, Dr. Seuss published *Oh! The Places You'll Go!* which quickly became favorite high school and college graduation gifts.

In his senior year, he was elected to Casque and Gauntlet, the Dartmouth senior honorary society. One member, Kenneth Montgomery, remember Geisel:

> *He was not gregarious in the sense of hail-fellow-well-met, there was no sense of self-importance about him. But when he walked into a room it was like magician's act. Birds flew out off his hands and endless bright scarves and fireworks. Everything became brighter, happier, funnier. And he didn't try. Everything Ted did seem to be a surprise, even to him.*

But Casque and Gauntlet voted him "least likely to succeed."

In April, 1925, he was caught with some bootleg liquor. The Dartmouth dean demanded that he write his parents telling them that he was on probation. He was also forbidden to contribute to the *Jack-o-Lantern*, but not banned from their offices. So he continued to contribute to the magazine, using a variety of pen names including Sing Sing, the name of the New York State penitentiary—and he also used Seuss.

Seuss was his mother's maiden name and his middle name. Since it was German, it should have been produced *Zoice*, but non-German speakers wouldn't know that, so *Zoice* quickly—and universally—was pronounced *Seuss*. Later he added Dr. because his father wanted him to either complete a doctorate or practice medicine.

When he was due to graduate from Dartmouth, he had no plans—no career, no job in sight. Back home, his father asked him what his plans were—what he was going to do. Geisel impulsively said that he was going to win a scholarship from Dartmouth to go to Oxford. Oxford. In England. *That* Oxford. But it wasn't true. He had applied for the scholarship, but didn't get it.

Before he could explain all that to his father, his father told the editor of the *Springfield Union* newspaper, who happened to live across the street from the Geisels. Ted Geisel remember it was on the front page:

GEISEL WINS SCHOLARSHIP TO GO TO OXFORD

When he finally told his father that he hadn't won the scholarship, he was met with cold silence; the silence was overwhelming. His father finally said that if Ted announced he would go to Oxford, he would go—friends and family would eventually forget the scholarship.

And so he went.

He majored there, in English, and writing, but later ruefully said:

English and writing was my major, but I think that's a mistake for anybody. That's teaching you the mechanics of getting water out of a well that may not exist.

True advise, ignored by thousands of English majors everywhere.

Again, he was the outsider; he was a Yank in a British university and he was of German extraction in a country which had not yet forgotten World War One.

He found Oxford life trivial, tedious or bizarre. And pompous. Very pompous. It had centuries of pomposity to live up to. Geisel was alternatively bemused or leery of it all. He attended lectures on Geoffrey Chaucer, who he called Jeff and doodled in the margins of his notebooks. Supremely bored by it all.

Then he met Helen Marion Palmer, who had graduated from Wellesley and had taught English for three years in Brooklyn before coming to Oxford.

Their first encounter: Geisel had—in his own way—illustrated great chucks of *Paradise Lost*:

With the imagery of Paradise Lost, Milton's sense of humor failed him in a couple of places. I remember one line, "Thither came the angel Uriel, sliding down a sunbeam."

I illustrated that: Uriel had a long locomotive oil can and was greasing the sunbeam as he descended, to lessen the friction on his coccyx.

"You're crazy to be a professor," Helen said, after a class. "What you really want to do is draw," and said, looking at his sketchbook, "that's a very fine flying cow."

She had picked him up.

Any woman who could appreciate Uriel and his oil can, and a flying cow and a drooling cow with a sagging udder, a Chaplinesque clown, dogs walking on high wires, a chicken with a windmill for a tail—that woman was for him.

He quickly fell in love with her and she, just as quickly, fell in love with him.

He was at the verge of giving up on Oxford. He and Helen spent some time in Europe—touring Switzerland, Munich, Nuremberg, Dresden and Berlin. In the village of Kleinschwarzenbach, they hosted a party for Seuss family members and 67 people attended.

He returned to Oxford and gave it one more try. It was useless. He returned to the United States in February, 1927. Once again he had no job, no prospects for a job, no talent for a job. And no degree from Oxford. He retreated to his father's desk and again drew the odd, misshapen, bizarre animals he had drawn before. They weren't frightening, just odd.

He journeyed to New York City, and later said:

I have trampled all over this bloody town and been tossed out of Boni and Liveright (publishing house), Harcourt Brace, Paramount Pictures, three advertising agencies, Life, Judge, (magazine) and three public conveniences ...

Finally one day he got an envelope from *The Saturday Evening Post*. He had submitted a cartoon of two American tourists riding camels and comparing themselves to Lawrence of Arabia. *The Post* bought it for $25. He had signed it Seuss.

On that thin blade of Seuss success, he moved to New York and got as job at the humor magazine *Judge*, for $75 a week. (On that salary he and Helen could get married. And they did, November 29, 1927.)

Shortly later he added *Dr.* to his pseudonym, because, he said, it made up for the doctoral degree he never got at Oxford, and, he also said, he wanted to us his own name for the Great American Novel he wanted to write. It was a dream; he never wrote that novel and never used his own name in print.

He always claimed that serendipity played a large part in his career. *Judge* was faltering as a magazine, but a financial windfall soon occurred. He said, later ...

> I'd been working for Judge about four months when I drew this accidental cartoon which changed my whole life. It was an insect gag.
>
> It was a picture of a knight who had gone to bed. He had stacked his armor beside the bed. Here was this covered canopy over the bed, and a tremendous dragon was sort of nuzzling him.
>
> He looked up and said, "Darn it all, Another dragon. And just when I sprayed the whole castle with ..."
>
> With what? I wondered.
>
> There were two well-known insecticides, One was Flit and another was Fly-Tox. So I flipped a coin. It came up Flit.
>
> So the caption read "... another dragon. And just when I sprayed the whole castle with Flit."
>
> Here's where luck comes in.
>
> Very few people read Judge. It was continually in bankruptcy—and everyone else was bankrupt too.

But one day the wife of Lincoln L. Cleaves, who was the account executive at the McCann-Erickson advertising agency failed to get an appointment at her favorite hairdresser's and went to a second-rate hairdresser's, where they had second-rate magazines.

She opened Judge while waiting to get her hair done and she found this picture. She ripped it out of the magazine, put it in her reticule, took it home, bearded her husband with it and said "Lincoln, you've got to hire this young man. It's the best Flit ad I've ever seen."

He said "Go away." He said, "You're my wife and you're to have nothing to do with my business."

So she pestered him for about two weeks and finally he said, "all right. I'll have him in and buy one picture."

He had me in. I drew one picture which I captioned "Quick Henry, the Flit!"—and it was published.

Then they hired me to do two more—and 17 years later I was still doing them.

The only good thing Adolf Hitler did in starting World War Two was a that he enabled me to join the Army and finally stop drawing "Quick Henry, The Flit!"

I had drawn them by the millions—newspaper ads, magazine ads, booklets, window displays, 24-sheet posters, even "Quick Henry, the Flit!" animated cartoons. Flit was pouring out of my ears and beginning to itch me.

Flit sales grew rapidly. A song was written about it. The only comparable campaign was the four-panel Burma Shave highway signs.

Geisel simply sailed financially through the Depression.

And his contract allowed him considerable freedom—all he had to do was submit his Flit material on time—otherwise, he could do 'most anything else, except, of course, Fly-Tox material.

He could, and did, complete a year's worth of Flit material in three months, leaving him the rest of the year free.

Readers of Dr. Seuss books may wonder about the fantastical creatures and the even more fantastical locales Geisel drew. He remembered the animals at the Springfield Zoo—and how he had drawn them misshapen, and, well, bizarre.

And the locales? He and Helen toured Greece during the spring of 1938 and toured elsewhere—for their first anniversary they traveled to La Jolla, a suburb of San Diego. Everything was fresh, new, clean, inviting. Flowers and plants in profusion everywhere. Views of the Pacific and California and Mexico. La Jolla had a Mediterranean / Spanish look. They were enchanted and vowed to return.

They later toured Peru.

Oh! The Places You'll Go!

In fact, Ted and Helen were world travelers. After nine years of marriage, they had visited 38 countries. *The Lorax* (1971) his *paean* to the environment, was conceived and developed during a visit to Kenya (with his second wife Audrey).

A collection of schoolboy gaffes was published, in England under the title *Schoolboy Howlers*. The Viking Press bought the United States publication rights and re-titled the book *Boners*. Geisel was hired to illustrate it—and a sequel, *More Boners*, this time American schoolroom mistakes, sent in to the Viking Press by U.S. teachers. Both were published in 1931. The illustrated work on these titles gave Geisel an epiphany:

> *That was a big Depression year. And although by Depression standards I was adequately paid a flat fee for illustrating these best sellers, I was money-worried. The two books were booming and I was not.*
>
> *This is the point when I first began to realize that if I hoped to succeed in the book world, I'd have to write as well as draw.*

He was encouraged by a review win the *American News:*

offhand ... we should have said this would be a flop. But the inimitable illustrations of the renowned Dr. Seuss of Judge, Life and Flit fame, are not unlikely to put this over. They are simply swell.

With that encouragement, he wrote and illustrated a children's ABC book, full of Seussian animals with seventeen colors of blue and three colors of red. He took it to publishers Bobbs Merrill, Viking Press and Simon and Schuster and others ...

... where it was promptly rejected. He abandoned it.

But many others—*many others*—had seen his Flit illustrations/ cartoons, over the years.

Flit beta Esso.

The Esso gasoline people hired him, and later Schaeffer Bock Beer, Ford, Atlas Products, New Departure Bearings, NBC Radio, and Holly Sugar all hired him. None ever asked that Seussian drawings ever be changed. None ever carried the byline Seuss; they didn't need to.

Serendipity again played a major part in his life.

In the summer of 1936, The Geisels sailed for Europe aboard the M.S. Kungsholm. They visited the Alps. Geisel saw intrepid Alp animals clinging to sheer Alp mountain outcroppings. They traveled to Germany and saw the chill of the coming Nazi tide. Geisel was then 32 years old and the storm clouds of European politics left him saddened.

They returned on the same ship—the Kungsholm.

And Geisel found himself caught in the drone of the ship's engine.

Da-Da-DA. Da-Da-DUM. Dum-De-Da. De-De-Da.

There was slight variations but the rhythm stayed in his head.

He was on the ship for eight days on the way back. Eight days of listening to the SAME engine rhythm.

> *The drone of the ship's engine became the driving energy of Dr. Seuss's career. It was as simple as that.*

Da-Da-Da. Da-Da-Dum. Dum-De-Da. De-De-Da. Geisel may not have known what he was hearing, but the rhythm was hypnotic. Once captured by it, he was hooked. The rhythm didn't leave his head.

He didn't know what he was hearing, but there was a name for it. He might have heard the name at Dartmouth, or Oxford; if he did, he probably forgot it.

He was hearing the rhythm of:

> *'Twas the night before Christmas ...*

... or ...

> *He flies through the air with the greatest of ease ...*

He was hearing anapestic tetrameter (or something close to it), which dates back as far as the ancient Greeks, who used it as a marching beat. And so he had the rhythm; now he needed text to match.

As he later recalled:

> *I was on a long stormy crossing of the Atlantic and it was too rough to go on deck. Everybody in the ship just sat the bar for a week, listening to the engines turn over; da-da-ta, da-da-ta-ta, da-da-ta-ta ...*
>
> *To keep from going nuts, I began reciting silly words to the rhythm of the engines. Out of nowhere I found myself saying, "And this is a story no one can beat; and to think that I saw it on Mulberry Street."*
>
> *And when I finally got off the ship, the refrain kept going through my head. I couldn't shake it. To therapeutize myself I added more words to it.*

Mulberry Street, was, of course, in his home town of Springfield.

Marrying text and rhythm and illustrations was not easy—what he perhaps knew instinctively, but did not or could not verbalize was: *the rhythm dictated the story and the rhythm galloped.*

And without knowing quite why, he may have guessed it was a perfect rhythm for a children's book.

And, as asides to the reader: all book text begins on a right side page; page 1, as in this book. Pages 2 and 3 are facing or double pages, 4 and 5 are double pages, and so on. In regular textual material, there is a a white "gutter" between pages. Geisel drew illustrations which were one picture for the facing or double pages—there was no separation between pages 2 and 3, pages 4 and 5, and on … more importantly, again, probably instinctively, he added two important concepts:

- *the action always moves to the right, to keep readers turning the pages;*
- *characters and situations grow more and more fantastical, stranger and stranger, page after page until the action ends, as "the balloon breaks," on the end page, leaving young readers to think or say wow! or whew!*

And to Think that I Saw It on Mulberry Street (1937);
McElliot's Pool (1947);
If I Ran the Zoo (1950) and
If I Ran the Circus (1956)

… all employ these techniques, as do many of the later Dr. Seuss books. When he did not use the anapestic tetrameter rhythm, his books were not quite as successful.

The rhythm gallops. Children can read it, Sing it, SHOUT IT! They can dance to it.

As one young reader once said, "he has an imagination with a long tail." Geisel replied, "that kid will go far."

Additionally, on the copyright page which is always "behind" the main title page (on a left page), there is a set of numbers, usually at, or toward, the bottom of the page:

12345678

If the number 1 is on the list, the book is part of the first printing; when the printing is exhausted and the book goes back to press, the 1 is deleted and the line becomes:

2345678

Or sometimes backward:

98765432

There is no indication of how many copies were printed in the first (and subsequent) printings; some books have an average of 3,000 copies per printing.

Many—most of—Dr. Seuss books have gone on and on and on. My copy of *McElligot's Pool shows:*

60 59 58 57

And my copy of *The Cat in the Hat* shows:

104 103 102 101 99

… which means there have been thousands and thousands, hundreds of thousands of copies of those books printed and sold.

It took Geisel six months before he was pleased with his book. And here the story turns into legend. He took it to children's book publishers in New York City, one, two, three publishers turned it down, four, five six. The rhyme scheme was too unusual, the drawings and characters far, far too unusual.

More and more rejections: *No. No. No.*

Finally, after 27 *rejections* (although Dr. Seuss, with a twinkle in his eye, changed the number from time to time), he decided to give up.

He was on a New York sidewalk one day, with his manuscript under his arm, when he chanced to meet Marshall McClintock, who had been at Dartmouth a year behind Geisel.

The conversation, went more or less, like this:
"Ted, how are you? And what have you got?"
"A book manuscript."

Twenty-seven rejections ...

Part of his text was:

... and this is a story no one can beat ...

... which became true.

McClintock had just been named editor at The Vanguard Press and they were standing outside its offices. McClintock invited Geisel into their offices, and he was introduced to James Henle, President of The Vanguard Press and Evelyn Shrifte, staff editor.

Later that same day he had a book contract.

Geisel's life was full of *ifs*:

- *If the wife of the MCann-Erickson ad executive hadn't seen his Judge magazine work he wouldn't have had years of work for Flit;*
- *If Geisel had taken a another ship to Europe and back he wouldn't have heard the anapestic tetrameter engine sounds which became his hallmark rhythm;*
- *If he had been five minute earlier on the street or five minutes later he would have missed Marshall McClintock and missed his chance at The Vanguard Press.*

Vanguard Press published *And To Think That I Saw It on Mulberry Street*. Reviews were exceptional:

> *They say it's for children, but better get a copy for yourself and marvel at the good Dr. Seuss's improbable pictures and the moral tale of the little boy who exaggerated not wisely but too well.*—The New Yorker.
>
> *Highly original and entertaining. Dr. Seuss's picture book partakes of the better qualities of those particularly American institutions, the funny papers and the tall tale. It is a masterly interpretation of the mind of a child in the art of creating one of those stories with which children often amuse themselves and bolster-up their self-respect—* The New York Times.

The New York Times review hits on a key to Dr. Seuss's success; *there are never any adults shown in the Dr. Seuss books.*

> *They are all the secret worlds of children;*
> *Their imaginations at play.*

How is it that Geisel, as Dr. Seuss, could remain "true to the imagination of a small boy?" Helen Palmer Geisel, from the perspective of a loving spouse, later said, "his mind has never grown up."

Ted Geisel published two books with The Vanguard Press: *And To Think That I Saw It on Mulberry Street* (1937) and *The 500 Hats of Bartholomew Cubbins* (1938). For that book he put aside the anapestic tetrameter he had discovered and used regular text.

Oh! The People You'll Meet!

Then Bennett Cerf entered his life.

Cerf, a native New Yorker, graduated from Columbia University and initially wanted to be a stockbroker. That career was not for him—he quickly realized. He then joined the publishing firm of Boni and Liveright, run by Horace Liveright. Part of the Boni and Liveright publishing lists was the Modern Library. Liveright was a speculator; the profits he made with the publishing company he lost financing Broadway plays. He seemed to always need additional capital for Boni and Liveright. Cerf bought into the firm for $25,000; he eventually contributed another $25,000, to keep the publishing house (as they are called) in business. Two years later, Cerf offered to buy The Modern Library. Liveright sold it to Cerf for $200,000, plus an additional $15,000 "adviser fee," which Liveright tacked on at the last moment.

Donald Klopfer joined Cerf, with an investment of $100,000. Two years after acquiring The Modern Library, they had recovered all their investment, including Liveright's "adviser fee."

A *colophon* is a publishing house's signature icon; a symbol that is usually used on the lower spine of a book, on the lower dust jacket for hardcover editions, sometimes on the main title page and in advertising and promotion.

Notable colophons are: a Viking ship for The Viking Press; a bantam rooster for Bantam books; a penguin for Penguin Books; a Borzoi dog for the Alfred Knopf firm (traditionally the most regal of all American firms); a castle for the Henry Regnery firm; a kangaroo for Pocket Books; and owl for the Henry Holt firm and there are others.

In his memoir, *At Random*, Cerf writes:

> *Rockwell Kent had become a good friend of ours after he did the end papers for the Modern Library. I would say he was at that time the leading commercial artist in America. One day Rockwell dropped in at our office. He was sitting at my desk facing Donald and we were talking about doing a few books on the side, when suddenly I got an inspiration and said, "I've got the name of our publishing house. We just said we were going to publish a few books on the side at random. Let's call it Random House."*

> *Donald liked it, and Rockwell Kent, said, "That's a great name. I'll draw your trademark." So sitting at my desk he took out a piece of paper and in a few minutes drew Random House, which has been our colophon ever since.*

Now with The Modern Library and their newly-minted colophon, which appeared in many variations over the years, Random House grew. Cerf brought in authors Eugene O'Neill and Robinson Jeffers, Marcel Proust, Gertrude Stein, W.H. Auden, Stephen Spender, Havelock Ellis, George Bernard Shaw, William Saroyan, Budd Schulberg ... and others.

Cerf bought the financially-struggling firm of Smith and Haas, and got its authors, including William Faulkner, Andre Malraux and Robert Graves.

And then Cerf entered Ted Geisel's life. At the urging of Cerf's wife Phyllis, he began a children book division; the author he most wanted was Geisel. But Geisel was legally obligated to The Vanguard Press, so Cerf did the easiest thing: Random House bought The Vanguard Press to bring Geisel to Random House.

Cerf didn't know what Geisel wanted to publish next and perhaps didn't care. Geisel's next project was not a success but first editions are now highly prized by Seuss collectors.

It was *The Seven Lady Godivas*; a retelling of the Lady Godiva fable, with not one but seven naked Godivas. But Geisel's naked ladies were as lumpy and malformed as all other Seuss creatures— in short, naked, but not one iota erotic. Adults weren't interested and librarians didn't want naked ladies in any form, in the *kiddie lit* shelves of their libraries.

Although it was the lowest point in Geisel's career, neither Cerf nor Geisel were discouraged.

Random Hours would be Geisel's publishing home for the rest of his career and bringing Geisel to Random House was eventually a huge coup for Cerf professionally and financially.

Bennett Cerf's gamble on Dr. Seuss would pay off, quite literally for decades.

Another aside for readers: books that stay in print more than one year are called "backlist" books; when they are first published, they appear in the front of publisher's catalogs, traditionally issued twice a year. As new seasons and new titles appear, the formerly new titles are pushed toward the back of the catalogs. Books that stay in print for more than one year are eventual goldmines for publishers as all the expenses associated with editing and printing the books are factored into the first year's sales.

Sales and profits from backlist books help pay for new titles. Publishers can't survive on books that have only limited, one-year sales.

(Books with year dates in the title are suspect—how many people buy a ten-year old *Farmer's Almanac*?)

Think of classic authors; Hemingway, Faulkner, others ...

John Steinbeck's *The Grapes of Wrath* was first published by The Viking Press in 1939 and stills sells in the millions of dollars each year; estimated six to ten million in sales per year, with very little effort by The Viking Press, except making sure there are copies in the warehouse to ship out and occasionally changing the hardcover dust jacket.

The second book for Cerf and Random House was *The King's Stilts*, and it also was in prose, not rhyme. While *The Seven Lady Godivas* was Ted Geisel's nadir, in sales, *The King's Stilts* was a close second. It sold 4,648 copies during the first year of publication, but only 394 copies the second year. Bennett Cerf must have thought, to himself, *Random House bought Vanguard Press to bring Ted Geisel to our new children's lit department, but his first two titles have been disasters ... was this all a huge mistake?*

But he was the very soul of tact to Geisel—waiting and hoping for better ...

Geisel was taking a break from work one day when a slight

breeze from an open window blew a drawing of an elephant across a drawing of a tree.

What would an elephant be doing in a tree? he thought. Hatching an egg, of oourse.

That led to feverish long-term work.

And To Think That I Saw il on Mulberry Street taught children that their imaginations were as real as Marco's—the little hero—and occasionally they should—or must—shield their imaginations from adults.

And so Dr. Seuss eventually finished *Horton Hatches the Egg.* It was in his galloping anapestic tetrameter; it had a hero, Horton, which children could identify with and he had made a promise (*He meant what he said and he said what he meant...*), but had trouble keeping it. It was in the first-person I form and children could *chant* it: *I said what I meant and I meant what I said ....*and they well understood: *if you make a promise you must keep it.*

The New York Times reviewed it thus:

> *A moral is a new thing to find in a Dr. Seuss book, but it doesn't interfere with the hilarity with which he juggles an elephant up a tree. To an adult the tale seems a little less inevitable in its nonsense, but neither young nor old are going quibble with the fantastic comedy of his pictures.*

Bennett Cerf and editors at Random House loved it. Back in La Jolla, Ted Geisel found an abandoned Army observation post at the highest point in La Jolla—long time residents assumed it was not for sale; Geisel bought it. He asked Cerf for an advance on his royalties of $500 which Cerf promptly sent. The purchase price in 1940 dollars—$8,000. (Imagine what a mountaintop La Jolla home with a view of the Pacific and Mexico would bring today?)

The La Jolla purchase was his permanent home; he seldom left it—and why should he? With commanding views of California and the Pacific and San Diego below, and Mexico ...

Then the coming war interrupted Dr. Seuss.

A drawing he had done was passed along by a friend to Ralph Ingersoll, who had left the staff of *The New Yorker* to start a very liberal newspaper, *PM,* for New York City. The very idea amused Dr. Seuss; *PM took no advertising,* which made it a sister to *Judge,* which *got no advertising.*

Dr. Seuss contributed editorial illustrations or cartoons—he called Charles Lindbergh "one of our nation's most irritating heroes," and he was a very early critic of Hitler.

His cartoons were acidic—very acidic. Australia was shown as a kangaroo with its tail being eaten by the Japanese and Nazis were depicted as dachshunds, at least until American dachshund owners protested.

His World War Two cartoons for *PM* have been published in book form: *Dr. Seuss Goes to War: The World War II Editorial Cartoons of Theodor Seuss Geisel* (New York: The New Press, 1999).

And what of *PM,* Ingersoll's experiment in ultra-liberal, advertising-free journalism? It lasted from June, 1940, to June, 1948, but during those years, besides Geisel, contributors included: Haywood Hale Broun; Dorothy Parker; Ernest Hemingway; James Thurber; Malcolm Cowley; Tip O'Neil (later Speaker of the U.S. House of Representatives); and Ben Hecht. Liberals all.

Geisel was subsequently inducted into the U.S. Army as a Captain and assigned to the Information and Entertainment Division, in Hollywood.

There he joined director Frank Capra *(It Happened One Night, Mr. Smith Goes to Washington; It's a Wonderful Life);* composer Meredith Willson *(The Music Man),* novelist Irving Wallace, animators Chuck Jones *(Bugs Bunny)* Friz Freleng and a gaggle of others.

Geisel worked on a team to produce training films.

> ... to teach G.I.s cleanliness, avoidance of VD and other military matters. Geisel and company learned if they showed average spokesmen in the films, recruits wouldn't listen; if they used Hollywood actors, the G.I.s jeered at the screen. They would pay attention to cartoons, so Geisel and his crew created Private Snafu to explain things.
> Snafu was, of course, Army slang for Situation Normal All F****d Up. They changed SNAFU to Situation Normal All Fouled Up. The G.I.s still loved it.

When World War Two ended and Geisel was free from the distractions of Private Snafu and such, he returned to his Dr. Seuss books. It became a near-annual event when he traveled from la Jolla to New York to hand-deliver a Seuss manuscript to the New York offices of Random House, and, like others whose experiences shape their craft, he simply got better and better. His most critical and financial successes came after World War Two.

* * *

Why does this analysis of Dr. Seuss begin with *McElligot's Pool*, as a title, instead of *The Cat in the Hat,* his perennially best-selling title or perhaps *Green Eggs and Ham* ?

It was his first title after the war. With it, he returned mentally and psychologically to his home town of Springfield and *To Think That I Saw It on Mulberry Street*, for his next book. There are striking similarities between *Mulberry Street* and *McElligot's Pool*.

McElligot's Pool contains the same *escalating sequences* or *escalating action* that Geisel used in *Mulberry Street,* and the same hero, the boy Marco.

He is told by a farmer:

> *"Young man,"* laughed the farmer,
> *"you're sort of a fool!*
> *You'll never catch fish in McElligot's Pool!"*

And, he says,

> *"When people have junk Here's the place that they throw it.*
> *You might catch a boot Or you might catch a can.*
> *You might catch a bottle,*
> *But listen young man*
> *If your sat fifty years*
> *With your worms and your wishes,*
> *You'll grow a long beard Long before you catch fishes."*

This is the first Ted Geisel—Dr. Seuss book that used paintings, instead of pen and ink drawings. And Geisel often uses the double pages 2 and 3, 4 and 5, as one spread for his art.

But young Marco imagines that ...

> *"This pool might be bigger Than you and I know."*

... and, he says ...

> *"This MIGHT be a pool, like I've read of in books,*
> *Connected to one of those underground brooks!*

And he imagines a natural underground aqueduct, flowing right under State Highway Two-Hundred-and-Three! and under the villages and on and on ... to the sea, where fantastical Seussian sea creatures would swim up from the sea into McElligot's Pool, and to Marco's hook. (Note—the worm is carefully only looped around the hook, not impaled.)

There are morals in many of Dr. Seuss books—in *McElligot's Pooh,* young (and older) readers learn: don't believe, or trust others, (maybe especially don't trust adults); trust your own judgment; be patient, things could happen ... and finally, *there is a unity to all nature*—McElligot's Pool is connected to the sea.

So why again, is *McElligot's Pool,* from 1947, featured in the title of this Seussian analysis, rather than *The Cat in the Hat* or *Green Eggs and Ham*—or others in the Seussian canon?

Dr. Seuss spoke to me, in that book.

McElligot's Pool was the first Dr. Seuss book I remember reading, going on five. I came from a family of educators; my father, mother and an aunt, were all educators. I largely taught myself to read before grade school, usually sitting on the carpet surrounded by books.

I remember to this day following the pictures of the underground aqueduct winding its way to the sea, thinking then: *it could happen just like that.*

We lived about 60 miles south of Lake Erie and we occasionally took day trips to the lake, on weekends. Some time after reading *McElligot's Pool,* I was taken by my parents from our home in north central Ohio, to The Blue Hole, a private park, for family picnics and group events, which I remember as being 35-40 miles from Lake Erie. I checked an Ohio map recently—in a straight line, The Blue Hole outside of Castalia, Ohio, is about 8-10 miles south of Lake Erie. I remember it as a crystal blue aquamarine spring. I couldn't see any fish. While we there there, a guide told us, "We don't know how, but we believe the The Blue Hole is connected underground to Lake Erie."

Just like Dr. Seuss said!

I remember thinking.

McElligot's Pool was connected to the ocean; The Blue Hole was connected to Lake Erie.

Augmented by my childhood visit to The Blue Hole, my memory of reading *McElligot's Pool* for the first time never faded. And that's duplicated, I am sure, by the millions of children who read Dr. Seuss books for the first time and think:

It could happen just like that! Just like Dr. Seuss said!

And I still have my childhood copy of *McElligot's Pool.*

* * *

After *McElligot's Pool,* came:

1948: *Thidwick, the Big-Hearted Moose*
1949: *Barththolomew and the Oobleck*
1950: *If I Ran the Zoo*
1953: *Scrambled Eggs Super!*
1954: *Horton Hears a Who!*

In 1954, Geisel learned that his alma mater, Dartmouth, planned to grant him an honorary degree.

But the same year his wife Helen felt pain in her feet and ankles. Two days later she checked into the Scripps Metabolic Clinic; she had numbness in her arms, hands and face and she could not swallow. She had Guillian-Barre Syndrome and was placed in an iron lung. She was unable to sit up without help.

Throughout his life, Ted Geisel has coasted along; he had a successful career and lived on a mountaintop. Except for his sister's death in Springfield, tragedy had never struck him. But this was *serious.*

Helen was moved to a rehabilitation center for extensive treatment. Geisel was left alone—everything she had done he now had to do alone—he had never balanced his checkbook or even made a pot of coffee.

A year after he heard about his Dartmouth honor, he bought an academic gown at a San Diego second-hand store, trekked to Dartmouth and received his honorary degree. (Along with Robert Frost), thus making Dr. Seuss legitimate. It should be *Dr. Dr Seuss,* he said. Helen was, by then, well enough to travel with him to Dartmouth.

He then began *If I Ran the Circus*, patterned after *If I Ran the Zoo*. He had been asked by William Spaulding, publisher of the firm Houghton Mifflin to write a children's book with no more than 225 words—but there was a problem—Geisel was legally bound to Random House. Spaulding would somehow have to work with Bennett Cerf and Random House to get Geisel. The resolution was ingenious: Geisel's book would be split fifty-fifty. Houghton Mifflin could have educational rights—legal rights to sell copies to schools and such and Random House would have "trade rights," rights to sell the book in bookstores and other non-educational outlets. To the "book trade," as it was, and still is, called.

With *If I Ran the Circus* completed, Geisel began the new book. It was very nearly impossible. Houghton Mifflin wanted a book better than any children's book ever published.

Impossible for Dr. Seuss and impossible even for Ted Geisel.

It took him a full year. He examined every word, every possible combination of the 225 words in the word list. He though he had a combination with Queen and Zebra, but discovered they weren't on the list.

He finally found what he was looking for:

> *I read the (word) list forty times and got more and more discouraged. It was like trying to make strudel without the strudel. I was desperate so I decided to read it once more. The first words that rhymed would be the title of my book and I'd go from there. I found "cat" and I found "hat." That's genius you see!*

Genius indeed. But wasn't it Thomas Edison who once said, "genius is one percent inspiration and 99 percent perspiration"?

Geisel slaved at that book—which changed children's literature forever. He worked and he thought and he thought and he worked—the Cat began to take over the story—a Cat wearing a red and white striped top hat. And a bow tie—tied with three loops, not two. And white gloves like early Mickey Mouse cartoons.

It didn't quite have his usual anapestic tetrameter, but the rhyme carried the story. In some of the Dr. Seuss books, the story begins with a daydream—*And To Think That I Saw it on Mulberry Street,* as an example—but in this book The Cat simply appears.

The Cat is a trickster figure, a technique as old as storytelling itself, as in the Kokopelli trickster figure of the American southwest. The Cat is magical and does not think logically—it appeals to the rebellious nature of all children.

But the Cat's wild nature is balanced by the two children—who are worried about what will happen and what their parents will say. Indeed, it's every child's nightmare that their house will somehow be demolished and their Mother will appear at the front door at just the wrong moment.

The Cat does demolish the house—pandemonium everywhere. Everything a mess. The children look on helplessly. The Cat brings out two creatures—Thing I and Thing 2—the Cat assures the children that they are harmless, but they make things even worse. Finally the Cat brings out a cleaning machine to straighten everything out.

The Cat in the Hat, published, in 1957, was an instant success. It was everything standard *kiddie lit* books were not: it was written from the child's point of view; every child could read it; it encouraged mayhem and making a mess of everything and it had no real moral.

Perfect!

And children could read it by themselves—without adult supervision.

Random House bookstore sales skyrocketed and quickly outsold the Houghton Mifflin education market.

> *Within three years, the book sold nearly a million copies and had editions in French, Chinese, Swedish and Braille.*

Reviews poured in: *The New York Times, The New York Herald Tribune, The Chicago Sunday Tribune* and *The Saturday Review of Literature*—all enthusiastic.

And then—it became the only book that established a whole publishing program. The next time Geisel traveled to New York and the Random House offices, Phyllis Cerf, Bennett Cerf's wife, took him to lunch. She proposed that *The Cat in the Hat* should be continue to be published in a large format—roughly 8 1/2 by 11 inches in hardcover, but that a whole new series should be published in mini-formats for pre-schoolers and even earlier.

Then the Cat—*The Cat in the Hat*—by itself begat Beginner Books, which became a separate room inside the Random House house, if you will. And very few cats can claim they established a publishing program by themselves.

Ted—and Helen Geisel—were both intrigued. They invested in Beginner Books, as did Phyllis Cerf, Bennett Cerf's wife.

And indeed, some child experts have suggested pre-beginner books—the babies would be read to *in the womb*—Ted Geisel, presumably, would agree.

But before Geisel could begin Beginner Books, he had to complete another title he promised too Random House.

Christmas…

Something about Christmas.

And for the first time he featured an adult. A bad guy, as children might say.

The Grinch.

He portrayed the Grinch with a remarkably apt description, which children—especially children—could understand;

> *The Grinch hated Christmas!*
> *The whole Christmas season.*
> *Now, please don't ask why.*
> *No one quite knows the reason.*
>
> *It could be his head wasn't screwed on just right.*
> *It could be perhaps, that his shoes were too tight.*

> *But I think that the most likely reason of all*
> *May have been that his heart was two sizes too small.*

And with that beginning, Geisel crated a fable just as endearing and timeless as "'Twas the Night Before Christmas." Geisel said that the Grinch had hated Christmas for 53 years—Geisel was 53 years old when he wrote it.

The Grinch steals all the presents from the Whos in Whoville—appearing again—but Christmas went on anyway; it isn't presents that make Christmas.

But Geisel had a problem—he didn't know how to end the book.

> *I got hung up getting the Grinch out of the mess. I got into a situation where I sound like a second-rate preacher or some biblical truism. Finally in desperation ... without making any statement wherever, I showed the Grinch and the Whos together at the table, and making a pun of the Grinch serving the "roast beast" ... I had gone through thousands of religious choices, and then after three months it came out like that.*

And the hard *GR* sound of Grinch is just perfect for a "bad guy." Like Lewis Carroll with his invented word *chortle*, Geisel added a new definition to the language:

> *Grinch: any sour, pessimistic person who dismisses love and attempts to deprive others of happiness.*

His moral in *The Grinch* ...

> *Maybe Christmas doesn't come from a store,*
> *Maybe Christmas ... means a little bit more!*

And while *The Cat in the Hat* was settling sales records, the first printing of The Grinch was ... 50,000 copies.

Critics again raved about a new Dr. Seuss book: *The Saturday Review of Literature; The San Francisco Chronicle; The New York Times; The New York Herald Tribune* and *Kirkus*, the book review service, were all overwhelmingly enthusiastic.

Thereafter, Geisel published *The Cat in the Hat Comes Back*, (1958) which was *good* Dr. Seuss but not *great* Dr. Seuss.

In 1957, Helen Geisel was taken to the nearby Scripps Clinic misdiagnosed with dizziness and confusion. The diagnosis was she had suffered a small stroke.

Geisel had covered Christmas with *The Grinch* … he subsequently tackled another holiday celebration which virtually guaranteed sales to, and for children; *Happy Birthday to You!* (Geisel liked to use exclamation marks in text and titles.) It was published in 1959.

Bennett Cerf had a thought—and made a bet—could Dr. Seuss write a book with only 50 words? Geisel had access to 225 words for *The Cat in the Hat*. Could he be as successful with just 50? The bet was for $50.

Geisel's eventual title: *Green Eggs and Ham*, an obvious play on ham and eggs.

Chuck Jones, of *Bugs Bunny* fame, clearly saw what Geisel was doing: he was using the reversal of a common phrase, but using it like the Pennsylvania Dutch, who are not Dutch at all but German. (Pennsylvania Dutch is a corruption of *Deutsch*, the German word for German); and he was using the phrase like the Yiddish language, which employed phrases like "throw your Mother from the train, a kiss."

> *Thet Sam-I-am!*
> *That Sam-l-am!*
> *I do not like That Sam-l-am!*
>
> *Do you like*
> *Green eggs and ham?*
>
> *I do not like them, Sam-l-am.*

Much later Geisel said it was the only Dr. Seuss book that still made him laugh.

And Ted Geisel won the $50 bet with Bennett Cerf.

The Cat in the Hat ... The Grinch...Green Eggs and Ham—all critical and financial successes for Dr. Seuss,

The price of fame: after *Green Eggs and Ham* was published and when Boy Scouts, Cub Scouts, Girl Scouts, Brownie scouts, various kids clubs, groups and such, all knew his la Jolla address, on his birthday, crew after crew came too his front door with platters of green eggs and ham.

"Vile stuff," he said.

One birthday, to get away, Ted and Helen and another couple decamped to Las Vegas. "They'll (the kids) never find me here," he said. The four had front row-seats to a splashy Las Vegas show. The first act was 20 nearly buck-naked women roaring onto the stage on 20 motorcycles.

"I can't tell what kind of motorcycles they are," Geisel said.

"I think you're missing something," his friend said.

In late 1961, the Geisel's got a call from Donald Klopfer, at Random House. The Geisel's had invested in Beginner Books. Klopfer told them that Grolier, another publisher, wanted to begin a children's book club and wanted Dr. Seuss books, among others.

The Geisel's refused; Grolier could have Dr. Seuss titles but no others—none from any other publisher. Klopfer was astonished, but the Geisels still refused. Grolier could distribute Dr. Seuss titles *and* other Beginner Books titles, but none from any other publisher. Eventually Grolier agreed. Forty years later, Grolier had paid more than forty million dollars to Beginner Books, and, in the process, had become the nation's largest children's book club.

Geisel had created another pseudonym; Theo. LeSeig, Geisel backward, and with that, he added a new line of books; he would write the text and others would contribute the illustrations. *Ten*

Apples Up on Top came first, then *I Wish I Had Duck Feet* and *Come Over to My House*—and others … They weren't quite top-of-the-line Seuss, but they did fit Beginner Books and they did sell.

Geisel later checked: his stock in Beginner Books had made him not just a millionaire, but a multi-millionare.

Cathy Goldsmith, president and publisher of Random House's Beginner Books said recently:" We sell more Dr. Seuss books today than we did when he was alive. The books stand the test of time."

To date, *The Cat in the Hat* has sold 16,000,000 copies. It has been translated into: Spanish; French; German; Dutch; Italian; Portuguese; Latin; Chinese; Japanese; Icelandic; Norwegian; Russian; Polish; Yiddish; Hebrew; Estonian, Serbian and Greek.

Whew!

Average annual sales in multiple languages: 500,000.

Random House staged a "60 and a Half" celebration of the publication of *The Cat …* in September, 2017.

"We know Ted would be overjoyed by *The Cat in the Hat's* enduring legacy, and tickled by this whimsical celebration of a book that he wrote to inspire children to love to read. *The Cat in the Hat's* impact has been extraordinary and we only wish Ted could be here to see it today."

Of the Seussian stories, she said: "There's always something unexpected; they're not formulaic. You remember them quite vividly. It's hard to get bored with Seuss. He's entertaining for the adult as wells the child."

Geisel had Dr. Seuss books, Beginner Books and now Theo LeSeig—and then Chuck Jones re-entered the picture. Jones, from Geisel's Private Snafu Army period …

> … believed that Dr. Seuss material could, and should be made into cartoon special for television, Typical negotiations followed, via Geisel's agents, potential sponsors, Ted and Helen Geisel and assorted friends and others.
>
> It was early in 1966 and the calendar made the choice: by the end of the year. Jones could have The Grinch … ready for holiday viewing.

> *Jones moved The Grinch ... into animation without using any of the slapdash techniques of the time. Typical cartoons then used abbreviated action—backgrounds repeated (the same trees would reappear behind running figures), for instance, and voices didn't quite match actions. Jones used full-action techniques: 25,000 drawings instead of a typical cartoon with 2,000 drawings.*

The Grinch had to be reinvented. Colors—which colors should be used? What kind of a voice? How would the Whos be animated? And the length?—typically the Grinch story could be read aloud to an audience in less than 15 minutes. It had be lengthened to almost a half hour (minus time for commercials). Would the plot have to be changed, or added to?

Geisel wanted the Grinch to be black-and-white—but Jones suggested his eyes to be a jealous green. A Grinch song was added:

> *You're mean one, Mr. Grinch.*
> *You really are a heel.*
> *You're as cuddly as a cactus,*
> *You're as charming as an eel.*
> *Mister Grinch! You're a bad banana*
> *With a greasy black peel ...*

And eventually narrating the story was—the man with the perfect Grinch-y voice—Boris Karloff. CBS-TV bought the Grinch, paying MGM $315,000. for two annual showings, in 1966 and 1867. Chuck Jones predicted it would run "for the next ten years."

He was wrong—*How the Grinch Stole Christmas!* has become an annual holiday event along with Dickens' *A Christmas Carol* and another cartoon classic, *Charlie Brown's Christmas* by Charles Schultz.

Some things should soon forever. *How the Grinch Stole Christmas!* is one—a holiday story with an obvious holiday moral, without being preachy or being overly religious. In other words, perfect for everyone.

And then … and then …

On the morning of October 23, 1967, their housekeeper entered the Geisel's home and found no one up. That itself was not unusual. Ted and Helen had separate bedrooms and he often slept late. The housekeeper, Alberta Shaw, entered Helen's room …

… and found her dead. Sometime during the night, she had taken her own life, over-dosing with sodium pentobarbital tablets.

No one knows how much pain she may have been in; she left a note for Ted, believing herself a failure.

Her death was published in the local newspapers and quickly sent across the country by the wire services.

As he had done with the death his sister decades before, in Springfield, Massachusetts, Geisel maintained a stoic silence. Always. Part of the Geisel fortune went to the La Jolla Museum's Art Reference Library, which was renamed in her honor. Her share of the Geisel royalties went to Dartmouth and other royalties and income went into the nonprofit Seuss Foundation. It was considerable.

Ted and Helen Geisel had known Audrey Dimond, a La Jolla friend.

In June 1968, Ted and Audrey traveled to Reno, where they spent the requisite period of waiting time and were married.

And in September, 1970, they traveled to Kenya. One afternoon, at the Mount Kenya Safari Club, he witnessed a herd of elephants passing on the horizon. He was galvanized into action. The result was *The Lorax* (1971), his *paean* to the environment. It became his most controversial book.

His readers would have never known that, by the 1970s, his heath was slowly fading. One morning in 1975, he couldn't see. He called Audrey in a panic. She feared cataracts; the diagnosis was cataracts *and* glaucoma. He endured five years of eye operations—which contributed to his 1978 book, *I Can See with My Eyes Shut*. Old age crept closer.

During a dental exam, a lesion was discovered at the base of his tongue—it was cancerous and potentially very dangerous. An operation placed an implant under his tongue to neutralize the cancer.

In 1985, he won the Pulitzer Prize.

"It was," he said, "usually given to adults. I'm a writer who has to eat with the children before the adults eat." And the same year, Audrey tricked him into going to Princeton University, where he received an honorary degree. When he got up to receive his diploma, the entire graduating class rose and chanted the entire text of *Green Eggs and Ham*.

He considered the health problems he had suffered through. The eye problems, the mouth cancer—and decided to write a book for adults. Those in the same lifespan as he; those with health problems or those who anticipated health problems. He had often said "adults are only obsolete children—and to hell with 'em."

But this book was for them. The title: *You're Only Old Once!* (He continued to use exclamation marks in his book titles.)

He recalled then—as now—the costs of modern medicine.

> *Just why are you here?*
> *Not feeling your best ...*
> *You've come in for*
> *An Eyesight and Solvency Test ...*

And here Dr. Seuss shows a progressively larger eye chart which reads:

HAVE YOU ANY IDEA

HOW MUCH MONEY

THESE TESTS ARE

COSTING

YOU?

Staff people at Random House were worried that adults wouldn't buy a Dr. Seuss book. Even the first- and second-generation of Dr. Seuss youngsters had probably forgotten about him long ago, they thought—the earliest readers were, after all, grandparents themselves by now.

But Ted Geisel *and* Dr. Seuss knew—they *knew* that young readers hadn't forgotten, as they grew older themselves. And he was right when Random House staff members—far younger than he—were decidedly wrong. The first printing was 200,000 copies. It hit the number one spot on *The New York Times* best seller lists and by the end of the first six months had sold 600,000 copies.

His mouth cancer problem had resulted in an infection of his jaw, impossible to eradicate. He became increasingly infirm with bouts of gout and loss of hearing and often turned down invitations outside La Jolla.

He then remembered the callow—the cynical—motto from his college years: "Oh! The places you'll go. The people you'll meet."

His next book *Oh! The Places You'll Go!* also hit *The New York Times* best seller lists and stayed there for more than two years. It sold, during that time, 1,500,000 copies. It was the last book published during his lifetime.

In 1991, critic Clifton Fadiman wrote, with sales over 200 million copies, Seuss "had become a part of the environment, a kind of public utility. Nothing in the history of books for children comes within hailing distance of this phenomenon."

* * *

In a feature obituary, "Audrey Geisel, 97, Dies; Dr. Seuss' Widow and Keeper of His Flame," Katherine Q. Seelye wrote in *The New York Times,* Dec. 22, 2018, that before Ted Geisel died, he told his wife that she would be in charge of the all the creatures he had created, including the Cat in the Hat, Horton the elephant and the Grinch. Seelye states:

> *Taking care of them became her mission. She developed and oversaw a global operation of publishing ventures, film projects, games and celebrations that kept Dr. Seuss' name, and his beloved stories in front of successive generations of children as they learned to read.*
>
> *She was deeply involved in the marketing and managing of all his material. Some people complained that her aggressive commercialism went beyond the wishes of her very private husband.*
>
> *"You use it or you lose it," she responded to San Diego Magazine in 2007 when asked about that complaint, "if we're not out there—if we don't keep up the reminders and remembrances—you fall off. And as long as I'm here, that isn't going to happen."*

In 1993, Seelye writes, she founded Dr. Seuss Enterprises, whose stated mission was to "protect the integrity of the Dr. Seuss books while expanding beyond books into ancillary areas." That meant keeping a sharp eye on copyrights and trademarks as Dr. Seuss merchandise and spinoffs are sold around the world.

She gave $20 million and thousands of her husband's drawings and manuscripts to the University of California, San Diego, where Geisel Library is named for both of them. She and her husband also donated millions over the years to what is now the Audrey and Theodor Geisel School of Medicine at Dartmouth, his alma mater.

… and … she would hold court every morning with aides at a hotel restaurant in San Diego, coming and going in a 1984 Cadillac with California license plates that read GRINCH.

She died late December, 2018.

* * *

Slowly Ted Geisel put his work away. There was no real pain, no real suffering. He began sleeping on a couch in his studio. He awoke once and asked his wife, "Am I dead yet?"

Theodor Geisel died quietly September 24, 1991, at 84.

But his legacy continued—there were additional Dr. Seuss books published posthumously; and the earlier titles were reprinted again and again.

His books will live forever.

from McElligot's Pool

    This MIGHT be a pool, like I've read of in books, *Connected to one of those underground brooks!*
    An underground river that starts here and flows Right under the pasture! And then ... *well, who knows?*

*   *   *

This *might* be a river,
Now *mightn't* it be,

    Connecting
      McElligot's
     Pool
      With
       The
        Sea!

Then maybe some fish might be swimming toward me

        (If such a thing *could* be,
        They certainly *would* be !)

Nineteen Eighty-Four
George Orwell / 1949

George Orwell's journey toward Big Brother

genre: dystopian science fiction

Like others before him, including Mark Twain—Eric Blair—born June 2, 1903 and died January 21, 1950—had world experiences fundamental to his writing.

He was born in India, to a family genteel but not wealthy. His father worked in the India Civil Service. A year after he was born, his mother took him and his two sisters to live in England, presumably for a better life. Blair saw his father briefly in 1907, when his father was on leave, but now again until 1912. Blair's school years were abysmal. He hated his first school, St. Cyrian's, in East Sussex. He described his next school, Wellington, as "beastly," but apparently was happier, when he reached Eton.

(His health problems, which would plague him throughout much of his life—eventually diagnosed as tuberculosis—may have begun, undiagnosed, during his time at Eton.)

Financially he couldn't afford further university work—moving from Eton to Cambridge University—without scholarship help, which, didn't look promising; he thus decided to leave England. In October, 1922, he traveled through the Suez Canal and Ceylon and arrived in Rangoon in November to join the Indian Imperial Police. He was posted in the Irrawaddy Delta area, then closer to Rangoon.

He gained responsibility there while young; while his contemporaries in England were still in school. He learned the Burmese language, but contracted dengue fever in 1927. He took leave, returned to England, examined his life and resigned from the Indian Imperial Police to became a writer.

Like Mark Twain, and others, he mined his travel experiences. His novel *Burmese Days* (to be cited later) was published in 1934.

Down and Out in Paris and London, 1933

In the spring of 1928, he moved to Paris where he lived in he Latin Quarter, where F. Scott Fitzgerald and Ernest Hemingway had also lived.

He fell seriously ill in March 1929 and was taken to a charity hospital.

Subsequently an encounter with a "trollop" (his words) led to his first book. He had taken this girl, or woman, to his quarters; she subsequently stole all his money, an incident, unfortunate at the time, which led to him taking jobs as the most menial of kitchen help in Paris restaurants …

Aside from the fact that he needed money immediately after the theft (the robber was described as an Italian male in the published book, not a trollop, so as not to offend his parents, still alive), why did he choose to work in the lowest-of-the-low dishwashing and kitchen help jobs in Paris, earning barely enough to stay alive day-by-day, week-by-week?

(Orwell uses the French word *plongeurs*; those who wash dishes and carry out other menial tasks in restaurants.)

It was a combination of work to stay alive and work to collect material for, well, for a book.

And why did he consider such a book about his lost days in Paris restaurant basements, in filth and heat, barely staying alive?

Four reasons, perhaps:

- The mad self-challenge of any writer and any writing project: *Can I do this? Will this work?*
- The chance to move as far as possible, psychologically, from his Eton-British background:

- It may have been a paean to Jack London, a writer he highly respect or even revered;
- It may also have been his personal atonement for his years in Burma helping prop up British Colonialism.

He returned to England and discovered he didn't have quite enough material for a normal-length book and subsequently added material about being a poverty-stricken tramp in England, thus the eventual title.

His descriptions of the effects of poverty are instructive—and striking:

> *It is altogether curious, your first contact with poverty.*
>
> *You have thought so much about poverty—it is the thing you have feared all your life, the thing you knew would happen to you sooner or later; and it is all so utterly and prosaically different, You thought it would be quite simple; it is extraordinarily complicated. You thought it would be terrible; it is merely squalid and boring. It is the peculiar lowness of poverty that you discover first; the shifts that it puts you to, the complicated meanness, the crust-wiping.*
>
> *You discover, for instance, the secrecy attaching to poverty. At a sudden stroke you have been reduced to an income of six francs a day. But of course you dare not admit it—you have to pretend that you are living quite as usual. From the start it tangles you in a nest of lies and even with the lies you can barely manage it.*

* * *

> *You discover what it is to be hungry. With bread and margarine in your belly, you go out and look into shop windows. Everywhere there is food insulting you in huge wasteful piles ...*

* * *

You discover the boredom which is inseparable from poverty; the times when you have nothing to do and being underfed, can interest you in nothing.

* * *

This—one could describe it further, but it is all in the same style—in life on six francs a day. Thousands of people in Paris live it—struggling artists and students, prostitutes when their luck is out, out-of-work people of all kinds. It is the suburbs, as it were, of poverty.

And, he writes—

Clothes are powerful things. Dressed in a tramp's clothes it it is very difficult, at any rate, for the first day, not to feel that you are genuinely degraded. You might feel the same shame, irrational but very real, your first night in prison.

And finally ...

And there is another feeling that is a great consolation in poverty. I believe everyone who has been hard up experienced it. It is a feeling of relief, almost of pleasure at knowing yourself at last genuinely down and out. You have talked so often of going to the dogs—and well, here are the dogs and you have reached them, and you can stand it. It takes off a lot of anxiety.

Orwell's first draft, without the down-and-out-in-London second part was sent to the British publishing firm Jonathan Cape, which rejected it. A year later, with the second part added, the manuscript was sent the firm of Faber and Faber, where T.S. Eliot was an editor. It was rejected there too. Finally, a chance encounter (as these things sometimes happen) gave the project a second life. A Blair family friend, Mabel Fierz and her husband, knew a literary agent, Leonard Moore. He sent the manuscript to a newly-established publishing firm, headed by Victor Gollancz; he wanted the manuscript. During the usual back-and-forth between author and editor ... *can we do that? should we do that?* Gollancz and then-Eric Blair had to decide on a title ... and Blair's by-line, his pen-name.

Gollancz's first suggestion was *Confessions of a Down and Out*. Blair was skeptical. Gollancz changed it at the last minute to the permanent title: *Down and Out in Paris and London*.

Then there was the question of Blair's by-line. He did not want the book published under his own name; he wanted to be a cipher, unknown, and thus able to investigate and write about, social-political issues which consumed him. Pseudonyms suggested were ""X," "P.S. Burton," the name he used during his forays into the depths of poverty and "H. Lewis Allways." Finally he settled on Orwell, from the river Orwell in Suffolk. And George, surely a quintessentially British name.

Down and Out in Paris and London was first published in January, 1933; it was subsequently published in the United States by Harper and Bros. Sales were slow until December, 1940, when Penguin Books printed 55,000 copies for sale in England.

(The idea of paperback publishing began in England before World War Two and in the United States largely after World War Two.) All Eric Blair's books were published under the George Orwell pseudonym.

And with the subsequent publication of *Animal Farm*, first published in 1945 and *Nineteen Eighty-Four*, first published in 1949, the pseudonym George Orwell became one of the four most university-recognized pen names in the world (the other three: Lewis Carroll, Mark Twain and Dr. Seuss).

Burmese Days—1934

George Orwell's first novel, *Burmese Days,* was a direct result of his five years' service—1902-1927—in the Indian Imperial Police in Burma (now Myanmar). At the time, Burma was part of British Colonialism; its was governed by Great Britain from India—Orwell saw it all ebbing away and was outraged by what he saw.

Burmese Days described "corruption and imperial bigotry" in a society where "after all, natives were natives—interesting, no doubt, but an inferior people." These devastating comments were on the outside back cover of an early paperback edition of the novel.

Critics have noted Orwell's debt to Joseph Conrad, Somerset Maugham and most particularly, for *Burmese Days,* to E.M. Foster.

Jeffrey Meyers, in a 1975 guide to Orwell's work, wrote ...

> Burmese Days *was strongly influenced by* A Passage to India *which was published in 1924, when Orwell was serving in Burma. Both novels concern an Englishman's friendship with an Indian doctor, and a girl who goes out to the colonies, gets engaged and then breaks it off. Both use the Club scenes to reveal a cross section of colonial society, and both measure the personalty and value of the characters by their racial attitudes ... But* Burmese Days *is a far more pessimistic book than* A Passage to India *because official failures are not redeemed by successful personal relations.*

And, Orwell later wrote, in *Why I Write* (1946):

> *I wanted to write enormous naturalistic novels, with unhappy endings, full of detailed descriptions and arresting similes, and also full of purple passages in which my*

words are used partly for the sake of their sound. And in fact my first complete novel, Burmese Days ... *is rather that kind of book.*

His protagonist, James Flory, has been described as "the lone and lacking individual trapped within bigger system that is undermining the better side of human nature."

As an Orwell friend, T. R. Fyvel, has written:

From Flory in his first novel ... to Winston Smith in 1984, his last, all his heroes are Orwell himself, suitably transmuted.

Orwell portrayed him as:

Flory was a man about thirty-five, of middle height, not ill made. He had very black, stuff hair, growing low on his head, and a cropped black mustache, and his skin, naturally sallow, was discolored by the sun. Not having grown fat or bald he did not look older than his age, but his face was very harried in spite of the sunburn, with lank cheeks and a sunken, withered look round the eyes.

He had obviously not shaved this morning. He was dressed in the usual white shirt, khaki drill shorts and stockings, but instead of a topi he wore a bettered Terai hat, cocked over one eye. He carried a bamboo stick with a wrist thong, and a black cocker spaniel named Flo was ambling after him.

All these were secondary expressions, however. The first thing that one noticed in Flory was a hideous birthmark stretching in a ragged crescent down his left cheek, from the eye to the corner of the mouth. Seen from the left side his face has a battered, woe-begone look, as thought the birthmark had been a bruise—for it was a dark blue in color. He was quite aware of his hideousness. And at all times, when he was not alone, there was a sidelongness about his movements, as he maneuvered constantly to keep the birthmark out of sight.

Flory's birthmark, or facial scar, which he turns away from those in front of him, is a stark foreshadowing of the denouement of the novel.

Topics in *Burmese Days* include British colonialism, and identity of those in Burma—the British officials tasked with preserving the British empire while in service there, trapped between British rule and the native Burmese culture. One of the characters calls the native Burmese people "black stinking swine."

Because of possible libel problems in England, *Burmese Days was* published first in the United States. Harpers published the novel in October, 1934, with a printing of 2,000 copies. In February, 1935, only four months later, 976 copies were remaindered, or sold off for pennies on the dollar. (The first British edition of *Homage to Catalonia* met the same fate, to be cited later.)

At the same time, in England, Orwell had to wrestle with his publisher Victor Gollancz, to publish the book. Gollancz first rejected it, based on legal problems he had with another author—not Orwell—although he had published *Down and Out in Paris and London* earlier.

The British publishers Heidemann and Jonathan Cape also rejected it. Finally Gollancz agreed to publish it after Orwell made assurances that names and situations could be changed so there would be no libel issues. The book was finally published by Gollancz in England June 24, 1935.

Some British hands still in Burma believed that Orwell "rather let our side down." Or, they implied, he was, as was oft-said of Franklin Roosevelt, "a traitor to his class."

In 1946, Orwell wrote, "I dare say it's unfair in some ways and inaccurate in some details, but much of it is simply reporting what I have seen." Orwell's reportage would come into exact focus in *Homage to Catalonia* later.

In 2013, the Burmese Ministry of Information named the new translation (by Maung Myint Kywe) of *Burmese Days*, the winner of the 2012 Burma National Literature award's "Informative literature" (translation) category. The National Literary Awards are the highest awards in Burma.

A Clergyman's Daughter—1935

After returning from Paris in 1929 from the experiences which led to Down and Out in Paris (finally published as *Down and Out in Paris and London*), Orwell lived in the home of his parents on the Suffolk coast. He subsequently spent two months, August and September, 1931, picking hops in Kent, lived like other hop pickers and kept a journal. Much of the journal appeared in *A Clergyman's Daughter*.

He began writing *A Clergyman's Daughter* in mid-January, 1934, and finished it in early October, 1934. It was his most experimental book, owing some to James Joyce and *Ulysses*. Christopher Hitchens, in *Why Orwell Matters* states that Orwell apparently took the title from *Ulysses*:

> *How now. Sirrah, that popped he lent you when you were hungry?*
> *Marry, I wanted it.*
> *Take thou this noble.*
> *Go to! You spent most of it in Georgia Johnson's bed, clergyman's daughter.*

In this novel, the heroine—if she may be called that—is Dorothy Hare, who was the weak-willed daughter of a disagreeable widowed clergyman. This is the old American Horatio Alger self-made success books, but in bleak reversal.

She suffers amnesia, and loses track of eight days. She, like Orwell, worked in the hop fields for very little wages. She travels to London, but as a single woman with no luggage, is not allowed to stay at respectable hotels. She is forced to sleep in the streets, much like Orwell in Paris.

Throughout the novel, she is a victim, psychologically dependent on others and without sufficient income to sustain herself. Orwell paints the same picture of deep, wrenching lower-class poverty he reveals in *Down and Out in Paris and London*.

He critiques the school system in England, where there are "good boys," whose parents can pay full fees and the others—which included Orwell himself earlier, whose parents pay part of the tuition and Orwell, then, is treated as barely a second-class boy.

Orwell's publisher, Gollancz released it in March, 1935, after some minor revisions to avoid any possible libel issues.

Victor McHugh, reviewing the book in the *New York Herald Tribune*, compared it to Dickens and George Gissing, whom Orwell admired.

> *Mr. Orwell, too, writes of a world crawling with poverty, a horrible dun flat terrain in which the abuses marked out by those earlier writers have been for the most part only deepened and consolidated. The stagers of Dorothy's plight—the coming to herself in the London street, the sense of being cut off from friends and the familiar, the destitution and the nightmare in which one may be dropped out of respectable life, no matter how debt-ridden and forlorn, into the unthinkable pit off the beggar's huger and the hopelessly declassed.*

Orwell himself was never satisfied with the book. In a letter to one friend he called it "tripe" and in another letter he said the book was worse than *Keep the Aspidistra Flying* and "I oughtn't to have published it, bit I was desperate for money."

He once stated that he didn't want the book to be reprinted after his death, but relented if it would "bring in a few pounds for my heirs."

In truth, if it hadn't been for his later worldwide critical acclaim (and financial success) with *Animal Farm* and *1984*, *A Clergyman's Daughter* and *Keep the Aspidistra Flying* would have—and should have—completely disappeared years ago.

Keep the Aspidistra Flying—1936

Orwell wrote this book in 1934 and in 1835 while living in a variety of flats in the London area; he mined his previous experiences at being down and out and the dismal life he experienced living near-penniless.

(The Aspidistra in the title is a medium-sized houseplant much prized during the Victorian era for its ability to to withstand inadequate heat and inadequate indoor light, but which became a long-running national joke later; a bit of "hurray for the middle class" sarcasm.)

Orwell's protagonist, Gordon Comstock gives up his career with an advertising agency "New Albion," to lead a life of genteel poverty (much as Orwell's life had been, up to this point)—and writing poetry.

Comstock had "declared war" on money and a respectable life. But, as he discovered, neither the war on respectability nor the poetry went well. Under the stress of his self-imposed exile from affluence, he became absurd, petty and deeply neurotic. He is obsessed with what he calls "the Money God." He has a girlfriend, Rosemary Waterlow, whom he met at New Albion, but their relationship is marred by his self-imposed poverty. She works late; they have little time together. She lives in a hostel and his landlady forbids female guests.

He sees money as the root of all evil and the root of everything that doesn't work in his self-imposed exile from middle-class respectability.

In the countryside, about to make love or have sex for the first time, she pushes him away—he was't going to use a condom—which engendered this diatribe:

> "Money, again, you see! ... You say you 'can't' have a baby ... you mean you daren't because you'd lose your job and I've got no money and all of us would starve."

Eventually he and she do have sex—then later she tells him she's pregnant. Neither want to have an abortion. He is then faced with a choice; leave her to remain in poverty—knowing the shame of her unwed pregnancy would bring to her family—or marry her and returned to a respectable job at New Albion. He chooses New Albion and returns to middle-class life. He throws away his poetry and returns to begin work on an advertising campaign for a new product to prevent foot odor.

And ... he buys an aspidistra for their new middle-class flat.

The plot is predictable; the characters predictable and the denouement even more predictable. Orwell's female characters are better realized than in previous books, but even that isn't saying much. (Orwell always had trouble with female characters up to and including *1984*.)

Orwell biography Jeffrey Meyers found the book flawed by weakness in plot, style and characterization (what else is there?).

Orwell himself said it was "one of two, or three books, of which he was ashamed."

Reviews? *The New Statesman* referred to it as "clear and violent language, at time making the reader feel as though he was in a dentist's chair with the drill whirring."

And Norman Mailer said "It is perfect from the first page to the last." *Really, Mr. Mailer, really?*

In order of excellence, from *1984* and *Animal Farm* through *Homage to Catalonia, Burmese Days, Down and Out in Paris and London,* and *The Road to Wigan Pier, A Clergyman's Daughter* and *Keep the Aspidistra Flying* surely rank at the bottom of the Orwell canon.

The Road to Wigan Pier—1937

Orwell turned in his manuscript for *Keep the Aspidistra Flying* to his publisher Victor Gollancz January 15, 1936 and almost immediately Gollancz offered him a new project—Orwell would investigate the coal areas and associated poverty in northern England.

Gollancz was not only a publisher, but a dedicated social reformer. In *Orwell: The Transformation*, Stansky and Abrahams write:

> *As a social reformer, a socialist, and an idealist Gollancz had an unquestioning, perhaps overly optimistic, faith in education; if only people could be made to know the nature of poverty, he thought, they would want to eradicate it, remove from power the government that tolerated it, and transform the economic system that brought it into being.*

If Orwell didn't accept the project with avidity—he must have surely recognized that the project would be a mirror image of the Paris section of *Down and Out in Paris and London*, which, in fact, it was.

Orwell traveled to northern England—a route that then took him from Birmingham to Manchester to Leeds and stayed in the same wretched quarters he had lived in, during his down-and-out-in-Paris experience.

He chronicled housing in those regions, mediocre at best; the plight of old-age pensioners, bereft of funds and security. He met local residents, talked, and observed the same type of squalor he saw in the lower depths of Paris and London.

What he saw and what he learned:

He went down into the coal mines and discovered he was far too tall to be a miner; they were short, muscular and worked for hours and hours and hours on their knees. (Orwell had to crawl through sections of some mines, on all fours.) When they emerged from the mines, they were invariably covered with coal dust, which caused eventual eye problems and other occupational ailments. He discovered that many seems to have odd misshapen natural "tattoos" on their noses or foreheads—if they were cut or bruised, coal dust would seep into the cut or bruise and eventually turn an off blue color. He learned that the braces for the mine shafts were all wood; if stressed, the wood would creak or groan before breaking, thus giving the miners at least a momentary warning before a tunnel collapse. Metal braces would simply snap without warning.

What he wrote:

In Chapter One, he described the Booker family, who had a bit more income than others in that locale, because they rented parts of their home to transients like Orwell, or more permanent guest-residents.

Chapter Two describes the life of coal miners, and includes Orwell's experiences going down into the mines. This is the most graphic part of the book.

Chapter Three discusses the average life of a coal miner; health and lack of financial security.

Chapter Four discusses the housing situation in the areas he investigated.

Chapter Five analyzes unemployment and employment statistics.

Chapter Six discusses food for the average miner—many

suffered from malnutrition. Food for the miners and their families, Orwell discovered, was also sub-standard.

Chapter seven describes how slag-heaps make the landscape a nightmare.

He writes:

> A slag-heap is at best a hideous thing because it is so planless and functionless. It is something just dumped on the earth, like the emptying of a giant's dust-bin. On the outskirts of the mining towns there are frightful landscapes where your horizon is ringed completely round by jagged grey mountains, and underfoot is mud and ashes and overhead the steel cables where tubs of dirt travel slowly across miles of country. Often the slag-heaps are on fire, and at night you see the red rivulets of fire winding this way and that, and also the slow-moving blue flames of sulphur, which always seem to the point of expiring and always spring out again.

Orwell saw nothing joyous, uplifting or positive in his journeys in northern England. Nothing at all.

The first seven chapters in *The Road to Wigan Pier* are Orwell's observation and reportage. The second part of the book, from chapter eight through chapter 13—are essays about Orwell's beliefs about socialism and why people should support it.

Gollancz, as a publisher, had based his publishing house on pacifist and socialistic non-fiction. He had established the Left Book Club, the first book club in the United Kingdom. He desperately wanted Orwell's book—but only the observational—reportage of the first half. He asked Orwell (and then perhaps his literary agent, or perhaps the agent first, then Orwell), to delete the second half of the book. Both refused. Orwell then left for the Spanish Civil War. Gollancz then wrote an Introduction, distancing himself, his publishing firm and the Left Book Club, from the book. His Introduction, one Gollancz biographer, Ruth Dudley

Edwards wrote, was "full of good criticism, unfair criticism and half truths."

Orwell's reportage from northern England resulted in him being placed under surveillance by the British government from 1936 to 1948—one year before the publication of *1984*.

Homage to Catalonia—1938

Orwell married Eileen O'Shaughnessy June 9, 1936.

Soon after the crises began that would lead to the Spanish Civil War. Orwell followed these developments avidly. He decided to go to Spain and fight on the Republican side against Franco and Hitler's legions, sent as a prelude or rehearsal for a later war.

The Spanish Civil War, 1936-1939, provided George Orwell the perfect opportunity to achieve his *true metier*; his reportage, observations and social-political criticism.

As biographer Peter Lewis writes:

When the Fascist forces, led by General Franco, rebelled against the Republican government of Spain on July 18, 1936, people of Left-wing sympathies everywhere felt passionately committed to the Republican cause. At that time the involvement of the Communists in the Spanish government and the arms it was soon getting from Stalinist Russia only confirmed to many the rightness of the cause. At last, it seemed to Orwell, democracy was standing up to Fascism. Two thousand volunteers from Britain went out to fight Franco in the International Brigade, in the spirit of crusaders for a new world, a dream of socialist brotherhood come true. They were a mixture of workers and intelligentsia, doctrinaire Communists and poets. Poets like Auden and Spender volunteered for service of a propagandist kind, others like Julian Bell and John Cornfield died in the fighting. Among the exalted waves of idealists, as soon as he had delivered the manuscript of Wigan Pier in December, Orwell went.

Orwell truly had discovered his *metier*, he only had to match subject and the self-examination he had experienced. He said:

> Every line of serious work I have written since 1936 has been written against totalitarianism and for democratic socialism as I understand it ... Looking back I see that invariably where I lacked a political purpose that I write lifeless books and was betrayed into purple passages, decorative adjective sand humbug generally.

Orwell reached Spain Dec. 26, 1936. He found almost impossible conditions there; the Republican side was rife with factions including Marxist groups and the United Socialist party, which distrusted each other.

He had first thought to be a war correspondent, but soon decided to join one of the militia units, then fighting Franco. He decided not to join the International Brigade nor Communist nor the Anarchist militias, but a small Marxist group, the P.O.U.M.; the *Partido Obrero de Unification Marxists* or Workers Party for Marxist Unity. Eventually it was not a wise choice.

Orwell did not know that two months before he arrived in Spain, the NKVD's (Soviet law enforcement agency) resident in Spain, Alexander Orlov, has assured NKVD headquarters, "the Trotskyist organization POUM can easily be liquidated"—by those, the Communists, whom Orwell took to be allies in the fight against Franco.

He was given two weeks' training and served with the P.O.U.M., from December, 1936 until June, 1937. That month, the P.O.U.M. was declared an illegal organization and the top officers arrested and imprisoned. Orwell was forced to hide for several days until he—and his wife—were able to flee Spain.

Orwell saw real action—in fact, he served with the P.O.U.M. in the Argon region for 125 days. He was granted leave and saw his wife Eileen in Barcelona. Returning to the front, Orwell was shot by a sniper May 20, 1937; hit in the neck, he was very nearly killed on the spot. His service in Spain effectively over, he was transferred from an aid station, then transferred to hospitals again and again, finally reaching Barcelona. On June 23, escaping from anti-P.O.U.M. forces, he and his wife boarded a train from Barcelona to Paris. It was barely in time; on July 13, a deposition was presented at the Tribunal for Espionage and High Treason, Valencia, charging both Orwell and his wife with "rabid Trotskyism" and being agents for the P.O.,U.M. Barcelona fell to Franco's forces January 26, 1939.

Orwell begins *Homage to Catalonia* with this remarkable portrait of a soldier he had just met—he pictures him much like an artist with a. sketch pad might have done:

> *In the Lenin Barracks in Barcelona, the day before I joined the militia, I saw an Italian militiaman standing in front of the officer's table.*
>
> *He was tough-looking young of twenty-five or -six, with reddish-yellow hair and powerful shoulders. His leaked leather cap was pulled down fiercely over one eye. He was standing in profile to me, his chin on his breast, gazing with a puzzled frown at a map which one of the officers had open on the table. Something in his face deeply moved me. It was the face of a man who could commit murder and throw away his life for a friend—the kind of face you would expect in an Anarchist, thought as likely as not he was a Communist. There were both candor and ferocity in it; also the pathetic reverence that illiterate people have for their supposed superiors. Obviously he could not make head or tail of the map; obviously he regarded map-reading as a stupendous intellectual feat. I hardly know why; but I have seldom seen anyone—any man, I mean—to whom I have taken such an immediate liking. While they were talking round the table some remark brought it out that I was a foreigner. The Italian raised his head and said quickly:*

> "Italiano?"
> I answered in my bad Spanish "No., Ingles. Y tu?"
> "Italiano."

He describes how the Communist hammer and sickle appeared as graffiti on nearly every wall in Barcelona and how the P.O.U.M. recruits seemed to be boys of sixteen or eighteen who lacked adequate weapons, who seemed to have no conception of *war*. And how everything seems to be put off until *mañana* (tomorrow).

In subsequent chapters, Orwell describes how he was supplied with ...

> ... *a German Mauser (rifle) dated 1886—more than forty years old! It was rusty, the bolt was stiff, the wooden barrel-guard was split; one glance down the muzzle showed it was corroded and past praying for.*

He was shot at for the first time near Zaragoza.

He describes the alphabet soup of names of trade unions and militia—which confused him:

> P.S.U.C., P.O.U.M., F.A.I., C.N.T., U.G.T., J.C.I., J.S.U., A.I.T.—*they merely exasperated me. It looked at first sight as though Spain were suffering from a plague of initials.*

On the east side of Huesca—he experienced nothing but boredom—and lice. One hand got infected and he had to spend two days in a "so-called" hospital, in Monflorite, where attendants stole everything he had.

And rats. *Rats !* that were "really as big as cats, or nearly." Orwell apparently had a phobia about rats (and who wouldn't, at that size?).

Orwell's rat phobia (and his memory of one obscure book, which he owned and had read, *The Woman Who Could Not Die*) clearly foreshadows one of the most horrific episodes in modern literature—Winston Smith's torture with the hungry rats in Room 101 toward the end of *1984*.

And, perhaps the most gripping episode in the book is Orwell's description of being shot by a sniper. He was near Huesca, where a bullet hit his neck—a fraction of an inch difference and he would have bled to death on the spot:

> *It was at the corner of the parapet, at five o'clock in the morning. This was always a dangerous time, because we had the dawn at our backs, an if you stuck your head out above the parapet it was clearly outlined against the sky. I was talking to the sentries preparatory to changing the guard. Suddenly, in the middle of saying something I felt— it is very hard to describe what I felt, though I remember it with the utmost vividness.*
>
> *Roughly speaking it was the sensation of being at the center of an explosion. There seemed to be a loud bang and blinding flash of light all-around me, and I felt a tremendous shock—no pain, only a violent shock, such as you get from an electric terminal; with it a sense of utter weakness, a feeling of being stricken and shriveled up to nothing. The sand-bags in front of me receded into immense distance. I fancy you would feel the same if you were struck by lighting, I knew immediately that I was shot but because if the seeming bang and flash I thought it was a rifle nearby that had gone off accidentally and shot me. All this happened in a space of time much less than a second, The next moment my knees crumpled up and I was falling, my head hitting the ground with a violent bang which, to my relief, did not hurt. I had a numb, dazed feeling. A consciousness of being very badly hurt, but no pain in the ordinary sense.*
>
> *The Americans entry I had been talking to had started forward "Gosh, are you hurt?" People gathered round. There was the usual fuss—"Lift him up! Where's he hit?*

Get his shirt open!" etc. etc. The American called for a knife to cut my shirt open. I knew that there was one in my pocket and tried to get it out, but discovered that my right arm was paralyzed. Not being in pain, I had a vague satisfaction. This ought to please my wife, I thought; she had always wanted me to be wounded, which would save me from being killed when the great battle came. It was only now that it occurred to me to wonder where I was hit, and how badly; I could feel nothing, but I was conscious that the bullet had struck me somewhere in the front of the body. When I tried to speak I found I had no voice, only a faint squeak, but at the second attempt I managed to ask where I was hit. In the throat, they said. Harry Webb, our stretcher-bearer had brought a bandage and one of the little bottles of alcohol they give us for field dressings. As they lifted me up a lot of blood poured out of my mouth, and I heard a Spaniard behind me say that the bullet had gone clean through my neck. I felt the alcohol, which at ordinary times would sting like the devil, splash on the wound as a pleasant coolness.

A personal friend, T.W.R. Fyvel, later wrote:

There was always a touch of Don Quixote about Orwell's knight-errantry. It was typical of his political individualism that, through accident, he joined not the International Brigade, but the so-called "Trotskyist" P.O.U.M., a Spanish Left-Wing opposition party later suppressed by the Spanish Communists.

It was typical too, that he was wounded, not in action, but on a quiet day, through sticking his head out of a trench. But he was wounded very badly ... and his life was saved only by a fraction of an inch and by the time he came out of the hospital the P.O.U.M. was proscribed as 'counter-revolutionary.' With a number of their British

I.L.P. friends under arrest, Orwell and his wife had to flee for their lives into France. From his experience of civil war, of death, dirt and military hospitals and prisons, Orwell returned with his faith in 'ordinary people' unimpaired, but with his eyes opened to one fact: Communist despotism could be far more ruthless than the earlier, milder tyranny which it overthrew. All of this he expressed in Homage to Catalonia *(1938), one of the most clear-headed books to come out of the Spanish Civil War, honestly and beautifully written, but which, partly because it was a book of the still unfashionable non-Communist Left, partially because this was Orwell's fate, sold only a few hundred copies over the next year or so.*

He received electrotherapy for his neck wound and was deemed unfit for further service. His time in the Spanish Civil War was over.

Back in England, his health collapsed—again. In March, 1938, he was admitted to the Preston Hall Sanatorium in Kent and diagnosed—initially—with tuberculosis.

Homage to Catalonia would not have fit Victor Gollancz's publishing house. Instead, Orwell and his agent turned to the firm of Secker and Warburg, which published it, and later, *Animal Farm* and *1984*.

In *George Orwell: The Road to 1984*, Peter Lewis writes:

He finished Homage to Catalonia *in January, 1938 and it was published in April while the war was still in the balance. Despite its brilliant reporting and important political analysis, it caused barely a ripple on the political pond," in the words of Fredric Warburg. Of 1,500 copies printed, 683 were sold the first six months and thereafter only a trickle. When Orwell died in 1950, there were still copies of the first edition lying unsold in the warehouse. Orwell had not even earned the 150 (pound) advance on his royalties.*

Only after Orwell's death was *Homage to Catalonia* acknowledged to be one of the most influential and significant books ever written about the Spanish Civil War.

Animal Farm—1945

His next book, written between November, 1943 and February, 1944, brought him international fame—it was, in fact, a perfect combination of, propaganda and art, philosophy and fable: *Animal Farm,* first published in 1945.

Orwell had seen Stalinist Communism up close in Spain and believed it to be a brutal dictatorship, built on terror.

How did Orwell conceive of the plot for this, which can be read both as fable and a cautionary political tale? A leap of insight, which writers sometimes find to their great benefit—and often to their surprise. In a Preface, Orwell writes:

> ... *I saw a little boy, perhaps ten years old, driving a huge cart horse down a narrow path, whipping it whenever it tried to turn. It struck me that if only such animals became aware of heir own strength we should have no power over them and men exploit animals in much the same way as the rich exploit the proletariat.*

And an even earlier genesis of *Animal Farm* as fable were his memories of his favorite book as a child:

> *I believe that* Gulliver's Travels *meant more to me than any other book ever written. I can't remember when I first read it. I must have been eight years old at the most, and it has lived with me ever since so I suppose a year has never passed without my re-reading at least part of it.*

The plot: most of the animals on the Manor Farm have names (just as in Clement Clark Moore's "'Twas the Night Before Christmas"—*on Dasher, on Dancer, on Prancer and Vixen ...*)

Old Major, an old boar, summons the animals together for a meeting in which he refers to humans as "enemies." They all learn a revolutionary song, "Beasts of England." When he dies two young pigs, Snowball and Napoleon, become leaders and prepare others for a coming revolution. (Napoleon can be read as Stalin and Snowball as Trotsky, with some elements of Lenin.) They forced the drunken farmer, Mr. Jones, from the farm and rename it Animal Farm. They adopt a dictum: the "Seven Commandments of Animalism."

The seven were:

1. Whatever goes upon two legs is an enemy.
2. Whatever goes on four legs, or has wings, is a friend.
3. No animal shall wear clothes.
4. No animal shall sleep in a bed.
5. No animal shall drink alcohol.
6. No animal shall kill any other animal.
7. All animals are equal.

The most important was: *All animals are equal.*

It becomes a commune, but later Napoleon and his pigs changed the commandments:

4. No animal shall sleep in a bed *with sheets.*
5. No animal shall drink alcohol *to excess.*
6. No animals shall kill any other animal *without cause.*

And most importantly,

7. All animals are equal but *some animals are more equal than others.*

Changing the Seven Commandments of Animalism, Orwell imitated, showed how easy it was to corrupt the system.

All the incidents in his fable directly matched the Russian Revolution and its aftermath:

The revolt of the animals against Farmer Jones is Orwell's analogy with the October 1917 Bolshevik Revolution. The battle of the Cowshed has been said to represent the allied invasion of Soviet Russia in 1918, and the defeat of the White Russians in the Russian Civil War. The pigs' rise to pre-eminence mirrors the rise of a Stalinist bureaucracy in the USSR, just as Napoleon's emergence as the farms' sole leader reflects Stalin's emergence. The pig's appropriation of milk and apples for their own use, "the turning point of the story," as Orwell termed it in a letter to Dwight Macdonald, stands as an analogy for the crushing of the left-wing Knonstadtrevolt against the Bolsheviks, and the difficult efforts of the animals to build the windmill, suggest the various Five Year Plans.

The puppies controlled by Napoleon parallel the future of the secret police in the Stalinist structure, and the pigs' treatment of the other animals on the farm recalls the internal terror faced by the populace in the 1930s.

In chapter seven, when the animals confess their nonexistent crimes and are killed, Orwell directly alludes to the purges, confessions and show trials of the late 1930s. These contributed to Orwell's conviction that the Bolshevik revolution had been corrupted and the Soviet system became rotten.

Orwell sought nothing less than a massive satire on the Stalinist system; to destroy the myth of Soviet superiority.

Then the unthinkable happened. Orwell's wife Eileen entered a hospital March 29, 1945 for as routine operation to remove uterine tumors. Routine, so very routine. But she died under the anesthetic. His subsequent death, alone and at 46 was tragic; her death equally tragic. When she died, she was not yet 40. Orwell was so stricken he seldom spoke of her death. And that left him a single parent to take care of son Richard, whom he and she had adopted.

Orwell and his agent had the same problems publishing *Animal Farm,* that they experienced with his previous books. Various publishing firms in England, including Orwell's previous publisher Victor Gollancz, rejected it; other publishers in England and the United States were skeptical of the premise of the book—was it too anti-Soviet at the time? (It is perhaps apocryphal that one American publishing firm was said to haver rejected it because "Americans won't read books about animals.")

Animal Farm was published August 17, 1945, less than five full months after Eileen's death; it achieved substantial recognition with the advent of the cold war, which began in 1947, when the Truman Doctrine offered economic aid to countries threatened by Communism; the Cold War did not end until 1989, with the fall of Communism in Eastern Europe, and finally in 1991 when the Soviet Union collapsed. *Animal Farm* became Orwell's first real financial—and critical—international success. Then came his masterwork.

1984—published in 1949

For many thousands—perhaps millions of readers—who came to *1984,* it has been a remarkable example of the *sui genesis* in literature. And for as many who who first read it decades ago—including this author—it remains as vivid and remarkable today as the day it was first read.

For those readers, with no antecedents or any *genetic history* to follow it has remained superbly iconic, standing by itself in twentieth-century literature.

But ... but ... writers borrow from each other all the time. Steinbeck's *Tortilla Flat,* as discussed earlier, is an exact chapter-by-chapter retelling of the Knights of the Round Table saga. It is said that Truman Capote based his bestseller *In Cold Blood,* 1966, on a previous book, *A Murder in Paradise* by Richard Gehman, published in 1954. (the murder in Gehman's book occurred in Paradise, Pennsylvania, near Lancaster.) And there are countless other examples, recognized or unrecognized by readers.

Consider these paragraphs by Paul Owens:

> *It is a book in which one man, living in a totalitarian society a number of years in the future, gradually finds himself rebelling against the dehumanizing forces of an omnipotent, omniscient dictator. Encouraged by a woman who seems to represent the political and sexual freedom of the prerevolutionary era (and with whom he sleeps in an ancient house that is one of the few manifestations of a former world), he writes down his thoughts of rebellion—perhaps rather imprudently—as a 24-hour clock ticks in his grim, lonely flat. In the end, the system discovered both the man and the woman, and after period of physical and mental trauma the protagonist discovers he loved the state that has opposed him throughout, ands betrays his fellow rebels.*
>
> *The story is intended as a warning against and prediction of the natural conclusions of totalitarianism.*
>
> *This is a description of George Orwell's Nineteen Eighty-Four ... but it is also the plot of Yevgeny Zamytin's We, a Russian novel originally published in English in 1924.*
>
> *Orwell's novel is consistently acclaimed as one of the finest of the last 100 years ... and it remains a constant bestseller.*
>
> *Should it alter our respect for it that Orwell borrowed much of his plot, the outlines of three of his central figures, and the progress of the book's dramatic arc from an earlier work?*

And, Owen writes:

> *The characters in We are numbers rather than named: its Winston Smith is D-503 and it Julia is 1-330.*

Its Big Brother is known the Benefactor, a more human figure than Orwell's almost mystical dictator, who, at one point, phones D-503. ("D-503? Ah ... You're speaking to the Benefactor. Report to me immediately!") Where Orwell's apartments come complete with all-seeing "telescreens," Zamyatin's buildings are simply made of glass, allowing each of the residents—and the "Guardians" who police them—to see in whenever they want. We's Airstrip One, or Oceania, is called OneState. Instead of puzzling over 2 + 2 = 5, its lead character is disturbed by the square root of -1.

... and ...

So does it matter that Orwell borrowed plot and characters from an earlier book? After all, it seems clear that he made a superior work of literature from them. Nineteen Eighty Four's *importance comes from not so much from its plot as from its immense cultural impact, which as recognized almost immediately when it won the 357 (pound) Partisan Review prize for that year's most significant contribution to literature, and which has continued to this day. Most of the aspects and ideas of the novel that will resonate so strongly are his own: newspeak, doublethink, thought crime, The Thought Police. Room 101; the extreme use of propaganda, censorship and surveillance; the rewriting of history; labels and slogans that mean the opposite of what they say; the role for Britain implied in the name Airstrip One. References to these things pervade all levels of our culture.*

In addition, unlike We, Nineteen Eighty-Four *is written with expert control in an accessible style about a world recognizably our own, and its twists of plot—including the existence (or not) of the Brotherhood resistance movement—are gripping, sophisticated and convincing. The dark, pessimistic tone of* Nineteen Eighty-Four *is also all Orwell's.*

If any aspect of We *takes the shine off* Nineteen Eighty-Four, *it's that Orwell lifted that powerful ending—Winston's complete, willing capitulation to the forces and ideals of the state—from Zamyatin. It's a wonderful, wrenching twist, in both books, and a perfect conclusion, though* We *and* Nineteen Eighty-Four *differ slightly in the fate of the female dissident:*

1-330 is killed without giving up her beliefs, whereas Julia is broken in the same way as Winston.

Perhaps We *deserves more recognition than it has had, but* Nineteen Eighty-Four *had never existed, it is extremely doubtful that Zamyatin's book would have come to full the unique place Orwell's work now occupies.* Nineteen Eighty-Four *is an almanac of all the political ideas no "right thinking" person would ever want their government to countenance, and the word Orwellian has come to signify a badge of shame intended to shut down any movement in that direction—with an imperfect record of success.*

So Orwell "westernized" *We*—taking it to London, not as a prediction but as a warning:

don't let this happen here.

For journalists, a book or article beginning is called the *lede*, (pronounced *leed*). Orwell's *lede* in *1984* is one of the most memorable literature:

It was a bright cold day in April and the clocks were striking thirteen.

In *1984* there are three world powers, constantly at war with each other. Oceania, the United States which absorbed the United Kingdom, and allies; Eurasia, the Soviet Union and allies and Eastasia, China and its allies. Alliances shift, sometimes quite suddenly and bewilderingly.

In London, Winston Smith is a minor functionary, working for the Party. Surveillance is constant. The Party's leader Big Brother is on billboards and everywhere else. The slogan

Big Brother is Watching You

... is everywhere. There is no escaping Big Brother.

The Party prohibits free expression, free thought, any effort to be an individual and even prohibits sex. The Party has crafted its own history and is working to implement its own language, *Newspeak*. Bad is now *not good*. If the Party can control language it can control history and government.

Smith works at the Ministry of Truth, (Minitrue) which works on historical revisionism; changing history to reflect the party line. Revisions are explained as fixing misquotations, but are, in fact, outright lies and forgeries. The Ministry of Truth destroys historical documents; if a document does not exist, there is no proof The Party is lying.

Smith knows how the Ministry of Truth is distorting history; he lives a shabby life in "Victory Mansions," subsisting on black bread, synthetic meals and "Victory gin."

Telescreens are everywhere—flat screens inset into homes and flats, which constantly broadcast Party victories and achievements, but can also see *into* everyone's homes and apartments—they can observe everyone and anyone, at any time.

Smith assumers the telescresns can observe *everyone all the time*.

The telescreens especially observe those who might challenge the Party's authority. Even children are encouraged by the Party to inform on their parents, relatives or friends.

There is no escape from the constant surveillance by the Party. Everything about the Party is a black reversal:

- The Ministry of Peace (Minipax) deals with war;
- The Ministry of Plenty (Miniplenty) deals with starvation;
- The Ministry of Love (Miniluv) deals with law and order;
- The Ministry of Truth (Minitrue) deals with propaganda.

Smith begins writing a journal, which he knows is a death warrant. He records his feelings about Julia, an acquaintance who works in the same office complex.

Julia subsequently hands him a note—she is in love with him. They meet upstairs above an antique shop, where Smith bought his journal. They assume there are no telescreens in the old shabby building, but they are betrayed by the owner of the shop, who is a member of the Thought Police.

Smith is taken to the Ministry of Love and is interrogated by O'Brian, who Smith knows; O'Brian is also a member of the party, but in a position slightly above Smith.

O'Brian subjects Smith to electroshock treatments and tells Smith that he can be "cured" of his insanity—his hatred of the Party—through conditioning. Smith "confesses" to "crimes" he has committed.

He is eventually taken to Room 101—the ultimate location for re-indoctrination—brainwashing.

It is every citizen's fear about the Party.

Smith betrays Julia when a wire cage with hungry rats inside is placed over his head.

"Do it to Julia," he says in abject panic.

Later he meets Julia on the street, in a crowd—she admits she betrayed him in Room 101, faced with the same wire cage with the hungry rats.

Eventually he is content to sit in a cafe, remembering a rare happy time with his family, but now believes it to be false.

He is content to love Big Brother.

* * *

Nazi rockets continued to rain down on London and elsewhere; one rocket fell near his flat; Orwell needed a safe place to take his son Richard, whom he and his wife had adopted, and finish his novel. He had contributed articles, essays, opinion pieces and reviews to a variety of British publications over the years—always earning little more than a meager income. He had worked for David Astor, publisher of *The Observer.* Astor offered him plane to stay.

His family owned an estate on the remote Scottish island of Jura, near to Islay. There was a house, Barnhill, seven miles outside of Ardlussa at the remote tip of this rocky finger of heather in the Inner Hebrides. Initially Astor offered it to Orwell as a holiday.

In May, 1946, Orwell, still picking up the shattered pieces of his life, took the train for the long and arduous journey to Jura. He told his friend Arthur Koestler that it was "almost like stocking up (a) ship for an arctic voyage."

It was a moonscape; it has been describes as:

> *... mountainous, bare and infertile, covered largely by vast areas of blanket bog, hence its small population. In a list of the islands of Scotland, ranked by size Jura comes in eighth, whereas by population it comes in thirty-first. Jura, in ancient Norse, means Deer Island.*

The house in Jura (biographer Jeffrey Meyers calls this his "Jurrasic Period") was scarcely more than just an isolated shelter to live and finish *1984.*

The Jura residents then knew him by his real name: Eric Blair, "a tall cadaverous, sad-looking man, worrying about how to cope on his own ... a specter in the mist, a gaunt figure in oilskins." His sister Avril then arrived to mange things. It was a godsend to Orwell.

His health was precarious before his trek to Jura, but he kept on, doggedly working on his book.

Then, an accident, a disaster for Orwell. In a boat with Avril, Richard and some friends, an infamous whirlpool capsized the boat. Son Richard remembered being "bloody cold." They were rescued by others. He did not go to a doctor after that incident.

Orwell went on.

Within two months he was seriously ill.

He kept on.

In *Why I Write*, he said:

> *Writing a book is a horrible, exhausting struggle, like a long bout of some painful illness. One would never undertaken such a thing if one were not driven by some demon whom one can neither resist or (sic) understand. For all one knows that demon is the same instinct that makes a baby squall for attention. And yet it is also true that one can write nothing readable unless one constantly struggles to efface one's personality. Good prose is like a window pane.*

He kept on. At Christmas, 1947, he told friends that he had been diagnosed with tuberculosis. Then, in March, 1948, he received reword from his publisher, Fred Warburg: "it's necessary from the point of view of your literary career to get it (done) by the end of the year and indeed earlier if possible."

Get it done by the end of 1948.

Or sooner. While battling tuberculosis.

Robert McCrum writes:

> *It was a desperate race against time. Orwell's health was deteriorating, the"unbelievable bad" manuscript*

needs retyping, and the December deadline was looming. Warburg promised to help, as did Orwell's agent. At cross-purposes over possible typists, they somehow contrived to make a bad situation infinitely worse. Orwell, feeling beyond help, followed his ex-public schoolboy's instincts: he would go it alone.

In fact, Orwell eventually worked on his project in bed, physically unable to get up.

The "unbelievable bad" manuscript: writers with some experience, who write (these days) a page on a screen and then print it out for proofreading, might be dismayed (or worse) to find three, four or five typescript errors on a page. *Nineteen Eighty-Four: The Facsimile* (manuscript edition), later published by Secker and Warburg, shows typescript changes *on every line of every page. Many manuscript pages are simply garble. That's how a masterpiece is revised and completed, but the hardship cost him dearly.*

McCrum suggests—or believes—that finishing the book with his health very much at risk cost Orwell his life.

The manuscript reached Orwell's publisher in mid-December. Fred Warburg recognized its importance immediately: it was, he said "among the most terrifying books I have ever read."

Orwell entered a TB sanitarium.

Nineteen Eighty-Four was published June 8, 1949 and was instantly recognized as a masterpiece.

Winston Churchill (Orwell, who had admired Churchill, named his protagonist Winston after Churchill) said he had read it—twice.

What had Orwell done in his book? He had transformed *We*—westernized it as a warning—and had made an indelible impression on readers for generations.

All the incidents and anecdotes in *Animal Farm* directly match the Russian Revolution and its aftermath.

How extensively did Orwell use the same techniques in *1984?* Consider these key elements:

- **Big Brother:** during World War Two in London, J,M. Bennett had a company, Bennett's, which offered correspondence courses for students. He appeared on billboards with he slogan "Let me be your feather." Later, after he died, his son took over and then billboard slogan became "Let me be your big brother."

Orwell worked for the British Broadcasting Company, the B.B.C., during World War Two, providing propaganda for the war effort. His superior was Brendan Bracken, the Minister of Information, M.O.I. staff members referred to him as B.B.

More tellingly, in political terms, Big Brother was most assuredly Joseph Stalin. Orwell described Big Brother as having a mustache, like Stalin.

- **Emmanuel Goldstein:** Big Brother's arch-nemesis said to have formed an underground resistance movement, The Brotherhood and who wrote The Theory and Practice of Oligarchial Collectivism. Goldstein was said to have been exiled by Big Brother, or otherwise fled.

Leon Trotsky born October 26, 1879, joined the Bolshevik ('majority") just before the 1917 October revolution. He ascended to top Party ranks and became one of the first seven members of the Politburo.

He served first as People's Commissar for Foreign Affairs, was a founder of the red Army and became a major figure in the Bolshevik victory in the Russian Civil War.

But after a failed struggle by the left against the politics of Stalin, he was removed as Commissar for Military and Naval Affairs, January, 1925, removed from the Politburo, October, 1926, removed from the Central Committee, October, 1927, exiled to Alma-Ata, January, 1928 and exiled from the Soviet Union February, 1929.

Trotsky was attacked in Mexico City August 20, 1944 by Ramon Mercader, a Spanish-bom NKVD agent wielding an axe handle. Trotsky died the next day; Mercader served 20 years in a Mexican prison. While in prison, he was awarded an Order of Lenin by Stalin, in absentia.

The description of Goldstein with a. "small goatee beard," evoked the image of Trotsky. The film of Goldstein during the Two Minute Hate is described as showing him being transformed into a bleating sheep. The same type of image was used in a propaganda film during the Kino-eye period of Soviet film, which shows Trotsky transformed into a goat. Goldstein's book is similar to Trotsky's highly critical analysis of the USSR, *The Revolution Betrayed*, published in 1939.

Leon Trotsky's birth name was Lev Davidovich Bronstein.

- **Oceania, Eurasia, Eastasia.** International spheres of influence were suggested by the Tehran Conference, November-December, 1943.

- **Sudden and dramatic shifts in alliances between Oceania, Eurasia and Eastasia;** based on the Nazi-Soviet Pact and the subsequent and unexpected invasion of Russia by Hitler in Operation Barbarossa.

- **"... the clocks were striking thirteen."** The 24-hour military clock was in universal use; thirteen is 1 p.m.

Orwell's remarkable *neologisms*—newly coined words or phrases—have long been a part of common usage and culture:

- **Big Brother**—any real or mythical dictatorial figure;
- **Thought Police—Thought Crime.** (Thinkpol in *1984).* So unlikely as to be unbelievable? Even in *1984*?

The Thought Police is based on the NKVD, which arrested people at random for "anti-Soviet remarks."

In the early twentieth century—specifically in 1911—the empire of Japan established the Special Higher Police, a political police force known as the *Shiso Keisho*, the Thought Police, who investigated and controlled native political groups whose ideologies were considered a threat to the public order of the countries colonized by Japan. In contemporary usage the term *Thought Police* often refers to the actual or perceived enforcement of ideological orthodoxy in the political life of a society.

- **Room 101.** The ultimate torture chamber; in *1984*, every prisoner's worse fears about the Party, where cage of live rats, was fitted over Winston Smith's head to force him to confess to anti-Party "crimes."

Orwell worked in a room 101 for the British Broadcasting Company during World War Two, where he detested the propaganda work he was doing.

- **Unpersons.** People who are erased from history.

During the Stalinist years, photographs which included officials who had fallen from favor were doctored to eliminate their images. Examples: Lavrentiy Beria—when he fell from power in 1953, and was subsequently executed, institutions and libraries which had encyclopedias with his picture were sent an article about the Bering Strait and told to paste it over the Beria material. And Nikolai Yezhov, who was shown in a photo with Stalin in the mid-1930s: when he was executed in 1940, his image was airbrushed out of the photo. They had become unpersons.

- **Doublethink.** The ability to hold twin contradictory concepts in mind at the same time—and to ignore the fact that they are contradictory.

- **Doublespeak** and **groupthink**—variations of **doublethink**.

- **Facecrime**, to inadvertently reveal anti-Big Brother emotions, which would lead to arrest or worse.

- **Memory hole**—when facts and history are deleted and permanently lost, they go down the memory hole.

… and finally …

- **Orwellian**—any reference to, or description of, a dictator or a totalitarian or dictatorial society.

* * *

And, a now-infamous wrought-iron Orwellian sign/slogan, over a gate at Auschwitz 1, the largest of there Nazi death camps read; **ARBEIT MACHT FREI,** roughly translated as *Work is freedom* or *Work makes you free.*

(The sign was also used at other death camps.) Prisoners at Auschwitz and other Nazi death camps well knew that they would likely die of overwork or starve to death. Prisoners with metal—working skills made the sign and in a subtle act of defiance, the B is ARBEIT was set upside down. It remains so to this day.

* * *

And another remarkably Big Brother statement—with the logic of 2 + 2 = 5—occurred during the Vietnam war:
We had to destroy the village to save it.
Zafar Sobhan summarized the story in *The Guardian:*

> *Be Tre is a city in the Mekong Delta in Vietnam, made famous by the statement of an unnamed US army officer to AP correspondent Peter Arnett in the aftermath of the crippling aerial assault it suffered at the hands of the US*

Air Force during the Vietnam war. It became necessary to destroy the town to save it.

The quote has since become distorted in the popular imagination and became immortalized in the familiar form used as the title of this piece, but, either way, it still stands as a classic statement of the folly of war and as a monument to the depths to which human idiocy can sink when we are blinded by our belief that we are in the right and the other side is in the wrong.

* * *

Outside the remarkable neologisms in *1984*, Orwell was the first to substantially establish the concept of the *Cold War*. The article "George Orwell and the origins of the term 'cold war,'" states:

> *On 19 October 1945, George Orwell used the term cold war in his essay "You and the Atomic Bomb," speculating on the repercussions of the atomic age which had begun two months before when the United States bombed Hiroshima and Nagasaki in Japan. In this article, Orwell considered the social and political implications of a "state which was at once unconquerable and in a permanent state of 'cold war' with its neighbors."*
>
> *This wasn't the first time the phrase cold war was used in English (it had been used to describe certain policies of Hitler in 1938), but it seems to have been the first time it was applied to the conditions that arose in the aftermath of World War II.*
>
> *Orwell's essay speculates on the geopolitical impact of the advent of a powerful weapon so expensive and difficult to produce that it was attainable by only a handful of nations, anticipating "the prospects of two or three monstrous superstates, each possessed of a weapon by which millions of people can be wiped out in a few seconds, dividing the*

world between them," and concluding that such a situation is likely "to put an end to large scale-wars the cost of prolonging indefinitely "a peace that is no peace."

Within years, some of the developments anticipated by Orwell had emerged. The Cold War (often with capital letters) came to refer specifically to the prolonged state of hostility, short of direct armed conflict, which existed between the Soviet bloc and Western powers after the Second World War.

The term was popularized by the American journalist Walter Lippmann, who made it the title of a series of essays he published in 1947 in response to U.S. diplomat George Kennan's "Mr. X" article, which had advocated the policy of "containment." To judge by debate in the House of Commons the following year (as cited by the Oxford English Dictionary), this use of the term Cold War was initially regarded as an Americanism; "The British government ... should recognize that the 'cold war' as the American call it, is on in earnest, that the third world war has, in fact, begun." Soon though, the term was in general use.

Orwell had graphically and dramatically shown the evils and cruelty of totalitarianism in *1984,* in ways *Animal Farm* could not, and did not; for some readers the Russian revolution references in *Animal Farm* were too obscure too be noticed or understood (re: the apocryphal American publisher whose said "American don't buy animal books.")

In October, 1949, in his room at University College Hospital, Orwell married Sonia Brownell. It was a moment of happiness—but only a fleeting moment.

Orwell suffered a massive hemorrhage January 21, 1950. He died alone, at 46.

In *Churchill and Orwell: The Fight for Freedom,* Thomas E. Ricks writes: "When he was alive his book sales were measured in the hundreds and thousands. Since his death an estimated 50 million copies of his books have been sold."

By 1989, *1984* had been translated into 65 languages throughout the world.

And sales spiked to the top of the best-seller lists with the advent of the Trump administration.

A half million copies were printed January, 2017.

from 1984

It was a bright cold day in April and the clocks were striking thirteen. Winston Smith, his chin muzzled into his breast in an effort to escape the vile wind, slipped quickly through the glass doors of Victory Mansions though not quickly enough to prevent a swirl of gritty dust from entering along with him.

The hallway smelt of boiled cabbage and old rag mats. At one end of it a colored poster, far too large for indoor display, had been tacked to the wall. It depicted simply an enormous face, more than a meter wide; the face of a man about forty-five, with a heavy black mustache and ruggedly handsome features. Winston made for the stairs. It was no use trying the lift. Even at the best of times it was seldom working and at present the electric current was cut off during daylight hours. It was part of the economy drive in preparation for Hate Week.

* * *

The Ministry of Truth—Minitrue in Newspeak—was startlingly different from any other object in sight. It was an enormous pyramidal structure of glittering white concrete, soaring up terrace after terrace, three hundred meters into the air. From where Winston stood it was just possible to read, picked out on its white face in elegant lettering, the three slogans of the Party:

WAR IS PEACE
FREEDOM IS SLAVERY
IGNORANCE IS STRENGTH

Night
Elie Weisel / 1960

The man and his work, acclaimed worldwide ...

genre: memoir/autobiography

If anyone has come to embody the Holocaust—the millions who were lost and those who survived—it has been Elie Weisel.

Weisel, was born Eliezer Weisel, September 30,1928, in Sighet, a Romanian Jewish *shtetl,* a hamlet. He had two older sisters and one younger sister. He began studying at a Jewish school at three, where he learned Hebrew, the Bible, and eventually the Talmud, the body of Jewish civil and ceremonial law.

In 1940, the Nazis turned Sighet over to Hungary; in 1942, the Hungarian government ruled that all Jews who could not prove Hungarian citizenship would be transferred to Nazi-held Poland and murdered. The only resident of Sighet who escaped and returned was his friend Moshe, caretaker in his synagogue.

In March, 1944, Germany occupied Hungary, which extended the Holocaust into Sighet. All Jewish residents were forced to wear the yellow star; the Nazis closed Jewish stores (the Weisel family owned a store in Sighet), raided their homes and created two ghettoes. The Weisel family had a Christian maid, who invited them to hide in a hut she had in the mountains, but they chose to stay with their Jewish community. In May, 1944, the Hungarian government, under pressure by the Nazis, began to deport the Jewish community to the Auschwitz concentration/death camp, where up to 90 percent were exterminated upon arrival.

In June, Weisel family members were among the last Jewish residents of Sighet to be loaded into cattle cars—with 80 people in each car—to Auschwitz. Elie Weisel was 15 at the time. He later wrote, "Life in the cattle cars was the death of my adolescence."

The train reached Auschwitz after four days. He followed the advice of a fellow prisoner and gave his age as 18, not 15, and told the Nazis he was a farmer and in good health. He and his father were sent to be slave laborers. His mother and sisters were shunted off elsewhere.

Weisel and his father survived first Auschwitz, then the Buna slave labor camp for eight months, enduring beatings, hunger and life-threatening labor conditions.

Weisel was given a tattoo on his left arm; he became A-7713.

On January 19, 1945, the SS forced all inmates in Buna on a death march. For 10 days the prisoners were forced to run and, at the end, were crammed again into cattle cars and sent to Buchenwald. Of the 20,000 prisoners at Buna, 6,000 reached Buchenwald

Weisel joined 600 children in Block 66 in Buchenwald.

On January 29, Weisel's father, Shlomo died of dysentery, starvation and exhaustion. Weisel was nearby. Years later, he told Oprah Winfrey his motivation was to survive—to save his father. "I knew that if I died, he would die." Wiesel remembered vividly the shame he felt when he heard his father being beaten and knew he could not possibly help without being killed himself.

Inmates in the camps eventually sensed the war was ending; on April 6, 1945, guards told prisoners they would no longer be fed and began evacuating the camp, killing 10,000 prisoners a day. On the morning of April 11, an underground movement inside the camp attacked the SS guards. The revolt was put down by the Nazis, but in the early evening the first American military forces, from the U.S. Third Army, arrived and liberated the camp.

Weisel had survived, but barely; he and the others liberated that day were *mussel men*,* the German/Nazi word for those close to dying of starvation, from brutality, devoid of expression—with no hope—little more than living skeletons.

After the liberation of Buchenwald, Weisel became ill with intestinal problems and while hospitalized he wrote an outline of his experiences during the Holocaust, but believed he was not mature enough to write it then; he wanted a perspective—he vowed to himself to write his memoirs ten years later.

Weisel joined a transport of 1,000 child survivors to Ecouis, France where a rehabilitation center had been set up; he subsequently joined a smaller group of 90-100 boys from Orthodox Jewish homes who wanted kosher facilities and a chance to rejoin their Jewish heritage. From 1945-1947, he was housed in different homes found for him by a Jewish group, the Children's Rescue Society. In 1946, he made an unsuccessful attempt to join the underground Zionist movement.

(By the sheerest chance his sister Hilda saw his picture in a newspaper; they were united in 1947. Later he was united with another sister Bea in Antwerp.)

Weisel then moved to Paris where he learned French and studied literature, philosophy and psychology, at the Sorbonne. He heard lectures by Martin Buber and Jean-Paul Sartre and read Dostoyevsky, Kafka and Thomas Mann.

By the time he was 19 he was a working journalist, writing in French and teaching Hebrew on the side. In 1949 he traveled to Israel and became a correspondent for the French newspaper *L'Arche* and also worked for the Israel newspaper *Yedoit Achronot*.

His life changed dramatically when he interviewed the French Catholic writer Francois Mauriac in 1954; for ten years Weisel had refused to write about the Holocaust. Mauriac, who had won the Nobel Prize for Literature in 1952, eventually became Weisel's friend and something of his mentor.

* The origin of that word may have been the word muslim, but how that transmuted into the Holocaust meaning of the living dead, is unclear.

During the interview Mauriac essentially focused on Jesus. It was an epiphany for Weisel. The dam broke.

"… ten years ago, not very far from here, I knew Jewish children every one of whom suffered a thousand times more, six million times more, than Christ on the cross. And we don't speak about them." He ran from the room. But Mauriac followed him, asked Weisel about his experiences and advised him to write them down.

(Much the same happened to Texan John Howard Griffin—without quite the emotional epiphany—and he eventually wrote *Black Like Me,* cited in the chapter about Griffin.)

Mauriac was a devout Christian and fought in the French Resistance during the war. He compared Weisel to "Lazarus rising from the dead," and saw in Weisel's tormented eyes "the death of God in the soul of a child." Mauriac convinced Weisel to write down his Holocaust experiences.

It took Weisel a full year to complete a 862-page memoir, *Un di velt hot geshvign (And the World Remained Silent);* written in Yiddish. It was published in abridged form, in 245 pages, in Buenos Aires.

It was published in French as *La Nuit.* It was translated into English and published as *Night* in 1960.

Sales were slow at first, but attracted interest from reviewers, which led to television interviews and meetings with Saul Bellow and others.

Night eventually was translated into 30 languages with ten million copies sold in the United States alone. At one point Orson Welles wanted to make a film of it, but Weisel refused; he believed it would lose its meaning if it was told without the silences between his words.

One wonders what Weisel would have thought of the highly acclaimed film version of Thomas Keneally's *Schindler's List,* produced by Steven Spielberg and released in late 1993.

Additionally, Branko Lustig, a Croatian Jew, worked for decades as a film producer. He had survived several concentration camps by the time he was 12. He applied to work on Speilberg's production of *Schindler's List* Instead of touting his previous film work, he applied in a more elemental way; he rolled up his sleeve and showed Spielberg his Auschwitz tattoo on his left arm. He got the job. Later, he, and two others, won Oscars for producing that film. "My number was A3317. It's a long way from Auschwitz to this stage," he said during the Academy Awards ceremonies. He later won a second Oscar for producing the Ridley Scott film *Gladiator,* in 2000. Branko Lustig died in Zagreb, Croatia, Nov., 13, 2019, at 87.

Night not only describes Weisel's harrowing experiences in the camps but also describes his loss of faith with death all around him.

He witnessed hangings in the death camps. Forced to watch. Standing in vast formations with all other death camp inmates forced to watch. One, the hanging of a young boy, surely the same age as Weisel, is described in the section: *from* Night, in the following pages.

With the publication of *Night* and his subsequent move to New York in 1955, Wiesel eventually became, quite simply, one of the twentieth century's most acclaimed citizens of the world.

In July, 1956, while crossing a street in Manhattan, he was hit by a taxi. He had to undergo a 10-hour operation; when he recovered he vowed to devote more time to his writing; he dedicated four hours each morning—from 6 am to 10 am—to his work. (All other writers fully understand his dedication ...)

He wrote a second novel, *Dawn*, about a concentration camp survivor, as a sequel to *Night,* and a third book, *The Accident,* was about a survivor hurt in a traffic accident, The three are now sold in one volume, under the title *The Elie Weisel Trilogy: Night, Dawn, The Accident.*

The Town Beyond the Wall (1962), *The Gates Of the Forest* (1964) and *Legends of Our Time* (1966); all chronicle Jewish suffering during and after the Holocaust. In those books he mixes tales and legends with testimony, recollection and lament, through the focus of the Talmud, Kabbalah and Hasidism, *The Encyclopedia Judaica* wrote.

In 1965, he visited the Soviet Union and the next year published *The Jews of Silence,* about the plight of Jews that he had seen there.

After the 1967 Israeli war, he published *A Beggar in Jerusalem,* about the Jews responding to the unification of Jerusalem. For that book, he won the Prix Medicis, one of France's top literary awards.

Although Weisel grew up in an Orthodox Jewish family, he later described himself as agnostic.

In 1969 he married Marion Erster Rose, a divorced woman from Austria, who had become the translator of his books. They had a son Shlomo, named after his father.

In 1977 he published *The Trial of God*, said to have originated when he witnessed three Jewish inmates of a concentration camp, conducting "a trial against God," accusing God of "hostility, cruelly and indifference," to the Jewish people.

Weisel not only wrote and spoke out about the Holocaust, but spoke about about injustices through the world; he protested against South Africa's apartheid and personally delivered food to starving Cambodians.

He and his wife established the Elie Weisel Foundation for Humanity in 1986. He served as chairman of the Presidential Commission on the Holocaust (later renamed the U.S. Holocaust Memorial Council), from 1978 to 1986 and spearheaded the building of the United States Holocaust Memorial Museum in Washington, D.C.

But … but … his Foundation had invested its assets with Bernard Madoff's guidance—later discovered to be a Ponzi scheme—and lost $13 million. Weisel and his wife also lost most of their assets. Madoff is still (at this writing—in March, 2020), in federal prison with his release date—2039 (if he lives that long).

Weisel was awarded the Nobel Peace Prize in 1986 for speaking out against violence, repression and racism. The Norwegian

Nobel Committee described him as "one of the most important spiritual leaders and guides in an age when violence, repression, and racism continue to characterize the world."

In his acceptance speech, he said:

> *Silence encourages the tormentor, never the tormented. Sometimes we must interfere. When human lives are endangered, when human dignity is in jeopardy, national borders and sensitivities become irrelevant.*

In 2003, he revealed for the first time that at least 280,000 Romanian and Ukrainian Jews had been massacred in Romanian-run death camps.

In early 2006, he accompanied Oprah Winfrey as she visited Auschwitz and, in 2009, he accompanied President Barack Obama and German Chancellor Angela Merkel as they toured Buchenwald.

Over the years he was awarded over 90 honorary degrees from a wide variety of colleges and universities.

They included:

- Doctor of Humane Letters, Lehigh University, 1985;
- Doctor of Human Letters, DePaul University, Chicago, 1997;
- Doctorate, Seton Hall University, New Jersey, 1998;
- Doctor of Humanities, Michigan State University, 1999;
- Doctorate, McDaniel College, Westminster, Maryland, 2005;
- Doctor of Humane Letters, Chapman University, 2005;
- Doctor of Humane Letters, Dartmouth College, 2006;
- Doctor of Humane Letters, Cabrini College, Radnor, Pa, 2007;
- Doctor of Humane Letters, University of Vermont, 2007;

- Doctor of Humanities, Oakland University, Rochester, Michigan, 2007;
- Doctor of Letters, City College of New York, 2008;
- Doctorate, Tel Aviv University, 2008;
- Doctorate, Weizmann Institute, Rehovot, Israel, 2008;
- Doctor of Humane Letters, Bucknell University, Lewisburg, Pennsylvania, 2009;
- Doctor of Letters, Washington University, St. Louis, Mo., 2011;
- Doctor of Humane Letters, College of Charleston, 2011;
- Doctorate, University of Warsaw, 2012;
- Doctorate, University of British Columbia, 2012.

And others. Over 90 in all.

He taught at Boston University, where he was a friend of University president John Silber; at the City University of New York; at Yale; he taught one semester at Eckerd College in St. Petersburg Fla.; and was the visiting Professor of Judaic Studies at Barnard College of Columbia University, from 1997-1999.

Boston University created the Elie Weisel Center for Jewish Studies in his honor.

He was the author of 52 books; nonfiction about the Holocaust as well as novels. Two of his most memorable were autobiographies: *All Rivers Flow to the Sea* (1996) and the sequel, *And the Sea Is Never Full* (1999).

Elie Weisel died in New York July 2, 2016, at 87.

from Night

 The SS seemed more preoccupied, more disturbed than usual. To hang a young boy in front of thousands of spectators was no light matter. The head of the camp read the verdict. All eyes were on the child. He was vividly pale, almost calm. Biting his lips. The gallows threw its shadow over him.

 This time the Lagerkapo* refused to act as executioner. Three SS replaced him.

 The three victims mounted together onto the chairs.

 The three necks were placed at the same moment within the nooses.

 "Long live liberty!" cried the two adults.

 But the child was silent.

 "Where is God? Where is He?" someone behind me asked.

 At a sign from the head of the camp, the three chairs tipped over.

 Total silence throughout the camp. On the horizon, the sun was setting.

 "Bare your heads!" yelled the head of the camp. His voice was raucous. We were weeping.

 "Cover your heads!"

 Then the march past began. The two adults were no longer alive. Their tongues hung swollen, blue-tingled. But the third rope was still moving; being so light, the child was still alive ...

 For more than a half an hour he stayed there, struggling between

---

* Lager: trans. camp. In this case, a labor camp, concentration camp or death camp. Kapo, lowest-level Nazi guard. Lagerkapo: Campguard. In this case, only one may have indicated chief or head Kapo. Lager not to be confused with current (lower case) meaning: lager, a type of beer.

life and death, dying in slow agony under our eyes. And we had to look him full in the face. He was still alive when I passed in front of him. His tongue was still red, his eyes were not yet glazed.

Behind me, I heard the same man asking:

"Where is God now?"

And I heard a voice within me answer:

"Where is He? Here He is—He is hanging here on this gallows."

That night the soup tasted like corpses.

Black Like Me
John Howard Griffin / 1960

... blind for ten years and then ...

genre: memoir/autobiography

1936
Tours, France

John Howard. Griffin, not yet sixteen, travels by himself from his native Texas to France.

Griffin was always autodidaetic. His mother ... had studied to be a concert pianist and gave piano lessons. His parents raised four children but only he had learned what his mother knew about music. At fourteen, he read of pianist Moritz Rosenthal, an eminent musician with degrees in medicine and philosophy; Griffin had found a role model, who "opened me up to a far more fascinating horizon." At fifteen, frustrated by the regressive public school system, he spotted an advertisement for a lycée (a French school that prepared students for university work), a boy's school in France and wrote a letter pleading for admittance.

Over four decades later, he remembered those days:

> *My father was a man that I will never understand. He was from Georgia. He was brought up in that fundamentalist religion which said that anything remotely pleasurable was sin. He set aside Sundays as a particularly sober time. He was brought up in an incredibly racist atmosphere. But he never implanted any of those ideas in*

me. My dad was a kind of miracle, a matter of pure grace. He was a wholly decent, uncorrupted human being.

It was a horrendous sacrifice on his part to send me to a French lycée at such young age. In those days, we didn't even have air mail. It was the belief in the south that France was utterly immoral and Catholic. They didn't know which was worse.

I had what they used to call a photographic memory. I could memorize a whole school course in one week. I was bored out of my mind, so they sent me to France, because in French schools you could advance as fast as you could learn. Also, there was a medical scholarship, and I was utterly impassioned by the sciences.

He sailed for France in search of an education he clearly could not receive in Fort Worth, Texas, in the 1930s. He was admitted to the Lycee Descartes in Tours (learning French in the process and presumably some Latin as well, to study medieval Gregorian chants) and, after graduation, obtained a scholarship to the University of Poitiers (campus at Tours) where he took literature courses. He also studied medicine at the School of Medicine at Tours. During his second year of pre-med., he also worked at the Asylum of Tours.

Medicine and music became his twin passions; both can be seen in obvious and more subtle ways in his early books.

He became as assistant to Dr. Pierre Fromenty, director of the Asylum of Tours. One of Fromenty's psychiatric techniques was to treat with, or at least expose psychiatric patients to, soothing Gregorian chants. Griffin became fascinated by these techniques. At the same time, he was studying music with Father Pierre Forger, an organist at Tours Cathedral. Griffin and Forger even co-authored a scholarly paper on music, *Interpretation of the Ornaments of the Music for Keyboard Instruments of the 17th and 18th Centuries,* privately published in 1939.

But World War Two changed everything.

Fromenty was drafted into the French Army and left and Griffin found himself in charge of 120 patients in the Asylum of Tours.

At nineteen, Griffin became an active member of the French Underground.

Griffin remembered:

> *I had worked in France smuggling Jewish people out of Germany until France fell. I was (then) twenty, a research assistant at the Asylum of Tours. When the war came, they conscripted all the doctors and medical students into the service. They couldn't conscript me because I was an American citizen. I was immediately ordered back to the U.S. I refused to go because France had formed me. How can I flee at this time of need?*
>
> *I was put in charge of the asylum. Then I got involved with the French underground, smuggling Jews out of Germany, across France, into England. We would use asylum ambulances, put the refugees in straitjackets and move them that way. They didn't have to speak. Many of them didn't speak French. They didn't have safe conduct papers, of course. We didn't know how to steal, we didn't know to forge (documents). We were infants in this, but we did the best we could.*

He, and others, moved German, Austrian and French Jews to safety.

> *The Nazis were moving in. I will be haunted to my death by those scenes. We brought the people inside those rooms and kept them hidden. We had to tell the parents who had children under fifteen that we weren't going to make it. Suddenly I experienced a double reality. The first, a parent said "It's all over for us. Take our children." We would move anybody under fifteen without papers. You*

sat there and realized these parents were giving their children away to strangers. The second: I could go downstairs into the streets and find perfectly good men who went right on rationalizing racism ....

Finally, Tours was over-run by the Nazis. Plans made by the French Underground were discovered by the Nazis. Before the time his Texas boyhood friends may have been celebrating their twenty-first birthdays, Griffins' name was on Nazi death lists and he was actively pursued by the Gestapo.

When one his of student friends was shot by the Gestapo, Griffin was forced to go into hiding.

"Having witnessed the tragic effects of the Holocaust, refined to hideous perfection by the Nazis, he never forgot the horror," Robert Bonazzi wrote, in the Introduction to *Scattered Shadows*.

These encounters with anti-Semitism may well have been one of the motivations for *Black Like* Me, decades later.

He was soon smuggled out of France, to England, to Ireland, and then to the United States.

Griffin returned to France in 1946, first to Fountainbleau, to study music with Nadia Boulanger, French composer, conductor and music professor (1887-1979). Griffin had hoped to become a composer. He was in good company. Among her other students had been Leonard Bernstein and Aaron Copland. He also studied with the French pianist and composer Robert Casadesus, whom he had met previously in Tours.

From Fountainbleau, he moved to Paris, where he spent some time in a monastery, until he was cleared to study at the Abbey of Solesmes, the monastery where the original Gregorian chants are catalogued in the *Paleographic Musicale,* and study with the Benedictine monks, the world's foremost musicologists of medieval plainsong. He had first wanted to be a composer, but eventually decided to become a musicologist specializing in Gregorian chants.

Life in a French monastery was grueling: dally rituals of meditation, prayers, mass and chores; living conditions were no more advanced than during medieval centuries. Eventually Griffin could no longer continue at Solesmes; his health became very much at risk in primitive monastic conditions.

Griffin had met the theater critic John Mason Brown in 1949 and Brown suggested that Griffin write about his experiences.

His monastic life in France gave him his first book, *The Devil Rides Outside*.

It is a first person novel-cum-memoir of an American who travels to France to study medieval musicology. The novel's focus, or fulcrum, is of the interior of the monastery, with lives devoted to Christ, rituals, masses, meditation and spartan life, contracted with carnal life outside the walls. The title is an old French proverb "La doable rode auto d'un monastere"—"the devil rides outside the monastery walls."

Griffin spoke the text of the novel into a wire recorder (in French) at night and then translated the tapes (into English) onto a typewriter the next day. The first draft of the novel was completed within seven weeks, although it was revised several times over the next two years. The eventual first hardcover edition was 596 pages.

The Devil Rides Outside has a musical foundation which may not be apparent to casual readers. Griffin based it on the form, or structure, of Beethoven's *String Quartet Opus 131*.

It was not only Griffin's first book, it was the first book of a new publishing company, Smiths Inc., established by two brothers Gordon and J. Hulbert Smith, in Fort Worth.

It was a surprising success; *The Devil Rides Outside* was chosen as a selection of the Book of the Month Club.

Critic Clifton "Kip" Fadiman wrote the review which appeared in Book of the Month Club flyers. Some of his review appeared on the back jacket of the hardcover edition of *The Devil Rides Outside:*

A staggering novel, in its length, its faults, and its qualities ... the hero is a young American ... He comes to a Benedictine monastery, somewhere in the north of France, to study manuscripts of Gregorian chant. The diary of his experiences there and in the neighboring village forms the narrative. At bottom this is a psychological confession novel turning on the most potent of all themes—the struggle within a single human soul between God, of which the monastery brothers are an emblem, and the devil, symbolized by the sensual temptations held out by the village plus the bias toward the flesh within the narrator himself. At the start he is a non-believer, but after ....intense soul-searching, arguments with the monks and sexual experiences described in torrid ... detail, he is at least driven, rather than led, to spiritual peace. Mr. Griffin's ... intense psychological analyses ... recall Dostoyevsky or Pascal. The pure doctrine of asceticism has rarely been so effectively demonstrated in twentieth-century fiction. The whole book is a kind of modern Temptation of St. Antony, without Flaubert's controlled art, but also without its frigidity. Mr. Griffin's baroque excesses are easy to ridicule but—at least to this reviewer—they seem the excesses of an intense temperament and possibly of a notable literary talent

Early in the book, Griffin reveals this as a *roman a clef*, the unnamed first-person narrator is Griffin's alter ego.

(The fictional Father Clement is based on Griffin's real mentor Friar Andre Hussar, who also had to be smuggled away from the Nazis when Griffin was forced to leave. Hussar's brother Jean later returned, joined the Free French Army and was killed in a firefight with the Germans. Jean was Griffin's best friend in Tours):

> *We talk of my trip to the monastery, of our interests in art and music, and of my background, first as a medical student and later as a musicologist He draws me out until I become conscious that for one of the few times in my life, I am taking freely and with complete honesty. Instinctive realization that there's no need to exaggerate here, no need to cover one's faults. Father Clement talks easily and intelligently as a man. He is particularly interested to know of my life as a medical student. And when he prepares to leave, much later, my impatience is largely gone. As he shakes my hand, I ask him about the life. What makes a man embrace such life? How can they accomplish what they do living under such a rigid schedule?*
>
> *"You will need to understand these things, gradually, my son," he laughs. "Tonight I will leave you some books. You may stay up as late as you like. You have everything? What about cigarettes?"*

And Griffin's protagonist reveals Griffin's continuing interest in medicine, when he is implored to save the life of a village child dying of untreated, or untreatable, epilepsy:

> *"What its it, Jacques? If I can be of any help—?"*
> *"The Chevissiers—you know, the family who works our farm—their little girl is ill. I think she's dying, but they refuse to spend a penny to call a doctor. Could you look at the child?*
> *"You told me you've been a medical student."*
> *"But, Jacques, I'm no doctor. I never got beyond pre-medical work."*

Griffin's narrator is unable to affect any cure for the child:

> *A gasp from the child as her left arm jerks into the air to fall half-back and be pulled up again on some drunken,*

invisible senseless string. Arms and legs tremble, slowly at first as in some macabre dance, becoming more frenzied gradually until the uneven rattle of her breathing grows labored, until the viscid mucus foams from her nose in gray bubbles to burst on the air. Her head moves slightly from side to side with great rapidity. Repeated short gasps come from her lips as we watch. The climax will take her. We know it but we work doggedly, hoping always that she may dance it out and still live. I heat the pads on her head and throat, wiping dampness from her colorless straw hair with a towel. Emaciated child against the strength of death. The dance continues.

The child is beyond help and does die. The narrator is furious that the parents never called a doctor sooner. Then he realizes that village gossips may well accuse him of letting the child die, gossip which he believes will eventually happen, perhaps sooner than later.

The narrator encounters monastic life far more primitive than he expects; no heat in the monastery, food little better than gruel, few comforts of any kind. Eventually he moves to a flat in the nearby village and journeys to the monastery library dally. In the carnal world of the village, he has a one-night affair with a French woman, then agonizes that she might be ostracized by other village women and driven from the village.

The female owner of the flat he rents as first appears to be polite and cordial, but eventually becomes—in his eyes—an absolute shrew.

Through the novel are extensive passages of theological debate between Griffin's unnamed protagonist and various Catholic monks. These passages may be more significant to Roman Catholic readers or, at least, deeply spiritual readers.

As Clifton Fadiman rightly observed in his review for the Book of the Month Club publicity, "he is at least driven, rather than led, to spiritual peace."

Monastic formality gives way to brief visits from many of the monks. There is a loneliness of rain and somberness within, that makes us feel the fringes of night during the day. Father G'seau knocks on the open door and bows his smiling way in, followed shortly by father Dutfoy, We talk of the monastic life and its history. Father Dutfoy, who is from the Midi, constantly mentions the tropics. He is always wiping his brow, on which there is only imaginary perspiration, and sighing, "Oh, how I should love to live in those places—and to be warm again."

The books come, are read and digested, and replaced by other books. The spell of the monastery begins to enter my blood, and the years of studying the outside world grow more remote. The reasons for the monastic life become more apparent as time passes, but a man is unable to live this way unless he believes, with St. Benedict, that God makes suffer only those whom He loves. For in his Regula* Benedict states that we must not only accept all hardships, and that above all we must never "murmur" against anything which arises in our monastic life, as such discontented murmuring is a sin. To live like this under the stringent vows of a monk, requires either a religious vocation of the highest order, or an interest, such as I have, in research. And yet I know that no amount of interest can give me the strength to continue this life for long ...

... he continues to wrestle with his own soul ...

"There, Father," I break in, "that's what I don't get, that's the reason I can't stand these books of piety. They're full of such dogmatic phrases—God's love, the devil's evil, and all that muck."

Father Clement looks at me.

"It is a good sign to see you like this, my son," he remarks very quietly. "If you were sure of your own disbelief,

out beliefs would not annoy you. It is because you became uncertain that you are troubled, it that not it?"

"I guess so"—disconsolately—"but I never accept."

"Will you let me say something that may appear very naive to you?"

"Say anything you like."

"Do not fight so hard to hold on. The moment the devil sees a sign of belief, he causes that belief to become so painful to you that you are in reality suffering from the devil, and not from God. Know that you are not essentially different than any of us here. None of us is struck, none of us is 'enlightened.' We struggle, and sometimes we lose. Few men have an unquestioning vacation. Like you, we are filed day by day, with unremitting temptation."

It does not become any easier for Griffin's narrator.

"My God, my God, forgive me. Forgive me and have mercy upon me. Make me love Thee, and make me love Thee despite myself. Force me, I beg Thee to want THY love." I lie in my prayer, but the words come and I cringe from them. "Make me want Thee above all other things. Forgive me my coldness. Let me learn the impossible grace; a faith, a belief, a love which is pure; a love which asks no questions, which compresses no doubts. Let me know why the other things are wrong, why they are really wrong. Let me, O God ..."

The prayer dies in my throat with the chill—suddenly—as I wonder to what I have been praying.

I waste my breath seeking an image that is false. No, no, they say it is real; it has to be real. But the doubt is there, and I cheapen myself and become a fake. I pray to a wall in which I have no belief because I think it may warm my belly with some trifling goodness of feelings. I utter idiotic prayers to a darkened vein of the soul.

Torn between the carnal and the chaste, the village outside the Benedictine Monastery overwhelms him. Griffin's alter ego nearly loses his moral and spiritual bearings; he discovers it is impossible to bridge the two worlds; physically so near and spiritually so distant. Ultimately, he make a decision, however reluctantly.

> *My sigh rasps loudly in the silence. Words seem to formulate themselves, sounding heavy and automatic.* "Can I come back here, Father?"
>
> "Do you really want to, my child?"
>
> "Yes," I say, tiredly, "I think I almost have to, now. I can't go on—*I shrug my shoulders and look at him.*
>
> "I know, my son." *He touches my arm again.* "Yes, by all means come back if it means that much to you. You may have your old cell this Sunday. I will help you move in."
>
> "Thanks Father." *I turn to go, but falter.* "Just one thing more, Father. You knew all this—why didn't you tell me sooner?'
>
> "You had to come to it yourself, my son."

The Devil Rides Outside is clearly an anachronism, as Clifton Fadiman observed; more closely related to Dostoyevsky, Pascal and Flaubert than to other contemporary twentieth-century novels.

Griffin subsequently said the novel "wrote me into the church." He was baptized as a Roman Catholic July 12, 1931, and became a Lay Carmelite, (before his book was published) even though it is far from clear that Griffin's alter ego in the novel is totally converted.

And only the readers who saw Griffin's photograph on the back dust jacket ever guessed what an achievement that book was for Griffin.

* * *

World War Two
The Solomon Islands and Morotai

Griffin fled the Gestapo, fled France, to England, to Ireland and then to the United States. In 1941, he enlisted in the Army Air Force, at a time when the Army and Air Force were not yet separate. After basic training, he was sent to the South Pacific, as an intelligence and language expert.

This became *life imitating art*; in 1943, he found himself as *Robinson Crusoe* in World War Two, Daniel Defoe's 1719 novel, about a castaway who spends 28 years on a remote tropical island near Venezuela, brought to life 224 years later. Griffin spent all of 1943 living in a native village on a remote island in the Solomon chain, assigned to study the indigenous culture, to translate the dialect of the inhabitants and gather strategic information on Japanese positions from the natives, allied the with United States.

He found himself isolated with a people that had no written language.

At first he viewed them as "primitives," as *Other*.

But after he was unable to navigate jungle trails without a five-year-old boy to guide him, it became obvious "that within the context of that culture, I was clearly the inferior—as a an adult man who could not have survived without the guidance of a child," he admitted, Robert Bonazzi later wrote, in the Introduction to *Scattered Shadows*.

Griffin's archives occupy 37 file boxes at Columbia University, New York, each at least two inches thick. Griffin was able to chart their language—for the first time—phonetically. The analysis of this dialect would place him in the Florida or Nggela islands, just north of Guadalcanal. His chart still exists in the Griffin archives, marked in pen ORIGINAL in the top right corner of the first page.

Some of his translations appear on page 15 in *The Man Who Changed His Skin, The Life and Work of John Howard Griffin*, 2011.

> *While living with the Pacific islanders, Griffin developed a friendship with John Vutha, Grand Chief of the Solomons, who was a strong ally of the Americans in battling against Japan's occupation. Vutha provided crucial information by tracking enemy movements and, when he had been captured and tortured by the Japanese, he refused to divulge allied positions. After 22 bayonet wounds, they left him for dead, hanging from a tree as an example. "There is little doubt that if he had given in and spoken," Griffin later writes, "the American victory at Guadalcanal would have been much slower in coming. Countless lives would certainly have been lost that were saved by his silence." For his heroism, Vutha received the highest awards accorded by the British and American governments,*

Griffin biographer Robert Bonazzi later wrote.

Grand Chief Vutha united all the Solomon Island tribes before the Japanese invasion. Griffin not only knew Vutha, but also "married" a naive South Pacific island tribal woman, in a ceremony traditional to the Solomon Islands. When Griffin began studying to become a convert to Catholicism, he told his spiritual advisor, Father Langenhorst, who decided that the marriage would not be considered "binding" in the Catholic church. Griffin did not mention this Solomon Island ceremony in any of his writings; biographer Robert Bozanni only heard about it years later, from Griffin's wife.

His experiences on the island led to his second novel, *Nuni*, eventually published in 1956. Griffin translated *Nuni* as *World*. He had a "next work," clause in his contract with Smiths, Inc., obligating him to offer that publishing firm his next project after *The Devil Rides Outside*. Smiths, Inc. had become inactive as a publisher by the time *Nuni* was ready. But on the strength of the Book of the Month Club success with *The Devil Rides Outside*, he was able to move to the mainstream publisher Houghton Mifflin. The main title page reads "Published by Houghton Mifflin Company Boston, in association with Smiths Inc., Dallas, Texas."

The Devil Rides Outside and *Nuni* share common characteristics: Both are first-person narratives. The narrator is never given a name in *The Devil Rides Outside,* in *Nuni,* his name is John Harper, literature professor, but it is only mentioned twice.

Both have musical motifs as foundation: Beethoven's *String Quartet Opus 131* in *The Devil Rides Outside*; the antiphonal structure form of the Gregorian chant in *Nuni* and both have anecdotes showing Griffin's passion for medicine.

Griffin's Gregorian chant motif appears toward the end of the novel, as a series of stream-of-consciousness passages, variations on a single theme:

> *Standing alone at the edge of the compound, looking at these sodden huts a phrase haunts my brain in repeated chantings:*
> driven along paths not of their own choosing *What are they? These beings that surround me with their sleeping. How is it they seem so dead and yet so move my affections, bound up as they are in the paraphernalia of snoring and flesh and hungers and salivas and hairs?*
> driven along paths not of their own choosing *Affection excites my heart with answers that cannot be formulated by the brain, truths from some far memory of the soul; intimate truths forever strangers to the intellect, truths stemming from:*
> driven along paths not of their own choosing

Griffin uses that phrase 19 times in 12 pages.

Readers might anticipate a resolution toward the end of the novel; a glint of metal in the sky, a seaplane gliding to a stop, a lone figure striding onto shore like General MacArthur returning to the Philippines or a lone figure crashing through the jungle with machete in hand and a hearty—"We finally found you ..."

There is no such denouement; no such resolution. John Harper has lost much of his memory of civilization and of time. He no longer knows whether a specific day is Thursday or Sunday, although he writes these words in the sand. There is virtually no hint that he might ever return to civilization.

After Griffin's success with *The Devil Rides Outside*, *Nuni* was judged exceptional and he was compared (by more than one critic) to William Faulkner.

A long essay/review about his work appeared in *The Dallas Morning News*, in 1956. It was part insightful criticism, part adulation (it was well known by then that he had served in the South Pacific). Written by Lon Tinkle, who had a very lengthy career as a critic, it is reprinted on pages 20-23, in *The Man Who Changed His Skin*.

Ultimately, *Nuni* could be described as "uneven, demanding and sometimes over-written," which could also describe *The Devil Rides Outside*. Griffin's first book is an anachronism; *Nuni* simply a curiosity.

In Griffin's body of work, *Nuni* surely ranks at the bottom (as well as later, *The Land of the High Sky*.) And, he admitted later, the indigenous tribe he lived with was far more humane than he pictured in *Nuni*.

After a year isolated on the island, Griffin was transferred to the landing base at Morotai. Much later he remembered those days:

> *By 1945, we had lost so many men and had been bombed so often that we had long ago learned to refuse any thoughts about death. Death did not exist for us except as a cold fact to be recognized and quickly dismissed. We had long ceased to mourn the deaths of our companions.*
>
> *In life, a warm and often devoted friendship existed between us. In death, nothing. They were there at the table one day, and then we saw them no more and that was all.*

Most of us in the 425th Bomb Squadron's radar section were in our third year overseas. Although our unit had been bombed often, this was the first time we were under a black alert. Now we were threatened with invasion from the enemy.

We stood, perhaps a dozen of us, in the radar tent on Morotai Island and drew straws. Pops Fendler drew first, and then Mills.

Each got a long straw. I was third in line and got the short one. Corporal Fred Kaplan cast me a glance of sympathy, tossed the remaining straws into the coral dust at our feet, and cursed.

The section captain told me I would go on duty at six this evening.

"Do you know what to do?" He asked.

"Not entirely."

He glanced up at the tent roof where rot holes let in thin rays of sunlight. "Intelligence has intercepted the Jap's orders. They are supposed to take the airstrip, kill the tower operators, and then proceed here to the radar tent, kill whoever is on duty, and take all our technical data before it can be destroyed. You'll have to have your gasoline ready to burn the place up. And you'll have the jeep outside to make a run for it. If they follow orders, they'll hit the tower first and you'll have some warning."

"The camp area had been evacuated when we reached our tents. Morotai had quickly became a ghost island. Rumors spread that the Japanese has amassed a force of 47,000 men across the bay, while our total remaining American and Australian forces were about a tenth of that.

Griffin took a jeep to his assignment, a radar tent:

Then the high, uneven rumble of airplane motors emerged from the silence. Hearing the 'Washing Machine

Charlies," as we called the Japanese bombers ... The motors drone louder, many of them.

Then I began to trot down the slope away from the radar tent toward a trench shelter we had long ago dug.

A massive pattern bombing began at the far end of the strip. I judged they were dropping one hundred pound bombs every twenty-five yards.

A spotlight caught one of them and other spots raked across the sky to converge on it from all angles and follow its flight. Anti-aircraft guns boomed and red splotches exploded high in the air around the bomber. The tiny fleck of silver did not swerve from its course.

As the bombers approached, I coldly concentrated on their height and the angle of the bombs' descent. Beneath me, as though detached from the upper body, my legs moved like pistons carrying me rapidly over the coral. A shell shirked downward and I threw myself to the ground.

Covering my head with my hands, I heard my voice boom back from the wet coral against my face—Mater misericordiae. While I cringed against the falling bomb, I felt astonishment that these words had burst into consciousness.

The shell exploded nearby and shrapnel whizzed unseen around my body. Relief and exhaustion overwhelmed the senses. The soaked ground chilled through my shirt and coral gritted between my teeth. I wanted to lie still and rest, to ignore some gigantic urgency in the atmosphere. Then a new wave of motors, ack-ack explosions, and shell screeches swept toward me. I hurried to my feet to run ahead of it.

The black edge of a ravine we used for an ammunitions dump brought me to a halt. I realized I missed our bomb shelter by a hundred years or more. I turned to go around the ravine, listening always to the planes and the pattern of explosions. Then I headed at the right angle.

If it dropped the bombs they would pulverize, me. I heard the high starting screech and fell intestines convulse. For an instant. I stood paralyzed, listening to the bombs hurtle toward me.

Without any voluntary movement on my own, I felt my body hurl itself over the cliff and crash into the ravine.

Two days later, when I regained consciousness, I lay naked on a bed.

Griffin had sustained a severe concussion, permanent loss of some memory and his vision had been damaged ...

* * *

1947
Texas

John Howard Griffin was blind.

His blindness did not happen when he awakened two days later, hospitalized from the horrific Japanese bombing. It did not happen a week after that, or two weeks later, but Griffin did become blind.

How had been in the Army for more than four years, in the Pacific for three years and three months. He was sent back to the states, to a mustering-out center near San Francisco. Griffin passed all the final physical tests, except for one; the vision test. He was told he had 20/200 vision.

I was stupefied. I felt I could see reasonably well and yet 20/200 meant that I could see at 20 feet what person with normal sight would see at 200 feet I was legally blind.

At the same time Griffin was told he had 20/200 vision, he witnessed an incident which, in a variety of circumstances, was being repeated again and again throughout the country:

We continued through series of interminable lines. Standing in the sunlight, I saw a tall, heavily decorated black sergeant who was being berated by the young white corporal who had charge of getting our group into the proper lines.

"You may be a damned hero overseas, but you'r nothing but a nigger here—and don't you forget it."

I approached the gathering group.

The sergeant, his body in a violent tremble, whispered, "I've been four years fighting for this motherfucking country. I'd damned if I am coming back to this shit. '"

"You're back in it alright," the corporal shouted back.

The armed forces weren't fully integrated until 1948 by President Harry S. Truman and the segregationist Jim Crow laws weren't broken until the Supreme Court decision Brown v. Board of Education in 1954.

Griffin returned to Texas where the diagnosis was confirmed by a neurosurgeon—his eyesight had become so inadequate, the neurosurgeon suggested that Griffin should give up the idea of a careering medicine. Griffin resolved to return to France and spent the rest of his sighted months in study.

He *had* been to France—studying the calming effects of Gregorian chants among psychiatric patients with Dr. Fromenty and studying music with Father Pierre Froger. And studying medicine, at least as far as pre-med. He wanted to return and spend the rest of his remaining sighted months in France, where had lived before the South Pacific, before the remote island, before Morotai, before the Japanese bombing, before traveling back to Texas.

He returned to Fountainebleau in the summer of 1946, and a began a deeply spiritual transformation.

I feared myself—feared that I would not be able to cope with the temptation to play the tragic figure, torn to become the noble sufferer accepting the world's pity.

> *I knew that my fiercest struggles would not be against losing sight, but against the assaults of public opinion about blindness that would judge my condition tragic.*
> *Faced with nothing, very little becomes everything.*

His declining vision was also accompanied by horrific headaches.

He eventually entered the Benedictine Convent of St. Jacques, to a world of routine little changed since the middle ages or before. It nurtured his soul, yet surprised him, at the same time.

> *I soon perceived that my stay would not be a matter of instruction. No one would seek to guide me in anything. I was left alone to absorb what I could from the atmosphere, from the rhythms of monastic life and from the liturgy. All needs were cared for.*
>
> *My deepest bewilderment—and edification—lay in finding that all my preoccupations of monastic formation were utterly false.*
>
> *I had imagined that men seeking union with God languished in a state of mystical trauma, soaring above the baser aspects of daily living. But here men lived in intimacy with the rich polyphony of philosophy and theology rather than with some lyrical emotionalism. The odors of cabbages and mop water no longer jarred against the fragrance of incense, but were complimentary.*

And he had long philosophical conversations with his mentor Friar Hussar, fictionalized in *The Devil Rides Outside* as Father Clement.

The horrific headaches became more frequent and his vision became increasingly blurry.

He journeyed to Tours, where he had lived in his previous sojourn in France. And Griffin met a blind man, a bookseller on the streets of Tours. "The Blind Man of Tours" became an integral part of his transformation and Griffin's essay by that name became one of his most famous publications of that period of his life. Griffin became curious how a blind man could sell books on the street; how he would know the titles and how he could accept the correct payment for his books.

Griffin found the man's flat; he wanted know what was like to be blind and, at first, then blind man was taken aback by Griffin's questions. The man had jazz playing in the background.

> "You didn't come for a book, though, did you?"
> "No sir."
> "Did you come to see a blind man?" He asked and leaned forward, his face covering my entire field of vision, consuming me.
> "Yes sir ..."
> The jazz raked across us.
> "Why?" His voice exploded, as though he dreaded the answer.
> I wished for silence. The room needed silence. But we were bombarded by the cheap upsurge of saxophones and clarinets.
> "Because I hoped to learn something from you ..."
> "From me?" He said in sneering disbelief. "What, for example?"
> "How you do things. How you live. What it's like ..."

When Griffin admitted that he was going blind, he saw a look of stunned anguish on the man's face. The blind man of Tours began to teach Griffin what he could ... Griffin offered to buy a book—*any* book—Griffin thought. At the end of an exceptionally evening, Griffin forgot to take a book along. And then he realized that he never knew the man's name—and the blind man of Tours never knew his name.

Griffin moved to the Abbey of Saint Pierre of Solesmes, living in a cell like all other monks. The stay would be all too brief. The Abbey was heated little better than during the middle ages. In

December, 1946, Griffin contracted malaria. He lay burning with fever in a freezing cell in the monastery. He fell unconscious.

The fevers reoccured so frequently that by January, 1947, he had to leave the Abbey. He simply could not withstand the constant cold and was not able to gain strength on the meager diet which sustained the monks. He rented a villa nearby (which presumably became the interior scenes in *The Devil Rides Outside*) and trekked back and forth to the Abbey. He found that if he wrote with a pen, he could see the lines only as a blur.

In the spring of 1947, at 27, John Howard Griffin became completely blind.

At that point, the overhead globe (of a light) appeared to him like candlelight seen through a dense fog. And he continue to wrestle with ... every aspect of blindness:

> *I knew that those I loved would suffer for more than I would suffer. I carried the responsibility of not only accepting what came, but also comforting them. And the best way to comfort them was to nullify the stereotypes of blindness, to work for skills that would dispel sadness and make them forget my condition, and even as I realized this, I was certain it was beyond my own capacities. I saw the enormity of the task and saw its would require help.*
>
> *I must be in perfect, voluntary obedience to a greater force, do out of obedience what I could not do from own own imperfect initiative. There was suddenly no alternative. If others were to be spared, I must make the last act of will ...*

He went to the chapel and may have silently said *le grand oui ...*

> *I forced the words out.* The Great Yes. *If you exist, take me for what I am. I hold nothing back. Show me what you want me to do. I'll obey no matter how repulsive it, is to*

> *me personally. I give you myself totally and without any reservation.*
>
> *And still navigating each day constantly presented challenges.*
>
> *When I tried to eat, either I speared my lip with the fork or the food dropped into my lap. When I reached for a glass, I often knocked it over. I lost my direction in the middle of the room and had to walk until I bumped into a wall to locate myself.*
>
> *My nerves jangled with each unexpected noise. I found myself cursing in solitude, trembling with impotent rage. The reality of blindness presented a thousand roadblocks altogether different from those I had attempted to foresee. I was thankful to have this initiation alone, to make the mistakes unobserved. How did a man comb his hair or find his clothes or shave? And what did he do during the hours except sit and wait for someone to come and take his arm and lead him somewhere.*

He discovered an old monk who was also blind. The monk offered wisdom from his decades of blindness:

> *Learn to search for a glass properly. Did it five hundred times and you'll never knock one over. Get yourself a lightweight fork and then you can tell by the weight if you bring it to your mouth empty or if it had food on it. You are a musician. You have already learned that a passage of music you cannot play the first time comes easily into your hands after practicing it twenty or a hundred times. I still learn this way.*
>
> *I am amazed all the time how quickly things come, and I've been without my sight for many years now, maybe twenty.*

Every part of daily life posed a problem. How would he ever urinate without making a mess? The old monk told him: learn to straddle a commode so he was touching it with the insides of both legs, then aim down between his legs.

Griffin wanted to shake his hand in friendship. But how? The old blind monk suddenly snapped his fingers. Griffin reached out to the sound and they shook hands.

He took a ship home and on board met a doctor from Guatemala. They spoke French together and Griffin received yet another lesson, a lesson from the doctor in musical terms he clearly appreciated.

> *"There are two main activities for you now.*
>
> *"First, there are the activities that do not involve seeing at all, like listening to the radio or a concert or lying awake in the dark. They are consonant situations.*
>
> *"However, if you were at a sporting event, you would be acutely aware of your lack of sight. That would be a dissonant situation."*
>
> *"Yes, that makes perfect sense," I said. Since the doctor was making a psychological distinction using music la metaphor and I was a musician who had studied medicine, what he said struck with precision.*
>
> *"Each of us must find some way to balance out the psychologically dissonant situations with consonant situations that allow tensions to resolve,"* he continued, *"or else your nervous systems collapse eventually. Now, without your sight, you still must live in a sighted world. You face many dissonant situations that people with sight are spared. Some of these will change into consonant situations as you learn to solve your problems and handle yourself better. Until you learn skills you will need, it seems to me that you have to avoid too many dissonant situations, or at least take time to recuperate from them by seeking consonant situations deliberately."*

Griffin returned home; his parents had always wanted to move to the country, so they had bought a farm outside Mansfield, Texas, 20 miles from Fort Worth.

Griffin had to face the fear of failure, to face the "paralysis of caution," to venture, to take a step, *to do*. Every step, every activity was a challenge to overcome, especially outside the farmhouse.

> *I felt into gullies, walked into low-hanging tree limbs, got lost It was worth the falls to kill the fear. To gain maximum freedom, my parents would frequently go into town. With the certainty no one watched, I began to develop astonishing speed, even running along pathways in the woods. I soon discovered I could locate myself by the feel of the terrain under my feet, by the sunlight on my face, by the direction of the wind.*

And Griffin simply refused to become *a victim*. Or a curiosity.

> *To most sighted people, blindness is simply the worst tragedy that can befall a man. The world tells you in a thousand ways that you are a pitiful figure. Few believe that you can be happy and interpret your own natural happiness as stoicism or bravery. To have people constantly whispering how pathetic you are becomes a grinding irritation ... most blind persons neither want pity for their "misfortune" nor applause for the simplest accomplishment.*

He journeyed into Fort Worth, to the Lighthouse for the Blind. He "learned all the Brailles."

He learned to raise livestock and bought chickens and Poland China hogs. He would feed, and judge them by feel:

> *I felt no loss of dignity when I sat in a farrowing pen in the middle of the night helping a sow farrow her pigs, drying them with a tow sack, clipping their umbilical cords*

and notching their ears before returning them. On the contrary, I felt satisfaction in doing it, or raking stockpens or plucking the geese for down or rendering lard in a huge iron kettle over a wood fire. I had lived at the Abbey of Solesmes. In both instances, in relative isolation and close to nature. I lived a simple, uncomplicated life. The liturgy, the chants, the silence were carried within when I worked. As it had been in France, so it was on the farm. Values held important by sighted society were supremely unimportant to me. I lived not behind cloister walls marked by bells but by the hunger of stock animals, by the woods in all their seasons and by the cycle of birth and death in nature.

He entered livestock competitions under a different name, so no one could claim he had an advantage because he was blind. He had stock shown in the Southwestern Exposition and Fat Stock Show in Fort Worth, and won prizes for his Poland China hogs.

He also raised Toulouse geese and Golden Roller canaries.

Other ranchers accepted him as an equal: he once overheard someone say "you don't need two feel sorry for him. He can do as good without his sight as the rest of us can with ours. He sure takes all the prizes."

He enjoyed the company of the other stockmen; after daily competition, they would go out to eat and play cards. None of them would play poker with him if he used a deck of Braille cards. They feared he could read their own cards with his fingers as he dealt them. He couldn't do that, but he never told them so.

He walked with a cane and he gave lectures on musicology to area colleges and universities.

In 1949, he went on a concert tour with Robert Casadesus, whom he had met previously in France. The tour began in Dallas, where he met professor and book critic Lon Tinkle; they conversed in French and subsequently became life-long friends. In New Orleans, he met Sadie Jacobs, who had been blind since three. She taught Griffin how to navigate the world, He learned to use a flexible white cane, instead of a heavy one he had used previously. He learned to walk the through the streets of New Orleans by himself.

> *She opened up a new world for me.*
>
> *Perhaps most importantly of all, she taught me to get rid of the "blind look." The sightless rarely look toward the person speaking to them. Like most, I tended to hold my head rigid and hold it too high, as if I was staring at the skies. The blind do this unconsciously. In some circles, it is brutally but accurately termed "the dumb look."*
>
> *"Aim you face directly at the speaker's voice," she instructed. "Animate your face. Show expressions. Move your head frequently. Remember to them you are not only Howard Griffin you are a symbol of all blind people in the world. They will judge others by you."*
>
> *Then she explained that "part of our problem now is that the sighted have seen too many beggars, too many ill-trained blind. So I want you to remember this: You will have succeeded only when you can make people forget you are blind."*

Griffin, who went by the name John or Howard, took her advice. (Before *The Devil Rides Outside* was first published he discovered there was another Howard Griffin, an active, published poet in England. He added the first name John to separate the two Howard Griffins.)

It was all part of his journey. He had been blind for two years when he met her. And when he returned to Texas, he met critic John Mason Brown, who urged him to become a writer. How? Griffin asked. "Get paper and typewriter and begin," Brown said, simply. *Surely it can't be that easy*, Griffin thought, but he returned to the Lighthouse for the Blind in Fort Worth and asked for typing lessons. He began on a Thursday, on an old Underwood typewriter. By Monday he knew how to type "with fair facility."

His father helped convert a feed room of their barn into a studio. It was scarcely three steps in each direction. It may have occurred to Griffin that his studio was much the same size as the cells he had lived in, while he was staying in the Benedictine monasteries in France, and used for much the same purposes—introspection and learning.

Griffin's ideas and words poured out, perhaps faster than he had anticipated. It was an *epiphany*.

> *The the characters, who at first seemed dead, began to come to life and acting with a vitality of their own.*
>
> *I wondered if this might be my true vocation, so casually stumbled upon. All of past situations seemed to have been a preparation for these long days and nights when I poured out pages of a first novel.*
>
> *My past training in giving up something beyond myself tempered life now. I immersed my being in the atmosphere, in the movements, and in the characters. The process became more hypnotically real than anything else. Soon the work took over so completely that I moved a cot into the feed room and lived there night and day.*

Griffin had to learn to judge his own sensibilities as a writer:

> *Each time I came to a passage where a truth appeared in conflict with current standards of good taste, I would ask myself if it would offend God. I soon discovered to my considerable amusement that God would appear to be much less narrow minded than those who pretended to act in His name.*

His background in music sustained him—in fact, his knowledge of the forms of music supremely aided his work:

> *In my first attempt at a novel, which became* The Devil Rides Outside, *I used the forms of Beethoven's String Quarter Opus 131, a work I knew intimately. The characters enter as Beethoven's themes enter and are developed*

in the same way. *The novel's four principal female characters were created as the embodiments of four sensual types as the protagonist reacted to them. But I responded to them as representatives of the four variations Beethoven had used in his quartet. When the theme of the novel did not match the music, I changed the novel.*

Griffin wrote *The Devil Rides Outside* as a first-pension narrative simply because that was the only technique he understood. He finished the novel in the summer of 1947 and immediately wrote *Handbook for Darkness*, a lengthy monologue/guide for the blind and their families, friends and colleagues. It was published by The American Foundation for the Blind in print and Braille editions.

In his student days in Tours, he began keeping a journal; he returned to it instinctively and discovered it greatly aided his work:

A private journal—with no thought of anyone else seeing it—allows the writer to rip the dull curtain off his thoughts, to record feelings, problems, emotions, reactions, temptations, and all of the private dramas and dreams. Most importantly, it is a way to recall those ideas and scenes that would soon escape memory unless set down on paper. If honest, it will contain the tremendous advantage of giving him a truer self-knowledge, which can be horrifying, sometimes overwhelmingly so, for it is humbling to see oneself without illusions. But this is the best way to compassion and wisdom.

The journal allows the writer to create directly and without wending his way through all the jungles of delusion and self-aggrandizement. The true writer, like the true painter, is an observer of all things, and quite especially of himself, but of himself in detachment, as though part of him stood away and appraised the rest, without love or partiality.

* * *

John Steinbeck used much the same method. Each day he wrote a journal/diary entry to "warm up" his pen—he wrote his novels in longhand because that method slowed down his writing and allowed him to concentrate on the flow and pace of his manuscript-in-progress. He kept a journal during the months he wrote *The Grapes of Wrath,* published in 1939, and that journal has been published as *Working Days: The Journals of The Grapes of Wrath* (1959). And later, he used the same method when writing *East of Eden,* published in 1952. *His Journals of a Novel: The East of Eden Letters* has also been published (1969). Both books of his journals/diary entries offer substantial insights about how a novelist views himself and his craft and how he visualizes and articulates his work.

* * *

The Devil Rides Outside was published the fall of 1952. When Smiths Inc. sent out review copies and publicity material, Griffin's secret was out. The back dust jacket photograph shows him outside, sideways to the camera on a giant rock, wearing black glasses and holding a white cane. Obviously blind.

It was a wonderfully perfect story for Texas newspapers. Headlines from those days tell the story.

> Blind War Veteran's Book
> To Be Sent to 300 Reviewers

> Blind Man Writes Way
> Into Catholic Church

> Blind Man's book Draws Praise
> From Nation's Literary Critics

> Blind author
> Off to Consult
> Literary Critics

> Success for Blind Author

> Novel Written in Barn at
> Mansfield Praised Highly

(All of these articles are in the Griffin archives at Columbia University, but the newspaper names had been inadvertently clipped off. Presumably all were Texas newspapers.)

An article by his friend Lon Tinkel, in *The Dallas Morning News* Sunday Oct. 12,1952 was headlined:

> Writing Farmer of Tarrant County
> Violates All 'Typical Texan' Rules

Readers outside the circulation areas of Texas newspapers knew nothing of this—outside Texas, only the readers who saw Griffin's photograph on the back jacket of the hardcover edition ever knew he was blind.

Years later, he told Studs Terkel:

> *I learned to type and wrote six books. They'd say "You're extraordinary." I'd say I'm not. It's just that I refuse to let them put me into a cloistered workshop. I resent very deeply the underchallenging of the blind, the young, the black.*

Six books. Written while he was blind. Or perhaps at least five. *The Devil Rides Outside* and *Nuni* were published during his lifetime. One other novel, *Street of the Seven Angels* was published posthumously. A fourth, *Passacaglia* remained unfinished. Another, a comic novel based on his father-in-law Clyde Parker Holland, was apparently lost.

Griffin claimed six books, his literary executor, Robert Bonazzi says he wrote five; Griffin did have long-term memory loss from the bombing on Morotai.

John Howard Griffin into only learned to adjust to his blindness, *he turned a handicap into enlightenment.*

The Devil Rides Outside sold out the first printing of 5,000 copies and a second printing was scheduled by October 27, 1952.

But Griffin had other concerns—he had met Elizabeth Ann Holland. She was a music student, studying with Griffin's Mother. She was 17, he was 32 and blind. But, as Griffin said:

> *I had always been considered controversial, yet I felt not controversial at all. I was sightless but refused to live down to the sighted view that I was handicapped. I was a writer who refused to spin out popular books. If I allowed myself to become average—a totally dependent blind man or an unscrupulous writer—I could never be normal or live naturally. That was not bravery on my part, but simply survival.*

He did not visualize himself as handicapped, neither did Elizabeth Ann Holland. They thought nothing of their age differences. They were married June. 2, 1953 and honeymooned in Mexico City. His new in-laws gave them 24 acres and a cottage on the Holland farm. Griffin wrote all his fiction in the barn studio at his parent's farm.

Griffin began to experience medical problems, which would plague him throughout the rest of his life; first a rare type of diabetes, difficult to control, and tumors on his feet. He had to use a wheelchair. In May, 1954, he began to lose the use of his legs, due to damaged nerves at the base of his spine.

By July, 1954, a diagnosis was confirmed; he could hobble around slowly, but might become paralyzed. Griffin began to have deep thoughts—why had he subjected Elizabeth Ann to a marriage to an older blind man, now barely able to walk?

Their marriage survived all of Griffin's medical crises points; they eventually had four children. The marriage was broken only by Griffin's death, in 1960.

Pocket Books printed a paperback edition of *The Devil Rides Outside* in 1954. Then it was censored in Detroit. It became a test case in obscenity. The Detroit ruling was based on a statute banning any book "containing obscene, immoral, lewd or lascivious language tending to incite minors to violence or immoral acts."

The ban was appealed to the Michigan Supreme Court, where it was upheld.

"The ramifications of such a statue are staggering," Griffin said, "because logically everything from the Bible to Shakespeare could be banned on this basis."

An Associated Press article distributed October 21, 1956, said, in part:

> "Some of the things I wrote in my novel make me sick to my stomach, but I had to write them to be honest.
>
> "But honesty in depicting a character is one thing, while obscenity is another. The problem could be solved if there were a clear legal definition of obscenity."
>
> The courts, Griffin said, have not come forward with an adequate definition so far, and he hopes the Supreme Court, ruling on his case later this year, will provide one.

Although Griffin expected a Supreme Court decision in 1956, it was not until February, 26, 1957, that a unanimous ruling by the Supreme Court was announced. *The New York Times* carried a frontpage headline:

High Court Voids Obscene Book Act

The Devil Rides Outside had been cleared of the charge it was pornographic. The landmark ruling, by Justice Felix Frankfurter, established several significant points in favor of authors, publishers and booksellers. It stated that book must not be judged pornographic on the basis of isolated passages taken out of context, but the entire work must be taken into consideration. It directed all states to revamp existing statues on pornography, protecting booksellers from future illegal incursions and clarifying the censorship battleground nationwide.

And, Frankfurter wrote:

> *It is clear on the record that appellant was convicted because Michigan made it an offense for him to make available to the general reading pubic a book that the trial judge found have a potentially deleterious influence upon youth. The state insists that, by thus guaranteeing the general reading public against books not too rugged for grown men and women in order to shield juvenile innocence, it is exercising its power to promote the public welfare. Surely, this is to burn the house down to roast the pig …. The incidence of this enactment is to reduce the adult population of Michigan to reading only what is fit for children.*

"A magnificent statement. How sweet is justice," Griffin said.

The Devil Rides Outside was not only a Book of the Month Club alternate election as his first novel, the Supreme Court ruling following the censoring in Detroit was a major victory for all writers, all publishers, all booksellers, all libraries and all readers.

Elizabeth Ann had become pregnant; on November 20, 1954, they had their first child, a girl, Susan Michelle.

In 1956, he became involved in a desegregation crisis in the Mansfield, Texas public school system. He co-wrote, with Theodor Freedman, of Houston, a lengthy monograph, "What happened in Mansfield." It was 16 single-spaced pages, and was "based on a series of interviews with residents of Mansfield and others directly connected with the local situation. Some of the interviews were recorded directly, in other instances, the interviewer recorded his impressions immediately after the interview." This encounter with segregation in the public schools of his hometown must surely have, again, reinforced his sense of injustice in the world.

In 1646, Griffin and Elizabeth had their second child, a boy, Johnny.

And beginning in January, 1956, Griffin began using two recording machines to complete *Nuni*—he transferred spoken text from one, along with edited changed into the second. This, he said, speeded up the process and eliminated tedious re-typing.

> *I had been very close to Nuni—aware perhaps that I had been putting the problems of my own life into the lap of Professor Harper, desperate for the narrator to solve them. I had stripped him of everything that men generally consider necessary to function at the human level—family, friends, even clothing—and plunged him into a world in which he was ill-prepared to live. My prospect was similar; though I never mentioned it out loud.*

When he finished the manuscript, Griffin faced the postpartum depression common to many authors when a major project is finished:

> *Now it is gone. They are really gone, all of these characters who have been more real than many people I knew during these past years, They walked out the door with stamps on them. Their existence disappears when words stiffen into print. The printed word is the tomb of human spoken utterance. The body of the speaker is elsewhere.*

* * *

Then an unimaginable—a most remarkable—event occurred quite suddenly and unexpectedly.

January 9, 1957 Mansfield, Texas

John Howard Griffin could see. His vision came back.
... as he was walking from his barn studio to his parent's house to begin lunch.

Redness swirled in front of my eyes. Then I thought I saw the back door, cut in portions, dancing at crazy angles.

Elements continued to dance and he had pain in his eyes and head.

Griffin's mental gyroscope, which had held him steady in the universe throughout the years, suddenly spun out of control.

He got to a telephone and called his wife. All he could say was "I think ..."

"What is it?"

"I think I can see," he said and began weeping.

I sat in a chair at the table. The room was broken up.

Triangles of color faded and swirled. Weird designs of floor and wall and ceiling fused. It was like being hit a terrible blow on my head. My system could not bear the shock.

Dimly I thought of all those sightless people who had for so long been my brothers and sisters. Was I actually leaving their world, to which I had been so accustomed?

I prayed for the presence of mind never to forget them, to do or say nothing that would build false hopes in them or hurt them. Was something happening to me that would never happen to them? Dear God, would this hurt them, would this make them feel more lonely? And I was concerned with my family. Was I really seeing? Would their hopes be built up only to crash when this incredible storm passed?

Another thought stuck me and almost twisted any brain.

Was ever a man in a stranger position? My own wife and children, people who were my life, and yet if I saw them in the street I would not even know them! From this swirl of my own confusion, I thought of how my wife must feel. Should she run immediately to me? Should she take time to dress, fix herself up, so I could see her first in the best possible light?

The doctor arrived, but Griffin could not see him—only a splotch of the blue in the corner. The doctor gave Griffin a shot and talked, presumably to soothe him.

I no longer remembered the words, for my mind was blotting out, trying to become unconscious. I sat, holding myself up, drained of all strength, all intelligence. The sedative made me withdraw into a deep calm, far from myself. It closed out the world. I heard myself asking what the sedative was.

"Demerol, a light sedative. I want you to be aware of everything. This is an experience few can have."

My wife and children. Would I know them? Would I know my parents, after all those years? Strange and twisted perceptions came to mind.

Later a car pulled into the driveway. He heard the door slam. Nerves simmered up from numbness. "Tell me who it is," he said to the doctor.

"Your parents."

I prayed vaguely and braced myself, prayed that this no be a deception for them. They had suffered too much, too gallantly on my account.

Then there was a swirl of movement. Faces drew close to mine. They were kissing me, talking in low tones. I had to pull out of it, to reassure them in some way.

"*Can you actually see me?*" *My mother asked.*

"*I can see you have on a green dress,*" *I mumbled.*

I couldn't control the vision enough to see their faces. I would see a portion of their clothes and instantly the ceiling or a wall—then haze.

Talk went on around me. I retreated into stupor until the sound of another car aroused me. I stayed seated at the table. At the door, I heard the voices of my wife and children. I staggered up from the chair. Susan ran forward and was the first to appear. I concentrated beyond strength to see all the radiant wisdom of her two-year-old face looking at me.

"*You beautiful little thing,*" *I said, touching her cheek.*

I saw her face clearly then it blurred.

Suddenly, Elizabeth was in my arms, her face beside mine. I glimpsed raven black hair. Johnny was tugging at my pantslegs. I reached down, felt his short-cropped hair, but could not see him. The first clear view of my daughter had been like looking at the sun, blinding me to everything else. That image remained in front of my face during the next dim hours. The effort of seeing her, or perhaps the emotion, had shattered me.

The next day, the psychic overload continued.

There were reporters and photographers, and the beginning of the nervous rigors that shook the whole body.

I concentrated on the blind, knowing that I must say nothing to hurt them or give them false hopes. I sat numb in the eye of a hurricane of activity. But. I had no recollection of their questions or my answers. I was collapsing without realizing it.

The press loved the story, because it was such an unexpected sequel to the blind man-writes-novel stories they had published previously:

> 'Suddenly I Could See':
> Novelist Regains
> Long-Lost Vision

> *Finally Sees Children*
> *Blind Author Regains*
> *Sight after 10 Years*

... and even the next day:

> *The next morning I was having hard rigors. No recollection of that day. I was virtually unconscious, although I moved and spoke. I saw a hall full of reporters and photographers, and I think I said yes to everything they wanted, but remembered no specifics. Then I was taken to the eye specialist. The press mob followed us. The specialist said he would have temporary glasses made immediately. My doctor was concerned about the pressure from the reporters and laid down the law.*

Senator Lyndon Johnson called, with a typical Johnsonian message: this was the only Texas miracle he could not take credit for. The articles continued:

> Author Still Glorying
> In Restoration of Sight

> His Sight's Restored,
> He's Still Dumbfounded

> *Griffin in Seclusion*
> *To Avoid Pressures*

Even *Newsweek* and *Time* had brief articles about him: in the *Newsweek* column "Newsmakers," the third week in January, under the title "Sand and Sight," and *Time* magazine, in the issue dated Jan. 21,1957, in the section, "Medicine," under a title "Second Sight."

Time wrote, in part:

> *Last week, as Griffin walked alone and unaided from his workshop to the house on his parent's farm outside Mansfield, Texas, he began to see again for the first time in ten years.*
>
> *Knowing that many cases of apparent blindness are relieved by a shock, Griffin explained: "There was no bump, no jar. Nothing happened. Suddenly everything looked like red sand in front of my eyes." By the time a doctor arrived, Griffin could make out the color of his blue shirt and read a prescription blank. Near shock from the experience, Griffin was put under heavy doses of sedatives, given "cylinder glasses" to help pull his eye muscles back to useful strength. His vision, Griffin estimated, was about 20/150.*
>
> *Although Griffin belittled the possibility, the only plausible medical explanation of his cases was that his blindness had been mainly, if not entirely hysterical, i.e., brought on by the emotional shock of bomb blasts. Dissolution of a long-standing blood clot could not explain his recovery, as such a clot would have soon caused irreparable damage to the eyes' nerves. Seeing his wife and children for the first time, he said, "They are more beautiful than I ever expected ... I am astonished, stunned and grateful."*

Doctors wanted him to go to a hospital where he could recuperate with proper rest and medication. Instead, he retreated to a sanctuary where he felt completely cloistered: a nearby Carmelite monastery.

> *Finally, the doctors decided to sequester me in a distant hospital. No more visitors, telephone calls or interviews. I requested that I be able to stay with the Carmelites instead of the hospital. The doctors thought that that would even be better.*
>
> *So I was taken to Mount Carmel and no one knew I was being hidden. What the doctors did not know was that the monks would be tougher than they had been. The monks promised that I would be totally secluded and that the drugs would be administered strictly. I knew I would be safe in the cloister.*

And he eventually answered a question many asked, who had heard of his remarkable transformation:

> *Many people wondered what it might be like to see against after a decade of blindness. Sight does not return full-blown suddenly. You have to learn to see again, like a newborn infant.*
>
> *You have to learn to use muscles, to focus. The adjustment back to sight was as complex as the adjustment to blindness had been. The simple mechanics of living had be learned over again.*
>
> *How to eat, to walk, how to look at people. I kept forgetting that I could see, and that in seeing I could do many things I had put out of my life.*

As the late Paul Harvey used to say on his syndicated radio show "Now you know ... the rest of the story ..."

* * *

Some months after my book *The Man Who Changed His Skin: The Life and Work of John Howard Griffin* was published in 2011, I was introduced to a black minister in Richmond, Virginia He was told my book "was the first full biography of Griffin, who wrote the American classic *Black Like Me*."

He said, "I read it years ago," which was the comment I have always heard. Millions have read it. He didn't, however, know about Griffin's decade of blindness. I described it briefly, in our conversation, adding, "No one knows how or why his eyesight came back."

After only a slight pause, the minister said, "God had different plans for him," which may be the only ultimate answer.

* * *

The answer of *why* he became blind may have been a severe concussion during the bombing at Morotai and undiagnosed diabetes. The *why* his eyesight returned, a decade later, is still unexplained to this day, except perhaps, for "God had different plans for him."

* * *

Back in the world of sight, Griffin's first major writing job in the summer of 1958, was a "work for hire" project in Midland, Texas. A "work for hire" in publishing, is an article or book that is sold on a one-time basis; the writer gets paid once, not yearly or semi-annual royalties. It is the publishing equivalent of selling a used car; once it is sold—it's gone. He was approached by the First National Bank of Midland; to celebrate a new bank building, Griffin was to be paid $10,000. to write a book—the history of the Midland area. The book was to be given away by the bank—there was little distribution beyond the Midland area, surely no copies in bookstores across the country or any major sales to libraries.

Griffin had led a hardscrabble life during his decade of blindness. He could surely use the money (it's a universal truth: *all writers always need more money—*).

Griffin's description of the vast plains (he camped out by himself to experience the vastness of that world) reads like John Steinbeck's description of his native California in the pages of *Of Mice and Men,* published in 1937, especially in the early pages where Steinbeck describes the hobo campsites along the Salinas River.

Griffin begins the chronicle of that land in 1849 and wrote of wagon trains, of Comanches, the *Llano Estacado* (the *Land of Staked Plains),* how that area was impacted by the Civil War, the need for water, cattle drives, buffalo hunting, the advent of the railroads, droughts and blizzards, cowboys and the cowboy life, cattle and cattle ranching and, of course, the rise of the banking business in that area. The growth of towns into cities, electricity, telephones, automobiles, discoveries of prehistoric life in that area, and much about the oil industry and the growth of Midland up to 1959.

At $10,000. the bank got its money's worth, but still he overcompensated. Returning to full sight and enthusiastic even for this "work for hire" project, Griffin's first draft exceeded 1,300 pages.

The final book, as printed was 180 pages. And, for what it was, *The Land of the High Sky* is still readable as a history of that area of Texas.

* * *

After regaining his sight, you would think—*you would think*—that Griffin would want little more than to sit on his front porch, enjoying his sight and with his wife and children.

But sometime after completing the Midland bank project, he told his wife, in effect, "Oh honey, there's something I need to do …"

"What is that?" she may have said, with the innocence of a lamb.

"I need to know what it's like to be black."

Her response is not recorded but may have been in the area of "You want do *WHAT?*" Or perhaps it might have been, in her astonishment, "You want to do *!@#$%A&** *WHAT?*"

* * *

October, 1959
Mansfield, Texas

Why did Griffin take the dangerous and yet courageous step of dying his skin black to make the journey throughout the south to eventually write *Black Like Me?* He could have answered this in any number ways, but the most succinct is told in Robert Bonazzi's *Man in the Mirror*:

> "The real story is the universal one of men who destroy the souls and bodies of other men (and in the process destroy themselves) for reasons neither really understand. It is the story of the persecuted, the defrauded, the feared and detested." This universal story of persecution—man's inhumanity to man—has been told in countless variations by every culture in all historical epochs—right up to the present.
>
> "I could have been a Jew in Germany, a Mexican in a number of states or a member of any 'inferior' group," he insisted. "Only the details would have differed. The story would be the same."
>
> *Black Like Me* is, of course, the historical record of what it was like to be a Negro in the Deep South prior to the civil-rights era of the 1960s. It is also an intensively lived experience, evoked by the immediacy of his vital, vivid prose, that has kept open a window on that historical time and place.

Why he did it, he later said, was a question black people *never* asked him.

(And he never mentioned his blindness in the book; it wasn't germane to the *Black Like Me* story.)

He also had to face the question of the *Other*. Griffin was always, by instinct, a cultural anthropologist, or ethnologist, and he encountered a wide variety of situations that raised the question, as he phrased it, of the *Other*. The outsider in a strange culture; oppressed minorities in a variety of cultures; the outsider unable to communicate; the sense of modem humanity lost in the world.

He had seen it as a young American in French schools (a benign version of *Other*-ness, easily conquered in large part by learning French); he had seen it during his stays in the monasteries in France, when he was the outsider in the close-knit priesthood of the Benedictine orders; he had seen it when the Nazis came for the Jews and other non-Aryans; he had seen it in the isolated island in the South Pacific when he was the *other*, led through the jungle by a five-year-old boy, unable to cope in a primitive world, as a twentieth century urban male. And he had surely become the *Other*, during his decade of blindness when he was trapped in a sightless world, an outcast, with his black glasses and white cane, stigmatized as helpless by the sighted world.

Now he would be the *Other* in the south, a stranger in a strange land.

* * *

Griffin began his odyssey October 28, 1959 considering the proposal, which was "suddenly mysterious and frightening." The next day he drove to Fort Worth and talked to George Levitan, publisher of *Sepia,* a general circulation magazine for blacks, that was designed like *Life* or *Look*. Griffin explained his proposal to Levitan, who was both surprised and skeptical. His reaction and the reaction of other staff members of Sepia was; *you don't know what you're getting into*. But Levitan agreed to underwrite Griffin's expenses and Griffin agreed to contribute articles about his experiences to *Sepia*. Griffin also met with FBI officials in Dallas. Their reaction was: it was out of our jurisdiction, they said and, oh yes, you don't know what you're getting into.

Griffin told his wife what was planning. After recovering from her astonishment, she said *if that's what you have to do, that's what you have to do.* He never offered to take her along. It would be altogether too dangerous; dangerous enough for himself, impossibly dangerous to take his wife along.

Griffin traveled to New Orleans November 1. He had a sumptuous meal at Broussard's, in the French Quarter, then, the next day, called three dermatologists and made an appointment with the first one.

A common question throughout the years always has been: how did he change his skin? The dermatologist used a treatment for vitiligo, a skin condition in which spots appear on the face and body. The chemical was Oxsoralen and the treatments should have taken six weeks-to-eight months to darken the skin, but Griffin decided he could not wait that kong and began accelerated treatments.

His treatment regimen was dangerous. He had be closely monitored and checked for liver damage. The dermatologist gave him a prescription for Oxsoralen and recommended lengthy sunlamp treatments. He spent up to 15 hours a day, for a week, under a sunlamp, wearing cotton pads to protect his eyes. The only side effects were fatigue and nausea.

(When he died years later, rumors persisted that he had been poisoned by the chemicals needed for this change—this was apparently not true.)

Griffin spent much of this time as a guest of Harold and Gladys Levy, who had previously introduced him to Sadie Jacobs; she, in turn, had taught him how to use a flexible white cane and how to navigate the streets of New Orleans, while he was blind.

He didn't live in the Levy's home, but rather a guest house which had been a former slave quarters. Becoming a black man while living in a slave cabin was an irony not lost on Griffin. He did not mention them by name in *Black Like Me*, to protect them from any possible consequences.

The last appointment with the dermatologist was November 7, 1959.

The dermatologist established the daily dosages of Oxsoralen and informed Griffin that if the dosage was discontinued, his skin would slowly lighten. If the dosage was begun again, his skin would slowly darken again.

He showed, as Griffin recalled, "much doubt and perhaps regret that he had ever cooperated with me in this transformation."

The doctor shook Griffin's hand and then said, with remarkable prescience, "now you go into oblivion."

* * *

The doctor suggested that Griffin shave his head; he simply didn't show the characteristics of being black, with his natural hair.

Alone, in the dark, Griffin began to shave his head by feel; he had learned how to shave while blind, so shaving his head offered no problem, although it was tedious. He applied coat after coat of stain, washing away the excess. He showered, washing away more excess stain. Only then, did he venture a look at what he had become:

> *Turning off all the lights, I went into the bathroom and closed the door. I stood in the darkness before the mirror; my hand on the light switch. I forced myself to flick it on.*
>
> *In the flood of light against white tile, the face and shoulders of a stranger—a fierce, bald, very dark Negro—glared at me from the glass. He in no way resembled me.*
>
> *The transformation was total and shocking. I had expected to see myself disguised, but this was something else.*

> *I was imprisoned in the flesh of an utter stranger; an unsympathetic one with whom I felt no kinship. All traces of John Howard Griffin I had been were wiped from existence.*
>
> *Even the senses underwent a change so profound it filled me with distress. I looked into the mirror and saw nothing of the white John Howard Griffin's past. No, the reflections led back to Africa, back to the shanty and the ghetto, back to the fruitless struggles against the mark of blackness. Suddenly, almost with no mental preparation, no advance hint, it became clear and permeated my whole being. My inclination was to fight against it. I had gone too far. I knew now there is no such thing as a disguised white man, when the black won't rub off. The black man is wholly a Negro, regardless of what he once may have been. I was a newly created Negro who must go out that door and live in a world unfamiliar to me.*
>
> *The completeness of this transformation appalled me. It was unlike anything I had ever imagined. I became two men, the observing one and the one who panicked, who felt the beginnings of great loneliness, not because I was a Negro, but because of the man I had been, the self I knew, was hidden in the flesh of another. If I returned home to my wife and children they would not know me. They would open the door and stare blankly at me. My children would want to know who is this large, bald Negro. If I walked up to friends, I knew I would see no flicker of recognition in their eyes.*
>
> *I had tampered with the mystery of existence and I had lost the sense of my own being. That is what devastated me. The Griffin that was had become invisible.*

The word in German is *doppelgänger,* the ghostly counterpart of a living person, *but doppelgänger* makes no reference to this sort of second self.

When Griffin went to the bathroom, waited for his eyes to

adjust to the dark and turned on the light and saw himself in the mirror, it was midnight.

He remembered thinking:

> *I was a man born old at midnight, into a new life.*
> *How does such a man act?*

Griffin clearly did not comprehend the moral complexities of what he had done; he continued to wrestle with the myriad of implications of his journey into the *Other.*

Biographer Robert Bonazzi wrote:

> *Through a crude but mysterious alchemy, his scientific experiment had been transformed into a life-study; the seclusion of midnight had changed into a secret human laboratory. Since it was "a new life" into which even this "man born old" entered, the inevitable results would be fresh and fascinating, because the manchild became both the experimenter and the body of experimentation.*

In a subsequent essay, "The Intrinsic *Other*," he explained how he continued to wrestle with the implications:

> *Almost the deepest shock I had came the first night I went out into the New Orleans night as a Negro. I went to a hotel in the ghetto and took the best available room— a tawdry miserable little cubbyhole. I sat on the bed and glanced at myself in the mirror on the wall. For the first time I was alone as a Negro in the community. That glance brought a sickening shock that I tried not to admit, not to recognize, but I could not avoid it. It was the shock of seeing my face in the mirror and of feeling an involuntary movement of antipathy for that face, because it was pigmented, the face of a Negro.*

* * *

> *I realized then that although intellectually I had liberated myself from the prejudices which our southern tradition inculcates in us, these prejudices were so in-dredged in me that the emotional level was in no way liberated. I was filled with despair.*

His first few hours had become an almost horrific version of the German idea of the *doppelgänger*—the ghostly second self.

The transformation into being a very, very black man, was horrifically traumatic enough for Griffin, but in public, he faced yet another:

> *He didn't know how to be black.*

During his sojourn as a black man, he lived in constant fear:

- that he would inadvertently do or say something that would reveal he wasn't black or …
- that southern whites, in the Klu Klux Klan or otherwise, would somehow discover what he was doing, kidnap and kill him.

He believed either was possible at any moment.

(See the final section … *from* Black Like Me …)

* * *

Griffin ended his sojourn after about five weeks, from fear, exhaustion and loss of self. He took a bus back to Texas. Once there, he feared that the Klu Klux Klan, then active in Texas, would discover what he had done. His skin tone back to normal, he took his family to Mexico for a year, where he wrote *Black Like Me*. When it was first published in 1960, it was judged an American classic and has remained so to this day—60 years later.

Key books about Griffin, in order of publication:

Man in the Mirror: John Howard Griffin and the Story of Black Like Me, Robert Bozanni, 1997.

The Man Who Changed His Skin: The Life and Work of John Howard Griffin, Thomas Fensch, 2011.

Reluctant Activist: The Spiritual Life and Art of John Howard Griffin. Robert Bozanni, 2018.

from Black Like Me

During his journey through the south, Griffin traveled from New Orleans east toward Alabama. While hitchhiking, he got a ride with a white man in a pickup truck. The incident remained seared in his memory:

"Where you from?"
"Texas."
"What're you doing down here?"
"Just traveling around, trying to find jobs."
"You're not down here to stir up trouble, are you?"
"Oh, God, no."
"You start stirring up these niggers and we sure as hell know how to take care of you."
"I don't intent to."
"Do you know what we do to troublemakers down here?"
"No, sir."
"We either ship then off to the pen or kill them."

He spoke in a tone that sickened me, casual, merciless. I looked at him. His decent eyers turned yellow. I knew that nothing could touch him to have mercy once he decided a Negro should be "taught a lesson." The immensity of it terrified me. But it caught him up like a lust now. He entertained it, his voice unctuous with pleasure and cruelty. The highway stretched deserted through the swamp forests. He nodded toward the solid wall of brush flying past our windows.

'You can kill a nigger and toss him into that swamp and no one'll ever know what happened to him."
"Yes sir."

Eichmann in Jerusalem: A Report on the Banality of Evil
Hannah Arendt / 1963

... the banality of evil ...

genre: nonfiction

The banality of evil ...
Adolf Eichmann ...
The two are now inextricably linked through Hannah Arendt's 1963 book and subsequent reprint editions.

Eichmann, Arendt, and the phrase *the banality of evil*—on her last page.

* * *

During his trial in Jerusalem, Eichmann displayed no emotion for his actions during the Holocaust; he was simply obeying orders—he was simply doing his job, a Nazi party worker, an officer obeying his orders—obeying his Führer, and those above his officer level.

He bore no moral responsibility for the deaths of millions, he said, he *was* simply following orders.

Earlier, in January, 1942, he attended the Conference of the *Staatssekretare,* (Undersecretaries of State); i.e., the Wannsee Conference, held in the Berlin suburb of Wannsee, where the objective was to co-ordinate all aspects of the Final Solution, to the Nazi's Jewish question. Eichmann was the lowest-ranking officer attending. It was a watershed meeting for Eichmann. As Arendt writes:

> *There was another reason that made the day of this conference unforgettable for Eichmann. Although he had been doing his best right along to help with the Final Solution, he had still harbored some doubts about "such a bloody solution through violence," and these doubts had now been dispelled. "Here now, during this conference, the most prominent people had spoken, the Popes of the Third Reich." Now he could see with his own eyes and hear with his own ears that not only Hitler, not only Heydrich or the "sphinx" Muller, not just the S.S. or the Party, but the elite of the good old Civil Service were vying and fighting with each other for the honor of taking the lead in these "bloody" matters. "At that moment, I sensed a kind of Pontius Pilate feeling, for I felt free of all guilt." Who was he to judge? Who was he "to have (his) own thoughts in the matter?"*

His Pontius Pilate moment, indeed. Who was he to judge?

* * *

ADOLF EICHMANN ....

Eichmann was born March 19, 1906 in Solingen, Germany. His father moved to Linz, Austria in 1913 to take a job with the Linz Tramway Company; the rest of the family followed year later. Eichmann's mother died in 1916 and his father remarried.

Eichmann was, shall we say, never a natural student. He attended the Kaiser Frank Joseph State Secondary School in Linz *(Staatsoberrealschule)* where Adolf Hitler had attended 17 years before. Eichmann participated in school activities, clubs and sports ... and apparently sometime along the way, joined the Y.M.C.A. He never graduated. His father pulled him out of that school and enrolled him in a vocational college, the *Hohere Bundeslehranstalt fur Elecktrotechnik, Maschinenbau und Hochbau*. He never graduated there either.

From 1925 to 1927 he was a sales clerk for a radio company; from 1927 to 1933, he worked in Upper Austria and Salzburg as a salesman for the Vacuum Oil Company.

Eichmann apparently had no sense of self; he couldn't feel fulfilled unless he was part of an organization. During the Jerusalem trial period, his attorney Robert Servatius said Eichmann had the personality of "an average mailman."

The Y.M.C.A didn't work for him; he eventually joined the S.S.; the *Schultz Staffel* (*Schultz*—Defense, *Staffel*—Echelon) . Early it was Hitler's bodyguard; later it grew into intelligence, security, police actions and exterminations.

Eichmann was clearly not the first; his membership in the S.S. was number 45,326.

He continued working for the Vacuum Oil Company; but lost his job in January 1933, in company employment cutbacks. The Nazi party was banned in Austria about the same time and Eichmann returned to Germany.

In December 1933, he was promoted to *SS-Scharfuhrer* (squad leader, equivalent to corporal) and assigned to a battalion quartered next to the Dachau concentration camp.

Bored there, he requested a transfer to the SD *Sicherheitsdienst* the Security Service, a division of the SS. He was assigned to create a museum of Masonic exhibits, including card indexes of all German Freemasons and Masonic organizations. It became extremely popular and visitors included Herman Goering, Heinrich Himmler, Ernest Kaltenbrunner and Baron Leopold von Mildenstein, who invited Eichmann to join his Jewish Department, section H/112 of the SD. It was Eichmann's big break.

He was tasked with completing reports on the Zionist movement and various Jewish organizations. He learned a smattering of Hebrew and Yiddish.

On March 21, 1935 he married Veronica (Vera) Liebl. They eventually had four sons: Klaus, born in 1936 in Berlin; Horst Adolf, born in 1940 in Vienna: Dieter Helmut, born in 1942 in Prague and Ricardo Francisco, born in Buenos Aires in 1955.

Eichmann continued being promoted, but never got higher then *SS-Obersturmbannfuhren,* lieutenant colonel.

Between 1933 and 1939 Nazi Germany pressured 250,000 of Germany's 437,000 Jews to leave the country. In 1939 Eichmann and his superior, Herbert Hagen, traveled to Palestine, then Haifa, then to Cairo (with forged press credentials) to meet with Feival Polkes, an agent of the Haganah; to encourage more Jews to leave for Palestine. They were unable to reach a deal with Hagen and were refused re-entry into Palestine.

The Jewish question changed dramatically when Germany invaded Poland September 1, 1939; voluntary deportation became forced deportation. Reinhard Heydrich, head of the SD, commanded that all Jews were to be collected in cities where they could be expelled by train from territories then controlled by the Third Reich.

Eichmann was posted to Berlin and assigned to the *Reichszentrale fur Judishe Auswanderung,* ie., the Reich Office for Jewish Emigration. He was assigned to organize the deportation of up to 80,000 Jews from the Ostrava district in Moravia and the Katowice district in Poland. On his own he began plans to deport Jews from Vienna.

It was too early in the Third Reich's plans for the Jewish question to be resolved easily. The plans which involved Eichmann were soon called off because Hitler needed the *Reichsbahn,* the German rail system, for other assignments.

In December, 1939, he was assigned to be Heydrich's "special expert" in charge of all deportations. He quickly developed a plan to deport 600,000 *into* Nazi occupied Poland, where they could be more easily controlled. His plan was blocked by Hans Frank, the governor-general of the occupied territories, who feared that transports would disrupt his plans for Germanization of the region he controlled. Herman Goering also forbade any transports unless he or Frank approved.

Transports did continue, but at a slower pace than Eichmann conceived; from the start of the war until April 1941, 63,000 Jews were transported as he planned and a third died in the boxcars, in transit.

He eventually planned deportations of one million Jews each year for four years, to be resettled on Madagascar, but as the British fleet controlled the Atlantic, the Madagascar idea was mentioned now and again by Hitler, but eventually ignored.

Hitler invaded the Soviet Union in Operation Barbarossa, in June, 1941, a massive campaign which appalled his generals; they knew such a campaign would surely fail, but no one dared broach that idea—the idea of failure—with Hitler.

Einsatzgruppen, task forces, i.e. killing squads, were sent behind the German divisions, to kill Communists, especially Communist leaders, all the Jews they could round up, homosexuals, gypsies and eastern Europeans, which the Nazis thought sub-human.

At the end of July, 1941, Herman Goering gave Heyrich orders to prepare for "the total solution of the Jewish question." The subsequent *Generalplan Ost* (General Plan for the East) called for deporting the population of Nazi-occupied eastern Europe and the Soviet Union to Siberia, to be exterminated or used as slave labor, but when the Nazi campaign in the Soviet Union stalled and when the United States entered the war, the plan became: exterminate all Jews in Europe immediately.

He was told in mid-September, 1941: Hitler ordered all Jews in German-controlled Europe be executed.

* * *

The Wannsee Conference, held in the Berlin suburb of Wannsee January 20, 1942, was the watershed, the turning point involving the Jewish Question: it was *The Final Solution*—and Adolf Eichmann was there, albeit the lowest-level officer attending.

Eichmann became the nexus of operations involving The Final Solution; he received regular reports of deaths associated with the Nazi killing squads.

Under Eichmann's direction, massive numbers of deportations began, to extermination camps at Belzdec, Sobibor, Treblinka and elsewhere.

He did not make policy, but directed the collection of Jewish victims, collecting their property for the Reich, and scheduled the trains to the concentration/death camps.

He was then promoted to lieutenant colonel, the highest rank he would ever achieve.

He visited Auschwitz and subsequently personally made arrangements to send victims to their deaths there, by rail.

When the war was winding down, he returned to Berlin and helped burn the records of Department IV-B4 (a task which intimately proved futile—parallel records and answering correspondence were eventually found in other Nazi departments).

He and his family were safely in Austria when the war ended.

He was captured by U.S. forces and spent time in several prison camps, eventually escaping with with papers that identified him as "Otto Heninger." He lived in safety—*for a while*—but at the Nuremberg Trials, beginning in 1946, Rudolf Hess and others gave incriminating testimony again him.

He was able to obtain new identity papers through an Austrian cleric; he became Ricardo Klement and traveled to Buenos Aires, arriving July 14, 1950. There he took various low-paying jobs, eventually running a laundromat. His income was meagre.

But Nazi hunters suspected he was still alive and Nazi hunter Simon Wiesenthal discovered he was in Buenos Aires. Eventually information was passed to the Mossad, the best, most secret and most efficient government spy agency in the world—then and now.

The Mossad found him and Israeli President David Ben-Gurion decided that Eichmann be brought to Israel for a trial. (He could easily be shot in Argentina, but the better choice would be put him on trial in Israel, to expose to the world his crimes against humanity) But how? He had to be kidnapped and transported to Israel, obviously against Argentine and international law.

The Mossad captured Eichmann May 11, 1960, outside his home in the San Fernando area, 12 miles north of Buenos Aires.

He was taken to a safe house. He had to be taken through the Buenos Aires International airport to a flight on Israel's El Al airline. The Mossad agents devised an ingenious plan. A doctor drugged Eichmann, he was dressed in an El Al flight attendant's uniform and carried through the airport, to the amusement of airport security people and other spectators, who assumed he was drunk, to an El Al airliner, without questioning—without incident. The ploy worked perfectly.

The Mossad—with Eichmann—on an El Al aircraft, reached Israel May 22, 1960 and David Ben-Gurion announced his capture the next day in the Knesset, the Israeli Parliament.

It caused a world-wide scandal; Argentina protested that the abduction was a flagrant violation of its laws. Anti-semitism broke out in Argentina and elsewhere.

Eventually Israel and Argentina issued a joint statement that the abduction *was* a violation of international law, but nothing further was to be made of the matter. An additional statement was issued that specified that the condition of his capture and transport to Israel would not be factor in his subsequent trial.

* * *

Eichmann was kept in a fortified jail cell in Yogur, in Israel for nine months; Israeli officials were reluctant to go to court without additional testimony (and documents). Eichmann was interrogated again and again and again, ultimately producing 3,500 pages of transcripts. When confronted by Avner Less, of the Israeli national police, Eichmann insisted throughout, that he had no responsibility as a Nazi officer and was only following orders.

Less observed that Eichmann seemed to have no real understanding of the huge morality of his crimes and showed no remorse at any time.

In a statement, released in 2016, Eichmann said, "There is a need to draw a line between the leaders responsible and the people like me forced to serve as mere instruments in the hands of the leaders. I was not a responsible leader and as such do not feel myself guilty."

His trial began April 11, 1961 and became one of the most famous—or infamous—news events world-wide of that year, or decade. It reverberates today, 59 years later.

A crucial aspect of the case: how could it be justified to put him on trial in Israel when that nation did not exist during World War Two? The ultimate answer: he was charged with crimes against humanity, which presumably had no borders and no time-frame regardless of when Israel was established. (It was, in fact, established as a nation in 1948).

He was charged with 15 criminal acts including, crimes against humanity, war crimes, crimes against the Jewish people and membership in a criminal organization.

His chief defense lawyer was Robert Servatius, a respected lawyer who came from Cologne, Germany, and represented Eichmann at the trial and for his appeal, and then returned to Germany and never spoke publicly about the case—ever. Why he decided to represent Eichmann, only he knows—or knew. (Israeli officials conceded that it would have been impossible find a lawyer in Israel willing to represent Eichmann, Jewish or non-Jewish, thus the choice of Servatius was at least acceptable.)

Servatius had been a Major in the Army in Germany, during World War Two, but was never a Nazi. Previously, he was a defense attorney during the Nuremberg war crime trials. Servatius died August 7,1983.

The prosecution of the case lasted 56 days, including hundreds of documents. Servatius was largely successful in blocking material about the Holocaust in general; material not germane to Eichman's case.

The prosecutions showed that Eichmann had visited the Chelmno extermination camp, Auschwitz, and Minsk where he witnessed a mass shooting of Jews—thereby proving he knew what was taking place.

Trial witnesses, including Hannah Arendt, remarked how very ordinary Eichmann appeared. He always insisted that he was only following orders, a defense which was given earlier by Nazis in in the Nuremberg trials. He explained that during the Wannsee conference he felt relieved—*his Pontius Pilate moment*—he felt relieved of any responsibility in the Final Solution.

At the end of the trial, he did admit he arranged transports—the trains to the death campus—but bore no responsibility of what happened otherwise.

When confronted with a statement he made earlier: "I will leap into my gave laughing because of the feeling that I have five million human beings on my conscience is for me a source of extraordinary satisfaction." He later amended that to mean "enemies of the Reich," (such as the Soviet Union) but still later said his original statement was true and that he did mean Jews.

Adolf Eichmann was found guilty December 12, 1961 of the following: 15 counts of crimes against humanity; war crimes; crimes against the Jewish people and membership in a criminal organization. He was found not guilty of personally killing anyone or supervising the activities of the *Einsatzgruppen*—the killing squads flowing behind the Nazi divisions striking east but he was also found guilty of crimes again the Poles, Slovenes and Gypsies.

The judges found that not only was he not just following orders, but was a willing participant in war crimes.

He was sentenced to death December 15, 1961.

His case was appealed to the five-member Israeli Supreme Court. His wife Vera flew to Israel and saw him for the last time in April, 1962.

The Supreme Court rejected all his appeals May 29; he, through his defense counsel Servatius, appealed for clemency to Israeli President Yitzhak Ben-Zvi.

At 8 pm., May 31, Eichmann was informed all his appeals were denied.

He was hanged just hours later, after midnight, early on June 1, 1962.

His execution was witnessed by a small group officials; four journalists and a Canadian clergyman, William Lovell Hull, who had been his spiritual advisor. (He refused to listen to Hull just prior to his execution.)

He is reported to have said:

Long live Germany. Long live Argentina. Long live Austria. These are the three countries with which I have been most connected with and which I will not forget. I greet my wife, my family and my friends. I am ready. We'll meet again soon, as in the fate of all men. I die believing in God.

I die believing in God, may be suspect, under the circumstances.

Raft Eitan, who accompanied Eichmann to the hanging reported—in 2014—that Eichmann also said "I hope that all of you will follow me."

Eichmann's body was cremated and his ashes scattered in the Mediterranean sea outside the territorial limits of Israeli, so there would be no gravesite as a place of worship for neo-Nazis.

* * *

HANNAH ARENDT ...

Ardent was born October 14, 1906 in Hanover, Germany, but raised in Konigsberg; her parents, Jewish, were progressives. Her father, who died when she was seven, had a large library which she consumed. She learned her social philosophy early; she later said:

My early intellectual formation occurred in an atmosphere where nobody paid much attention to moral questions; we were brought up under the assumption Das Moralische versteht sich von selbst, *moral conduct is a matter of course.*

Her family was basically non-religious but she went regularly to a Reform synagogue.

Her Mother raised her to read the complete works of Goethe, including the lines from *Wilhelm Meister's Apprenticeship* (1796) :

Was aber ist deine Pflicht? Die Forderung des Tages.

Just what is your duty? The demands of the day.

When World War One began the family left Konigsberg for Berlin to flee the advancing Russian forces; they returned after ten weeks when it appeared safe to do so.

She subsequently studied in Berlin, at the University of Berlin, where she decided to make philosophy her major field. She then moved to the University of Marburg.

There she met philosopher Martin Heidegger, who became the sun in her universe. She described him as "the hidden king (who) reigned in the realm of thinking." They began a long affair; she was 17, he was 33, married with two sons. She later was criticized for this affair, as he (later) supported the Nazi party. The affair did not become public knowledge until 1982, after both had died.

She then moved to the University of Heidelberg, where she completed her dissertation.

In 1929 she met Gunther Stern, whom she had known earlier. They were married September 26.

They moved to Berlin and in the years 1931-1933 she became focused on her Jewish identity; she discovered that Heidegger had been speaking at National Socialist (Nazi) meetings. She asked him to deny it, in effect, he didn't. Worse, as a Jew in Germany, she was unable to make a living at that time. She became convinced that as a Jew, she would be a pariah for ail time and this theme would become universal in all her writings about being Jewish.

Adolf Hitler had become Chancellor of Germany in January, 1933; the Reichstag fire occurred in February Suppression of civil rights came next.

Arendt used the Prussian State Library for research on anti-semitism in Germany, for a planned speech to be given at the Zionist Congress in Prague, but such research was forbidden; a librarian denounced her and she—and her mother—were both arrested by the Gestapo. Her notebooks were in code that could not be deciphered. She was released pending trial, but knew she was in danger and fled to Geneva, then to Paris.

She found herself an *emigre,* stateless; she had fled Germany, had no papers, no home, no anchor. She took menial jobs and to help support herself, learned some French, Hebrew and Yiddish.

Her husband moved—or fled—to America in 1936. She was then stripped for her German citizenship. In 1936 she also met Heinrich Blucher; they were married January 16, 1940. (He died in 1970.)

In May 5, 1940, the Gouvernur General of Paris ordered all "enemy aliens" from 17 to 55 to be interned. Her mother was over 55 and was allowed stay in Paris. Men were sent to Camp Vernet, in southern France; the women to Camp Guts. France capitulated and signed the armistice with Nazi Germany June 22. Guts was in Vichy France and she and others—in considerable chaos—were able to get papers allowing them to leave the camp. She was part of 200 who left.

She eventually got travel permits and traveled by train through Spain to Portugal, and eventually by ship to New York. She, her husband and mother reached New York in 1941; once ensconced there, she lived in New York until her death in December, 1975.

She became involved in Jewish rights causes, including becoming Executive Director for the Commission on European Jewish Cultural Reconstruction; in 1946 she left that position to become editor at Schocken books, which later published some of her titles. (She returned to the Commission in August 1949, where she worked in Germany, Britain and France, negotiating the return of archive material from the Germans. She found this frustrating, but stayed with that assignment.)

At various times, she taught at: the University of Notre Dame; the University of California, Berkeley; Princeton; Northwestern

University; the University of Chicago; Yale, Wesleyan and the New School in New York City.

She became know one of the world's twentieth century experts on philosophy and political thought, although her emphasis was difficult for most to quantify.

Hannah Arendt published over 15 books; notable in her canon were:

- *The Origins of Totalitarianism*, 1951;
- *The Human Condition*, 1958;
- *Eichmann in Jerusalem*, 1963;
- *On Revolution*, 1963;
- *Men in Dark Times*, 1968;
- *On Violence*, 1970;
- *Crises of the Republic*, 1972;
- *The Jew as Pariah*, 1978;
- *The Life of the Mind*, 1978.

Eichmann in Jerusalem became her highest-selling book; estimates of sales for the first 35 years since its first publication range from 260,000 to 300,000 copies.

Publication of *Eichmann in Jerusalem* in 1963 ignited furious controversies for an entire decade, controversies and debates which reverberate today, a full 57 years later (cited in the Conclusions section, following).

There have now been 50 books which focus on her or substantially cite her work.

Hannah Arendt died in New York December 4, 1975, at 69.

* * *

Eichmann in Jerusalem, the book …

The are four key categories which should be considered regarding Arendt's book: Style; her Work Ethic; Sources and Conclusions.

Style ...

Arendt was a political-social science philosopher and, as such, *writes as an essayist*. She never had any training (or perhaps never cared to have) any training in nonfiction writing. I read *Eichmann in Jerusalem* years ago and came back to it for this book. Her writing style made my eyes glaze over. Literally, not figuratively. The paragraph sizes—and the type size of the Penguin paperback—made me wipe my eyes with kleenex regularly and (reluctantly) plunge back into the text.

I felt reading this was like being chin-deep in a quagmire of political thought and Nazi dogma. Her paragraphs are often almost one page long.

Like John Hersey and the first publication of his *Hiroshima*, Arendt negotiated with *The New Yorker* for an assignment to cover the trial. Eventually, *Eichmann in Jerusalem* was first published in *The New Yorker* magazine. The entire text of *Hiroshima* occupied one issue of the magazine, *Eichmann in Jerusalem* was a five-part series.

One wonders if any editors at *The New Yorker* thought to edit her text to, say, three paragraphs per manuscript page ... or if editors at The Viking Press, which first published the book in hardcover, thought to do the same?

As an example: a new paragraph begins as the bottom five lines on page 286 (in the Penguin paperback edition); the same paragraph runs completely through page 287 and continues through the first 14 lines of page 288, almost the top half of page 288.

Any reader may be forgiven to be exhausted at such a Niagara of text in one single paragraph. (And not to say eye strain, at the type size in the paperback edition).

It might not have been asking to much for Arendt and her editors, first at *The New Yorker,* then at The Viking Press, for the hardcover, and perhaps at Penguin Books for the paperback editions, to re-set her text In shorter, more readable paragraphing size. Don't you think?

Her Work Ethic ...

The Eichmann trial lasted approximately nine months; Arendt apparently spend *only five weeks witnessing the trial* and then apparently used the trial transcripts for the rest. The language of the courtroom was Hebrew; she used the English version of the transcripts, indicated that the German translation was unreliable but that the English version, and perhaps the French version, were acceptable.

In his book 2006 book, *Becoming Eichmann: Rethinking the Life, Crimea and Trial of a "Desk Murderer,"* Writer David Cesarani says Arendt witnessed *only four days* of Eichmann on the stand in the trial.

She thus missed nuances of the court proceedings and the atmosphere or flow of the trial. Spectators screamed, cried and tried to kill Eichmann in the courtroom; he was protected inside an enclosed glass booth.

(In 1968, Robert Shaw published a fictionalized account of Eichmann as a play titled *The Man in the Glass Booth*. It is available in hardcover and paperback versions. The play was released on DVD in 2003 with Maximilian Schell in the lead.)

Arendt doesn't use any of this courtroom drama (and probably didn't know about these incidents).

Isn't this cheating? Not only cheating herself, as a writer, but essentially cheating the reader.

After reading Hersey's *Hiroshima*, with the *eye of the reporter* on every page, I wonder how Hersey would have covered the Eichmann trial.

Sources ...

Arendt's book has an Epilogue, Postscript, a substantial Bibliography and an Index, but no listing for Sources.

The text beginning "Adolf Eichmann went to the gallows ..." on page 252 of the Penguin edition (the last text page) is nonfiction reportage.

What he did.—drank an half bottle of red wine, what he also did—refused the succor of a Protestant minster, and walked to the gallows with great dignity (cited later).

Who witnessed this? A small group of Israeli officials, and four reporters, and the executioners. It is beyond doubt that Arendt was *not there—*

Where did she get this material? From what source?

The ethics of the writer and in fairness to the reader—she could have indicated in a Sources listings where this came from. It clearly wasn't her reportage from the scene of Eichmann's last moments.

Conclusions ...

Did Arendt really "buy into" Eichmann's professed innocence—his "I was only following orders" rationale? Did she believe this—too much? As she stated in the book, "He did his duty ... he not only obeyed orders, he also obeyed the law ..."

The firestorm of controversy and criticism lasted a decade and is still alive today.

She infers that he was semi-educated, almost illiterate, a very drab man—and scarcely—if at all—understood how he was complicit in the mass murder of millions.

There are others who don't believe Arendt's analysts of Eichmann. Christopher Browning, Deborah Lipstadt, Yaaciov Lozowick and David Cesarini all believe that Eichmann was not the unthinking Nazi drone that Arendt pictures.

Simon Wiesenthal, in his 1988 book *Justice Not Vengeance,* created the concept of the *desk murderer* (a term David Cesarini used in his later, 2006 book):

> *The world now understands the concept of desk murderer. We know that one doesn't need to be fanatical, sadistic or mentally ill to murder millions; that it is enough to be a loyal follower eager to do one's duty.*

In her 2011 book, *Eichmann Before Jerusalem*, Bettina Stangneth argues that Eichmann was, in fact, an ideologically motivated anti-Semite and lifelong committed Nazi who intentionally built a persona as a faceless bureaucrat for the trial.

Was he that cunning? He admitted routing trains to the death camps, but declared no responsibility of what happened thereafter.
Or was Arendt simply misguided in her analysis of Eichmann?

Ultimate review: tedious reading; her questionable analysis/evaluation of Eichmann.

from Eichmann in Jerusalem

Adolf Eichmann went to the gallows with great dignity. He had asked for a bottle of red wine and had drunk half of it. He refused the help of the Protestant minister, the Reverend William Hull, who offered to read the Bible with him: he had only two more hours to live, and therefore no "time to waste." He walked the fifty yards from his cell to the execution chamber calm and erect, with his hands bound behind him. When the guards tied his ankles and knees, he asked them to loosen the bonds so that he could stand straight. "I don't need that," he said when the black hood was offered him. He was in complete command of himself, nay, he was more: he was completely himself. Nothing could have demonstrated this more convincingly than the grotesque silliness of his last words. He began by stating emphatically that he was a Gottgläubiger, *to express in common Nazi fashion that he was no Christian and did not believe in life after death. He then proceeded: "After a short while, gentlemen, we shall all meet again. Such is the fate of all men. Long live Germany, long life Argentina, long life Austria. I shall not forget them." In the face of death, he had found the cliche' used in funeral oratory. Under the gallows, his memory played him the last trick; he was "elated" and he forgot this was his own funeral.*

It was as though those in last minutes he was summing up the lesson that this long course in human wickedness had taught us—the lesson of the fearsome, word-and-thought-defying banality of evil.

Slaughterhouse-Five
Kurt Vonnegut Jr. /1969

... Billy Pilgrim ... unstuck in time ... So it goes ...

genre: mixed / fictionalized autobiography satire, fantasy, black humor

Elie Weisel was a prisoner of the Nazis in the death camps, finally Buchenwald—until that camp was liberated by American forces April 11, 1945. In 1954, he met French writer Francois Mauriac who urged him to write about his experiences. It took him a year to write an 862 page manuscript—in Yiddish which was first published in Buenos Aires under the title *And the World Remained Silent*, then in France under the title *Night*, then in the United States, finally, under the same title, in 1960.

It took him years to gain perspective of what he had been through—and to establish a cohesive narrative—a straight-line account.

Primo Levi spent almost a year as a prisoner in the Auschwitz death camp complex until it was deserted by the Nazis and subsequently liberated by the Russian army, January 18, 1945. Upon his return to Italy he eventually began *If This Is a Man*, which was first published in 1947. It clearly did not take him as long as Weisel to write his prisoner memoirs, but he, too, had to wrestle with content and narrative structure.

Like Weisel's *Night*, Levi's *If This Is a Man* is a straight-line chronological narrative.

Kurt Vonnegut, as a young American G.I., became a prisoner of the Nazis during the Battle of the Bulge, and was eventually transported to Dresden, where he was housed (if that can be the word) deep in the bowels of *Schlachthof-fünf*—from the German—Slaughterhouse-Five, an underground meat locker.

Dresden, Germany, had no military value whatsoever, but was firebombed by the Allies in four raids between February 13 to February 15, 1945. 722 heavy bombers from the British Air Force and 527 United States Air Force bombers dropped more than 3,900 tons of bombs on the city; 22,700—25,000 Dresden citizens were killed.

Subsequently, a U.S Air Force report justified the bombings as a necessary strategic operation; opponents claimed Dresden was little more than a cultural landmark. Much later, right-wing critics in Germany called it "Dresden's Holocaust of Bombs."

Over 1,600 acres in central Dresden were destroyed—turned to ash.

Deep underground Kurt Vonnegut heard the bombs explode. When he was able emerge from Slaughterhouse-Five, Dresden was a moonscape.

Both Elie Weisel's *Night* and Primo Levi's *If This Is a Man* were eventually linear, chronological narratives.

Vonnegut wrestled with this—how to render his own experiences into a book-length project.

He wrestled with this problem for years. *Years.*

* * *

Kurt Vonnegut was born in Indianapolis ,November 11, 1922; his parents spoke fluent German, but the anti-German feelings in the U.S. during and after World War One caused them to question or perhaps abandon their German heritage. (The same happened to the family of Theodor "Dr. Seuss" Geisel). Vonnegut's mother's family, the Leibers, had been brewers, but the brewery closed during Prohibition (the same also happened to the Geisel family in Massachusetts).

When his family lost their German heritage, Vonnegut remembered feeling "ignorant and rootless." (Theodor "Ted"

Geisel wondered, during World War One, "why are we (now) 'the other?'")

Vonnegut attended Cornell University but dropped out to join the Army in January, 1943. The Army sent him to study engineering at Carnegie Institute of Technology (now Carnegie Mellon University) and then sent him the University of Tennessee.

On leave from Camp Atterbury, south of Indianapolis, Vonnegut had returned home for Mother's Day to discover his mother had committed suicide the night before by overdosing on sleeping pills.

The Army then sent him overseas to fight in the European theater.

He, and about 50 other American G.I.s, were captured by the Nazis December 22, 1294, during the Battle of the Budge and subsequently housed underground when the British and U.S. Air Force firebombed Dresden.

Finally released, he wrote to his family May 29, 1945. They apparently knew little more than he was "missing in action." In part, he said (reprinted in Vonnegut, *Armageddon in Retrospect*, 2008):

> *I've been a prisoner of war since December, 19th, 1944, when our division was cut to ribbons by Hitler's last desperate thrust through Luxembourg and Belgium. Seven fanatical Panzer Divisions hit us and cut us off from the rest of Hodges' First Army. The other American divisions on our flanks managed to get out: We were obliged to stay and fight. Bayonets aren't much good against tanks: Our ammunition, food and medical supplies gave out and our casualties out-numbered those who could still fight—so we gave up. The 106th got a Presidential Citation and some British Decoration from Montgomery for it, I'm told, but I'll be damned if it was worth it. I was one of the few who weren't wounded. For that much thank God.*

Well, the supermen marched us, without food, water or sleep to Limberg, a distance of about sixty miles. I think, where we were loaded and locked up, sixty men to each small, unventilated, unheated box car. There were no sanitary accommodations—the floors were covered with fresh cow dung. There was not room for all of us to lie down. Half slept while other half stood. We spent several days, including Christmas, on that Limberg siding. On Christmas eve the Royal Air Force bombed and strafed our unmarked train. They killed about one-hundred-and-fifty of us. We got a little water Christmas Day and moved slowly across Germany to a large P.O.W. camp in Muhlberg, South of Berlin. We were released from the box cars on New Year's Day. The Germans herded us through scalding delousing showers. Many men died from shock in the showers after ten days of starvation, thirst and exposure. But I didn't.

Under the Geneva Conventions, Officers and Non-commissioned Officers are not obliged to work when taken prisoner. I am, as you know, a Private. One-hundred-and-fifty such minor beings were shipped to a Dresden work camp on January 10th. I was their leader by virtue of the little German I spoke. It was our misfortune to have sadists and fanatical guards. We were refused medical attention and clothing: We were given long hours at extremely hard labor. Our food ration was two-hundred-and-fifty grams of black bread and one pint of unseasoned potato soup each day. After desperately trying to improve our situation for two months and having been met with bland smiles I told the guards just what I was going to do to them when the Russians came. They beat me up a little. I was fired as group leader. Beatings were very small time—one boy starved to death and the SS Troops shot two for stealing food.

Vonnegut was put to work carrying corpses from air raid shelters and was pelted with rocks by surviving Dresden citizens. Eventually he got to the Saxony-Czeckoslavakian border and even more eventually to Le Havre and total safety.

After the war, he married Jane Marie Cox; they had three children. He later adopted his sister's three children after she died of cancer and her husband was killed in a train accident.

He published his first free-lance fiction article in *Collier's* magazine February 11, 1950, while working for the General Electric Company in Schenectady, New York, as a publicist. He was encouraged by *Collier's* fiction editor, Knox Burger, who later became a highly successful literary agent. Vonnegut was paid $750 for his first article, then $950 for his second *Collier's* article. On that thin blade of success, Vonnegut quit G.E. to freelance; Knox Burger was horrified—he wanted to encourage Vonnegut, but not that that extent. Burger knew full well what Vonnegut perhaps did not—how grueling and usually unproductive the life of a free-lancer was (then and now).

Vonnegut published his first novel, *Player Piano*, in 1952, when he was 30. It was not commercially successful. Then came *The Sirens of Titan*, 1959, *Mother Night*, 1961, *Cat's Cradle*, 1963, and *God Bless You Mr. Rosewater*, in 1964.

Many of the techniques he used over and over throughout his canon, were developed in *Player Piano*—science fiction—in this case, post-World War Three; alien visitors to Earth and dystopian worlds. *Player Piano* was generally classified as science fiction and Vonnegut relegated to the science fiction shelf as author; a category then largely dismissed in literature, and an identification he resented.

In *The Sirens of Titan* he introduces time warps—of becoming "unstuck in time" again and again—and the planet Tralfamadore, which he revisits in *Slaughterhouse-Five*.

In *Cat's Cradle*, Vonnegut introduces Ice-9, a substance that turns all the world's water solid; when all the world's water becomes solid, most of mankind is wiped out. Vonnegut invents a religion, Bokononism, and quotes its holy books through the novel, as an attempt to save the world from the disasters of science.

None of these books were commercially successful, nor was *God Bless You Mr. Rosewater*, published in 1964. Vonnegut contemplated giving up his writing career, but to his surprise he got a job teaching at the University of Iowa's highly acclaimed (then and now) Writer's Workshop, the pioneering graduate-study program for aspiring novelists and poets.

That job saved him—it was a lifeline to a drowning man, he later said.

* * *

Eventually his *Slaughterhouse-Five* was first published in 1969, and *Slaughterhouse-Five* is nothing whatsoever like *Night* or *If This Is a Man*, except the anguish, the horrific experiences, the implied anti-war sentiments, the survival—by accident of war—of all three—Wiesel, Levi and Vonnegut.

Vonnegut's phrase *So it goes* ... , which appears again and again through *Slaughterhouse-Five* appears to be Vonnegut wrestling with how to explain the unexplainable, boiled down to three words.

And it may have indicated his undiagnosed PTSD, (Post Traumatic Stress Disorder) later diagnosed with Vietnam veterans in vast numbers (in World War Two—and before—it was simply called "shell shock") .

And Vonnegut's protagonist, Billy Pilgrim, becomes "unstuck in time," veering wildly between the war, the present—after the war—and Tralfamadore, a planet light years away from the earth, where he was transported and kept in a geodesic dome as a zoo exhibit for residents of Tralfamadore. (The natives of Tralfamadore, Vonnegut writes, "look like toilet plungers.") *Slaughterhouse-Five* is widely original and—in its originality, has been called a novel of "unmatched moral clarity," and "one of the most enduring antiwar novels of all time." It is also one of the most unlikely books ever to be on public school reading lists.

It was first published *24 years* after his experiences under Dresden as it was firebombed.

* * *

Vonnegut's crucial character in *Slaughterhouse-Five* is Billy Pilgrim—the name comes from, we can easily suppose, John Bunyan's *The Pilgrim's Progress,* written between 1677, the first part and 1679, the second part. It has been constantly in print since that time, translated into more than 200 languages and is said to be the world's first novel written in English.

The Pilgrim's Progress is surprisingly pre-Vonnegut. The author Bunyan could be called the Vonnegut of 343 years ago. It is a quest—in a dream sequence—of the main character Christian—an everyman—on a journey from his hometown, the "City of Destruction," toward the "Celestial City," or Heaven, on top of Mount Zion. Christian is burdened by his knowledge of sin—which he came to believe originated from reading "the book in his hand," (which was the Bible.) He knows he must seek deliverance from the burden of his knowledge of sin.

The characters in *The Pilgrims' Progress* include:

- Christian—his journey toward the Celestial City is the focus of the plot;
- Evangelist, who puts Christian on the path toward the Celestial City and shows him a book, which readers would assume to be the Bible;
- Obstinate and Pliable, two characters who attempt to return Pilgrim to the City of Destruction;
- The Slough of Despair, a bog composed of all the filthiness of sin / a swamp that make the fears and doubts of the past and present real. (Anyone read Washington, D.C. here?);
- Mr. Worldly Wisemen, who lives in a place called "Carnal Policy," who attempts to veer Christian away

from religion into the world—he has ruined many innocent pilgrims;
- Beelzebub, one of the devil's assistants;
- Shining Ones, presumably angels;
- Formalist and Hypocrisy, two false prophets, from the "Land of Vainglory";
- Prudence, Piety and Charity, three maidens who appear in the second part of *The Pilgrim's Progress*.

Whew! Vonnegut from 343 years ago.
But wait, there's more:

- Old Honest, a pilgrim from the frozen town of Stupidity;
- Giant Slay-Good, a Giant who is killed hy Mr. Greatheart;
- Mr. Ready-to-Halt … and …
- Madame Bubble, a witch whose enchantments make the Enchanted Ground magical with an air that makes foolish pilgrims sleepy and will never wake up again. She is an adulterous woman mentioned in the biblical *Book of Proverbs*. Mr. Self-Will went over a bridge to meet her and never *came back again.*

The only topic missing is Vonnegut's planet Tralfamadore.

* * *

Slaughterhouse-Five was Kurt Vonnegut's first commercial and critical success. Although he based it on his experiences in Dresden, it was published—in 1969—during the height of the Vietnam war.

Similarly, the book *MASH*, (Mobile Army Surgical Hospital) written by Richard Hooker (pseudonym of Dr. Hiester Richard Hornberger Jr.) was successful for the same reasons; he had been a MASH doctor in Korea. His book, rejected by a variety of publishers (have we heard this before?) was finally published by the Wm. Morrow firm in 1968. It led to the television series M*A*S*H which ran from 1972 to 1983. The end episode is said to be one of the most highly watched single shows in television history. About half the country's television viewers watched, an audience of approximately 125 million. M*A*S*H is still in reruns on cable. (And only half of the M*A*S*H cast members are now still alive.)

Slaughterhouse-Five was about World War Two; the book *MASH*—and the television series M*A*S*H—were about the Korean war, but both books and the television series reached their zenith during the Vietnam debacle, when the nation exploded into protests, young men burned their draft cards and threw their war medals over the White House fence.

* * *

Kurt Vonnegut survived Dresden, returned to the United States, married, had children, adopted his sister's three children after she died of cancer and her husband was killed in a train accident. He became a cultural icon with *Slaughterhouse-Five*, now in print for more than 50 years—taught at the universe level, wrote 14 novels, 13 collections of short stories, nine books of non-fiction, received numerous awards for his work. He and his first wife divorced; he remarried—to photographer Jill Krementz—in 1979, attempted suicide in 1984.

In 2007, he fell in his home in New York and hit his head.

He died April 12, 2007—several weeks later—of substantial brain injuries suffered in that fall. Kurt Vonnegut was 84.

Survived the firebombing of Dresden but died after a fall in his own home.

So it goes.

from Slaughterhouse-Five

He was down in the meat locker on the night that Dresden was destroyed. There were sounds like giant footsteps above. Those were sticks of high-explosive bombs. The giants walked and walked. The meat locker was a very safe shelter. All that happened down there was an occasional shower of calcimine. The Americans and four of their guards and a few dressed carcasses were down here, and nobody else. The rest of the guards had, before the raid began, gone to the comforts of their own homes in Dresden. They were all being killed with their families.

So it goes.

* * *

A guard would go to the head of the stairs every so often to see what it was like outside, then he would come down and whisper to the other guards. There was a fire-storm out there. Dresden was one big flame. The one flame ate everything organic, everything that would burn.

It wasn't safe to come out of the shelter until noon the next day.

When the Americans and their guards did come out, the sky was black with smoke. The sun was an angry little pinhead. Dresden was like the moon now, nothing but minerals. The stones were hot. Everything else in the neighborhood was dead.

So it goes.

A Desert Daughter's Odyssey
Sharon Wanslee / 2000

Survival Rules for a longer life ...

genre: memoir/autobiography-self-help

This is Sharon Wanslee telling her own story—the beginning paragraphs from the first chapter, "Fort Apache Wisdom," in *A Desert Daughter's Odyssey:*

> *Tucson to Texas—*
>
> Nearly all the advice my wise and witty cowboy father gave me about life was true. He was wrong only once—maybe twice—that I recall, but maybe that's because times have changed so much since he grew up on my grandfather's ranch.
>
> As early as I can remember he used to tell me, "Nothin's constant except change," and "Whatever you do, treat ever-body exactly like you'd want'a be treated goin' up the ladder o' life, 'cause you're sure gonna meet ever' one o' those sonovaguns cornin' back down"—all delivered in his soft West Texas drawl.
>
> Actually my grandfather's ranch lay between the forks of the Black and White Rivers in central Arizona, adjacent to the Fort Apache Indian Reservation, but all the ranchhands were from West Texas, so my dad grew up talking just like them. My grandmother 'Rene and my aunt Florence used to get so tickled when they'd tell me about "Baby Clyde Dear" standing out by the corrals with

the cowpunchers, scuffling his boots in the sand, laughing and leaning over to spit as though he had a "chaw" of Bull Durham in his mouth just like the big boys. He not only picked up their soft, easy drawl, he absorbed their dry piercing wit, summing up worlds of philosophy, experience and home-spun psychology in just a few colorful, understated words.

Most of his sayings were about the business of living, but once in a while he'd throw in one about business—"If you can't make money off your friends and relatives, who the hell can. you make money off of?" And it was funny how anybody who did business with my dad became a friend so well did he treat them—from monsignors and millionaire cowboys to men down to their last dollar and less hope. He was even right about the business of dying when he'd say with a rueful grin—"One thing's for sure, there ain't any of us gonna get outta this alive." But my all-time favorite expression of his was one I heard all throughout my awkward growing-up years, whenever a streak of bad luck seemed to hang on longer than seems fair—"The sun don't shine on the same dog's back ever' day," he'd tell me.

* * *

Sharon Wanslee was a fourth generation native of Arizona—a "daughter of the desert"—she used to call herself, but the phrase "my awkward growing-up years," is only a polite fraction of the truth.

Her father and mother divorced when she was two—and she only ever saw her mother once, years later, for one afternoon, when her mother was dying of cancer.

Her father remarried and for a whole decade—from when she was six to 16, she was mistreated again and again and again by the stepmother. She tried and tried to tell her father, but he either won't listen or it didn't register. In 1978, Christina Crawford published a book, *Mommie Dearest*, about her mother, actress Joan Crawford. In that book Christina called her mother "ruthless, unstable and violent." The book caused a sensation. A decade later, Christina Crawford published a sequel, *Survivor*.

Sharon Wanslee lived a *Mommie Dearest* life in Arizona for 10 years.

Her father sold Fords in Tucson, but wasn't an authorized Ford dealer. He somehow got new Fords from a dealer across town and often didn't want to be bothered with the little girl. He would say, "you're going to stay with Aunt Sally and Uncle Fred for a while."

They weren't relatives at ail, but acquaintances he could park her with for a few days at a time.

It almost goes without saying: he was never Father of the Year.

She remembered waiting hours and hours alone, for him come back for her.

One morning, when she was 16, the stepmother was beating her with the flat side of a hairbrush. The stepmother assumed Sharon's father had gone to work. Instead he was quietly shaving. He came out of the bathroom just in time to see the scene.

"I'll be damned ..." or "Oh, my God ..." was all he could say, instantly realizing that what Sharon had been trying to tell him *for ten years*—was all true.

The stepmother was out of the house and gone the same day.

Sharon almost, kinda, maybe, forgave her father for the decade of neglect. She had a younger brother Patrick, who had always known what was happening to Sharon, but never said a word about it. He was the Little Prince and didn't want—somehow—to upset his own applecart. She forgave her father, almost ... kinda ... maybe ... , but never forgave her brother.

When she was about 16, she met her own mother—for one afternoon. She had assumed her mother had moved 'way out of the Tucson area. She, in fact, had only moved across town. Sharon had been active in high school and had her picture in the local papers from time to time—her mother kept a scrapbook of clippings about her. Sharon saw her own mother only that one afternoon—when the mother was dying of cancer.

She lost herself—buried herself—in education.
After high school she attended the University of Arizona.
And got "A" grades in every course she ever took.
Every one.
All "As."
She didn't go into a university class and do a little curtsey and say to the professor, "give me an 'A' please." She worked at "A" grades. She read and took notes and read more, non-required supplemental books and wrote perfect term papers and never missed a class. All of it. She worked for every "A" grade.
She graduated above Phi Beta Kappa (yes, there is such a category.)

When she was at dating age, and had met a boy, her father said, "You oughta marry that ol' boy—he'd be good for you."

After the decade of *Mommie Dearest* and neglect from her father—who shunted her off to acquaintances and claimed they were relatives—she had no real concept of a solid—*loving*—marriage, as brilliant as she was—that was beyond her experiences.

So she said "Yes, daddy ..." and married—and the marriage didn't work.

More than one marriage didn't work—for the same reasons—eventually Daddy died and she didn't have to say "yes Daddy" anymore and could follow her own instincts ... and more of that in a minute.

In the 1970s—cancer touched her—personally.
She wrote:

Some say autumn naturally brings sorrow. Even Hemingway once wrote that you expected to be sad in the Fall, that part of you died each year when the leaves fell from the trees. Part of me died then—in that time of harvest, that time of rich maturity that should have reflected the fulfillment of all that had gone before—for that's when the stalking nightmare finally confronted me. Nineteen years earlier, my beautiful gentle mother, Sara, died—lingeringly—of cancer. At the age of 35, 1 was struck by the same reaper's blade, in the same place—over the heart— The terror of that specter gripped me, immobilized me.

Even though I like to think of myself as a writer, words would not come. Before, words flowed freely, easily, spontaneously, whether writing for small town newspapers or spilling impressions of life's paradox into journals—I'd been keeping them for 17 years. But that October day I put away my pen. I couldn't write. I couldn't even talk.

She was determined to find the right person—a cancer specialist she could trust. She was, after all, putting her life in someone else's hands—and expertise.

She found the right specialist—Dr. Luis Campos, practicing in Houston. Houston is one of the best locales in the world for cancer research and treatment. Originality from Arequipa, Peru, his father was a doctor and his grandfather a doctor. She called him a "Latin Peter Ustinov," and "Arequipa's gift"—Apequipa's gift to the world.

His philosophy, she quoted, could be summed up in two paragraphs:

In my early days, I made an effort not to become engaged emotionally with my patents—to protect myself. I was wrong. I was fighting the natural tendency to become close to them and when I realized that as what I should do, I became much happier. And I am certain I did a better job.

You have to be aware that you are the last stop for these patients and families and if you are not there maybe everything else is gone.

The last stop.

She devoted a chapter in her book to him, a chapter titled "Apequipa's Gift."

(The first time she met Campos in his office he charted her family history. What did your Mother die of? What did your father die of? When she said *both* parents died of cancer, he turned white. Cancer was deep in her DNA.)

And she found someone else—a psychologist to talk to. Ken Kopel, also in Houston. She thought he looked like a young Tom Hanks.

She wrote:

> *... by the end of that first session, I knew I had found a friend.*
>
> *Before long, I would discover that, although he may have looked like a young Tom Hanks, he proved to be as compassionate and wise as a mature King Solomon. He was a born psychologist—brilliant, intuitive and infinitely compassionate. And very funny.*
>
> *Like Campos, he knew as early as the eighth grade what his vocation would be, when he chose "psychologist" on "career day."*

She devoted a chapter in her book him too, a chapter titled "True Friend."

Her book: she grew up in a Mormon family in Arizona, but converted to Catholicism as an adult. The Catholic church was a far, far, better fit for her than the Mormon church.

Her book has 37 chapters; each a slice of her life. Each led to a Survival Rule—how to survive cancer. Each is a *homily,* a conversational sermon in the Catholic Church (and also in other churches).

She uses fitting quotations: the Hemingway anecdote, Emily Dickinson; Edna St. Vincent Millay, Robert Frost, Catholic monk Thomas Merton, The Jerusalem Bible …

... each chapter begins with a significant quotation, the text is a homily and each chapter ends with a Survival Rule.

(She had a operation early in her cancer struggle and went on with her life, convinced at least instinctively, that her own Survival Rules were much more beneficial than the operation itself.)

It is quite remarkable; comparable to *A Book of Great Worth*, by Dave Margoshes—in another chapter. But his *A Book of Great Worth* is fictionalized family history; Sharon Wanslee's is true memoir.

And self-help.

The manuscript found its way to the University of Iowa Press, where it was read by Albert Stone, advisory editor. His endorsement appears on the back cover:

On nearly every page I find words, images, scenes, insights and intuitions that ring true to the survivor self who writes them. Both personally and historically, this is an important record.
I recommend this timely and powerful text.
　　　　—Albert E. Stone, Ph.D. professor emeritus
　　　　The University of Iowa

The rest of the Iowa Press staff did not concur; her manuscript was returned, only because the Press had never published a book like this before.

In the fall of 1993, she was living in east Texas, north of Houston. She saw a notice: the local university would be offering a free, open enrollment, short course at night on book publishing.

She came into the first session 20 minutes late with a. "sorry I'm late" shrug and took a seat toward the back of the lecture hall.

The professor thought at the time his heart had just stopped.

She was fully six feet tall, jet black hair and worn an ankle-length swirling "broomstick skirt," so named because they could be wrapped wet, around a broomstick to maintain their swirling, crinkled look. Almost a peasant or western look. She usually wore a variety of colorful broomstick skirts (jeans and white Nikes in the summers). And western boots. She was the only woman he had ever seen who looked perfectly comfortable—and appropriate—in western boots. (He didn't know, at that time, of her fourth generation "daughter of the desert" heritage).

And a radiant smile.

He was stunned. (These days he may have thought to himself, the internet slang *O.M.G.: Oh My God.*)

At a mid-session break, she came to the lectern.

"I'm Sharon Wanslee and I was late because ..."

"Because ... ?"

"I have a dog that I had to rush to an emergency veterinary hospital in Houston."

The faculty member teaching the short course had a dog *he* had taken to the same emergency veterinarian hospital the week before.

After the class they talked about dogs; she had two classic police-dog type German Shepherds from the same litter, Merlin and Gypsy. He had two and Sally, a buff-colored Cocker Spaniel was the one he had to take to the emergency vet hospital.

After each session they talked about dogs ... and books. Books ... and dogs. He learned that she was married, although she hinted, not happily.

Oh well, he said to himself ruefully, *oh well, what might have happened* ... between the two of them. *Oh well ...*

After the short course he lost track of her for almost a year.

Then he got a call—would you like to meet?

They agreed to meet at a local beer-and-burgers place. He lived out of town in a golf course community (although he didn't play golf).

On the way driving into town, he had a remarkable epiphany:

She is going to tell me her marriage is over.

He got to the burgers-and-beer place first, found a booth toward the back and sat facing the door.
She came in, found him and sat down. Her hands were shaking.

My marriage is over, she said.

He took her hands. And he really never let go.
Weeks and weeks later, long after her divorce was finalized, they were standing in his kitchen, when he said quietly, apropos of nothing what-so-ever: *"would you marry me?"*
She shrieked and threw herself at him. They both fell against a wall. That was a *Yes*.
They eloped and flew into New Mexico and were married in Santa Fe, in the summer of 1994. The ceremony was deeply moving for them and Santa Fe fascinating—the art galleries, one after another, the restaurants, the mix of Indian, Spanish and Anglo cultures … Santa Fe was a thriving village years and years before the Pilgrims got to Plymouth Rock.
They toured Georgia O'Keeffe country (there is now an O'Keeffe museum in downtown Santa Fe). And they drove into the high New Mexico mountains and visited Los Alamos, where the first atomic bomb was engineered. He was fascinated—she hated it: "Bad karma here," she said.
All Sharon Wanslee ever wanted in her life was someone to love her—her college professor-husband loved her beyond all measure—*to the moon and back* as they say—and she knew it.

Two years after they were married, the *Unthinkable Happened*. her cancer came back. It had been over 20 years since her first cancer experience and with Dr. Campos—with her own Survival

Rules to guide her—20-plus years her doctors never though possible. But her cancer came back. She returned to Luis Campos, in Houston: first prescriptions, which did little, then drip therapy, with an IV in her arm. Then radiation therapy, at a regional hospital near Houston, with a door to the radiation chamber so thick it looked like a bank vault. She may have known that she wouldn't survive this second battle. She never told her husband.

Sharon Wanslee fought her second cancer battle for three and one half years. She died of metastatic breast cancer before dawn in a Houston hospital February 5, 2000. She was barely 60. She and her husband never got to their sixth wedding anniversary. He was with her, holding her hand when she died.

Some couples never talk of "what about *after*—" He knew that she had no thoughts of a casket that would never decompose in the ground. He knew what to do and never mentioned his decision beforehand to relatives or friends. He had her cremated and eventually took her ashes to the Saguaro National Park, west of Tucson. Saguaros are giant cactus plants, with "arms," native only to Arizona They can't be transplanted—if anyone tried to transplant one, it will die. They live 175 years.

He found a thriving Saguaro with four arms. The trunk represented Sharon and the four arms represented her husband, her son, his wife and Sharon's grandson, Clinton. He buried Sharon's ashes under the Saguaro and took a color photograph, had it framed and gave it to her son, Morris and his wife Vickie—they instantly called it "Sharon's cactus." A natural tombstone.

Sharon will always be warmed by the Arizona sun. Around her are the changing seasons and above her the stars and the vast wonder of God's universe.

She was home.

Sharon's book, *A Desert Daughter's Odyssey,* was published after her death, with the sub-title "For all Those Whose Lives Have Been Touched By Cancer—Personally, Professionally or Through a Loved One." Her husband made sure: *It will always be in print.*

from A Desert Daughter's Odyssey

Survival Rule # 8*

Anger, even rage, is vital part of the recovery process. Allow the anger to rise, to spew out, so that it does not stay seething within, blocking the healing process. Your system needs all the equilibrium and strength it can find to heal you.

Deal with rage in productive ways. In the CMT process, one learns that the combination of large muscle movements and verbalizing is most conducive in neutralizing stress; i.e. long, stomping curse-darn-swearing walks, throwing cheap dishes at a rock wall while voicing your anger.

Therapy—many kinds of therapy are good—art, dance, music therapy—and sometimes it's helpful to simply be alone and write out your pain and frustration about being betrayed by your own body. The CMT process proved most successful for me; up to that point it was the only acceptable place to vent my anger.

Whatever you do, DON'T SUFFER IN ANGELIC SILENCE. MARTYRS DO NOT SURVIVE.

---

* Sharon Wanslee discovered that her Survival Rules for conquering cancer were equally valuable for those battling other major illnesses and largely appropriate for divorce situations as well.

Survival Rule # 15

Love is the Great and Unequaled Comforter. If you have no one who loves you with unconditional acceptance, find someone. They are there waiting for you—in your family, among your friends or acquaintances, in a support or prayer group. If, on assessment, you realize you have no one. *Get help fast.* Seek a counselor, priest, minister or psychologist and build from there.

If you still find no one who loves you, maybe you are not being lovable enough. Maybe you need to seek the second greatest comforter first—forgiveness. Forgive others. If you cannot find it in your heart to do it for them, do it for yourself. Without it there can be no true healing from within. Then forgive yourself. Forgiveness leads inevitably to Love.

Maybe you need the great unconditional lover—a dog—the best of all earthly examples of how to love and be loved.

Survival Rule # 18

(The end of the chapter "Arequipa's Gift," about her doctor, Luis Campos)

Utmost confidence in your doctor is imperative. With it you can win. Without it, all the medical procedures in the world will be sabotaged by the lurking doubts in your mind. If you do not have such full trust, search until your find the physician not only worthy to be in charge of your prognosis, but of your hope as well.

Survival Rule # 21

*(The end of the chapter "True Friend,"
about her psychologist Ken Kopel)*

Find a counselor worthy to be called True Friend. And if you can, see your counselor before any major treatment or medical procedure. That fortification will surprise you with its strength.

Then find a new notebook and reserve it for all those thoughts that are life-giving and filled with hope, for all those ideas that come to you while reaching out to Life, for funny sayings, cartoons or happenings, or for inspiring ones. Refer to it often. Call it your "Survival Journal."

The Plot Against America
Philip Roth /2004

*Lindbergh in the White House ...
Prejudice in New Jersey ...*

genres: *fictionalized autobiography; alternative American history*

Philip Roth—born March 19, 1933—is regarded as one of the most highly acclaimed living American writers.

He graduated from Bucknell University, magna cum laude, was elected to Phi Beta Kappa. He attended the University of Chicago and received an M.A. degree in English Literature in 1955 and taught briefly at Chicago. He subsequently taught at the University of Iowa and at Princeton. He later moved to the University of Pennsylvania, where he ended his teaching career in 1991.

His first book, *Goodbye, Columbus and Five Short Stories* won the National Book Award in 1960; he followed that with two novels, *Letting Go* and *When She Was Good*.

Portnoy's Complaint, published in 1969, brought him critical and commercial success.

Sabbath's Theater, published in 1995, won him his second National Book Award.

He was awarded the Pulitzer Prize for fiction for *American Pastoral*, published in 1997.

I Married a Communist, 1998, examines the McCarthy era; *The Human Stain*, 2000, examines identity politics in America in the 1990s.

Roth published 27 novels between 1959 and 2010. His total awards include:

- *Goodbye Columbus,* 1960, National Book Award;
- *The Counterlife,* 1986, National Book Critics Circle award;
- *Operation Shylock,* 1993, PEN/Faulkner Award for Fiction;
- *Sabbath's Theater,* 1995, National Book Award.
- *American Pastoral,* 1997, Pulitzer Prize for Fiction;
- *I Married a Communist,* 1998, Ambassador Book Award;
- *The Human Stain,* 2000, PEN/Faulkner Award for fiction, *W. H. Smith Literary award;*
- *The Plot Against America,* 2004, Sidewise Award for Alternative History.
- His plots often focus on Jewish protagonists and Jewish issues. *The Plot Against America* is unique, even among novels.

The protagonist of the novel is Roth himself, as a young boy. Others in the novel include his brother, father and mother and their extended family, living in New Jersey,

The novel begins with the presidential election of Charles Lindbergh defeating Franklin Roosevelt. Roth's first paragraph:

Fear presides over these memories, a perpetual fear. Of course no childhood is without its terrors, yet I wonder if I would have been a less frightened boy if Lindbergh hadn't been president or if I hadn't been the offspring of Jews.

These three paragraphs are the best summary of the novel:

Lindbergh's first act is to sign a treaty with Nazi Germany and Adolf Hitler, promising the United States

will not interfere with German expansion in Europe (known as the "Iceland Understanding," after the place it was signed), and with Imperial Japan, promising noninterference with Japanese expansion in Asia (known as the "Hawaii Understanding"). The new president begins to take a toll on Philip's family, Philip's cousin Alvin joins the Canadian army to fight in Europe. He loses his leg in combat and comes home with his ideals destroyed. He leaves the family and becomes, a racketeer. A new government program begins to take Jewish boys to spend a period of time living with exchange families in the south and midwest in order to "Americanize" them, Philip's brother Sandy is one of the boys selected and after spending time on a farm in Kentucky he comes home showing contempt for his family, calling them "ghetto Jews."

Philip's aunt married Lionel Bengelsdorf and becomes a frequent guest at the Lindbergh White House, even being invited to a dinner party for German Foreign minister Joachim Von Ribbentrop. This causes further strain in the family. A new government act is installed relocating whole Jewish families to the western United States. Many of Philip's neighbors move to Canada. Philip's shy and innocent school friend Seldon Wishnow, an only child, is moved to Kentucky with his mother. To protest against the new act, radio broadcaster Walter Winchell openly criticizes the Lindbergh administration and is fired from his station. He then decided to run for President and begins a speaking tour. His candidacy causes anger and antisemitic rioting in southern and midwestern states, and mobs begin targeting him. Making a speech in Louisville, Kentucky, he is shot to death. Winchell's funeral in New York City is presided over by Mayor Fiorello La Guardia, who praises Winchell for his opposition to fascism, and openly criticizes President Lindbergh for his silence over the riots and Winchell's death.

> *After making a short speech, Lindbergh's personal plane goes missing. Body hunts turn up no results and Vice President Wheeler assumes command. The German State Radio discloses "evidence" that Lindbergh's disappearance, as well as the kidnapping of his son, were part of a major Jewish conspiracy to take control of the American government. This announcement causes further antisemitic rioting. Wheeler and Ford, acting on this evidence, begin arresting prominent Jews citizens, including Henry Morgenthau, Jr., Herbert Lehman and Bernard Baruch, as well as Mayor La Guardia. Seldon calls the Roths when his mother doesn't come home. They later discover Seldon's mother was killed by Klu Klux Klan members who beat and rob her before setting fire to her car with her in it.*
>
> *The Roths eventually call Sandy's exchange family in Kentucky, and have them keep Seldon safe until Philip's father and brother drive there and bring him back to Newark. Months later, he is taken by his mother's sister. The rioting stops when first lady Anne Morrow Lindbergh makes a statement asking for the country to stop the violence and move forward. With the body searches called off, former president Franklin D. Roosevelt runs as an emergency presidential candidate and is re-elected. Months later the Japanese attack Pearl Harbor and America enters the war.*

In the article, "Roth on Trump," in *The New Yorker*, Jan. 30, 2017, Judith Thurman writes:

> *Many passages in "The Plot Against America" echo feelings voiced today by vulnerable Americans—immigrants and minorities alarmed by Trump's election as the Jews of Newark are frightened by Lindbergh's. The book also chronicles their impulse of denial. Lindbergh's election make clear to the seventeen year old "Philip Roth"*

that "the unfolding of the unforeseen was everything. Turned wrong way around, the relentless unforeseen was what we schoolchildren studied as 'History,' a harmless history, where everything unexpected in its own time is chronicled on the page as inevitable. The terror of the unforeseen is what the science of history hides, turning a disaster into an epic."

from The Plot Against America

June 1940—October 1940

Vote for Lindbergh
Or Vote for War

Fear presides over these memories, a perpetual fear. Of course no childhood is without its terrors, yet I wonder if I would have been a less frightened boy if Lindbergh hadn't been president or if I hadn't been the offspring of Jews.

When the first shock came in June of 1940—the nomination for the presidency of Charles A. Lindbergh, America's international aviation hero, by the Republican Convention at Philadelphia— my father was thirty-nine, an insurance agent with a grade school education. Earning a little under fifty dollars a week, enough for the basic bills to be paid on time but for little more. My mother— who'd wanted to go to teachers' college but couldn't because of the expense, who'd lived at home working as an office secretary after finishing high school, who'd kept us from feeling poor during the worst of the Depression by budgeting the earnings my father turned over to her each Friday as efficiently as she ran the household—was thirty-six. My brother Sandy, a seventh-grader with a prodigy's talent for drawing, was twelve, and I, a third-grader a term ahead of himself—and an embryonic stamp collector inspired by millions of kids by the country's foremost philatelist, President Roosevelt—was seven.

I Heard You Paint Houses
Charles Brandt / 2004

What does "paint houses" really mean ...
... and whatever happened to Jimmy Hoffa?

genre: true crime

It has been the most perplexing crime in twentieth century America. What happened to Jimmy Hoffa? The ultimate unsolved and unsolvable disappearance. Hoffa, the famous—or infamous—leader of the Teamsters Union, at a time when the Teamsters were allied with various mob families, was last seen July 30, 1975; was missing for 44 years, 5 months and 18 days and declared legally dead July 30, 1982.

No trace of Hoffa or his remains were ever found. Over the years some FBI agents and officials believed they knew *approximately* what happened and *approximately* who was involved, but the case was eventually closed without any known results.

* * *

Frank Sheeran was born October 15, 1920 to an Irish Catholic family near Philadelphia. He had little interest in achievement, no ambition for education. He enlisted in the Army in August 1941 and was eventually assigned to the 45th Infantry Division, known the Thunderbirds or The Killer Division. Sheeran served 441 days in combat when the average was 100 days. He learned two life lessons; the first was: obey orders. The second—which he also learned in the 45th Infantry Division—kill without remorse.

The Killer Division was an apt name; apparently it *was* wildly accepted in that division that Nazi POWs were not to be kept long. Sheeran would be shown a group of Nazi POWs and was told "take these guys around the corner and come back as soon as you can." The message was clear and Sheeran obeyed orders. He later claimed to have participated in *"numerous massacres and summary executions of Nazi POWs"* (italics added).

Sheeran later said the war haunted him for years—perhaps the rest of his life. He said he seldom slept more than about four hours each night, although it was never clear that the combat, the stress, the 411 days or the POW orders were involved.

Out of the Army, Sheeran returned—to odd jobs—working here and there, scrambling, doing enough to stay alive, without ambition, with any real aim in life.

He drove trucks lull of beef and chicken, but diverted some of it to sell some himself to restaurants. When his truck once broke down at a gas station in Pennsylvania, a stranger offered to help. The stranger fixed the dead engine. And he and Sheeran became friends—indeed, lifelong friends. The stranger's name was Russell Bufalino, the first of many Italians that Sheeran, the Irish Catholic would know.

And here Sheeran's life took a turn toward the sordid from which he never recovered: now in civilian life, he followed orders and eventually killed without remorse.

Bufalino was a mobster; he later become known as the organizer of the Apalachin Conference, in 1957, a meeting of top mob families at a rural home in upstate New York to hammer out disagreements among mob families: the territory they each controlled; what they could (or usually could not do) in each other's territory. Police became aware of the mob conference and raided it; thus the nation became aware—for the first time—of the mob families that controlled organized crime nation-wide, or nearly so.

Sheeran didn't know—perhaps at least at first—that Bufalino was a mob figure; Bufalino was quiet, reserved. But Sheeran took a step—a turn toward Bufalino and his world. (It was said that—similarly—as a young man Adolf Hitler was once refused admission to an art school in Vienna and turned, relatively soon thereafter, to the nascent organization that would eventually become the Nazi party.)

Apparently, Sheeran's first stateside murder was that of Whispers DiTullio, a gangster who hired Sheeran to destroy the Cadillac Linen service in Delaware for $10,000. Unknown to Sheeran, Angelo Bruno, who was the boss of a mob family that controlled Pennsylvania and southern New Jersey, was a silent partner in that business; Sheeran had been seen outside the business. Bruno was dead set on killing Sheeran, Russell Bufalino intervened with Bruno. Bruno told Sheeran to go find DiTullio.

Sheeran told Whispers where to meet him.

The next day Sheeran read the papers:

> *The next morning was front page. He was found lying on the sidewalk. He had been shot at close range with something like a .32, the kind of gun the cops used to call a woman's gun because its was easier to handle and had less of a kick than even a .38. Being a smaller caliber it didn't do the damage a .38 does but all you need is a little hole, if you put it in the right place. The good feature is that it makes a little less noise than a .38 and a whole lot less noise than a .45. Sometimes you want a lot of noise, like in the middle of the day to scatter bystanders; sometimes you don't want a lot of noise, like in the middle of the night. What do you want to go around disturbing people's sleep for?*

Sheeran also thought later, while reading the paper, "that could have been me."

Mob families in those days: who wronged who; who pays the price?

Sheeran later described mob murders as the same as authorized killings in the Army: "It was just like when an officer would tell you to take a couple of German prisoners back behind the line and for you to 'hurry back.' You did what you had to do."

One of the most famous killings occurred in 1972; Joseph "Crazy Joe" Gallo, known to enjoy high society company, was a member of the Columbo mob family After a dispute between mob families Gallo was a celebrating a birthday with family and friends in Umberto's Clam House in the Little Italy section of Manhattan. Shots were fired, patrons screamed, tried to run out the doors, hid under tables. Gallo staggered outside and died on the sidewalk. Witnesses described a lone gunman. Police let it be known they thought there were three gunmen; a ruse meant to weed out bad tips and confessions that were clearly false.

A mob killing in a busy New York restaurant in plain sight.

Years later Frank Sheeran admitted he was the sole shooter who killed Crazy Joe Gallo.

Sheeran eventually met—or at least knew about—all the crime bosses and top mobsters of those years; Sheeran was one of the very few who was not Italian. Sheeran's nickname, along all the others, was "The Irishman."

One of the others was Anthony "Tony Pro" Provenzano, who was a "short stocky and ham-fisted man who bore the scars of his young years as an amateur boxer," according to his obituary in *The New York Times,* which described his "shadowily world of associates whose talents lay in beating other men with hammers, in selling labor peace to the trucking industry, in garrotes and guns and the clever use of garbage grinders and incinerators to make enemies disappear."

... the clever use of garbage grinders and incinerators to make enemies disappear ...

Provenzano and Jimmy Hoffa, once friends, turned on each other while serving time in the same prison, the Lewisburg Federal Penitentiary, in Pennsylvania.

Jimmy Hoffa had no other work in his lifetime except the Teamsters Union, formally known the International Brotherhood of Teamsters (IBT). And his connections with organized crime families dated back to his earliest days with the union.

Essentially, he needed the *muscle* that organized crime could provide, to intimidate his opponents and advance his plans for the Teamsters.

He was born on February 14, 1913 in Brazil, Indiana; his family moved to Detroit in 1924, where he lived for the rest of his life. He began organizing while working for a grocery chain which paid substandard wages; by 1932 he was invited to become a labor organizer with Local 299 of the Teamsters. In 1933, the Teamsters had 75,000 members; membership grew to 170,000 by 1936; by 1939 it had 420,000 members It grew steadily during the war years and after, and had over a million members by 1951.

Organized crime families controlled their own geographical areas; for Hoffa and the Teamsters to grow he had make arrangements with, and essentially continue to work with, the crime bosses.

He got a deferment during World War Two by claiming that his leadership in the Teamsters was needed so that freight could move smoothly for the war effort. He was selected as vice-president of the Union in 1952; in 1955 the Union moved its headquarters from Indianapolis to Washington D.G. Hoffa took over for president Dave Beck in 1957, when Beck was convicted and imprisoned for fraud, in a trial held in Seattle. During the trial Beck took the fifth amendment 140 times.

That same year, the AFL-CIO voted to expel the Teamsters, because of Hoffa's corrupt leadership; at the time, the Teamsters union contributions to the AFL-CIO were $750,000 annually.

Hoffa's most famous—or infamous—*fait accompli* was competed in 1964, the National Master Freight Agreement, which brought all the over-the-road truck drivers into one major contract. Hoffa subsequently tried to accomplish the same with airline workers, but found little success there.

When John Kennedy was elected president in 1960 he appointed his younger brother Robert, to become Attorney General. This was essentially the beginning of the downfall of Hoffa. Robert Kennedy began a strong attack on organized crime which he carried forward with a "Get Hoffa" squad. In turn, Hoffa always referred to him as Booby Kennedy.

As Brand writes in *Paint Houses,*

> *When RFK took over the Justice Department in 1961, there had been 35 organized crime convictions in the year before. In 1963 there were 288 and rising rapidly. Among those 288 conditions in 1963 was the "highest paid labor boss in America," the Genovese capo Tony Provenzano, who went down for extortion, selling labor peace to trucking companies. It cost Provenzano his pension and led to a mortal rift with Hoffa.*

Brand also writes, that during the Johnson and Nixon administrations,

> *Congress enacted three weapons of mass destruction to target the Mafia nationwide: (1) the authorization of wiretapping and bugging whose tapes could be used as evidence; (2) an expansion of the witness protection program to entice cooperating witnesses and, more important, (3) The RICO statue that created a new kind of conspiracy; making it illegal to belong to the Mafia.*

RICO is the Racketeer Influenced and Corrupt Organization statute, making it illegal to be a part of a criminal conspiracy; i.e., to be a member of a Mafia crime family.

Hoffa was indicted in May, 1963 for jury tampering in Tennessee; on March 4, 1964, he was convicted in Chattanooga, of attempted bribery of a grand juror during an earlier 1962 conspiracy trial in Nashville. He was sentenced to eight years in prison and a $10,000 fine; while out on bail during an appeal on that sentence he was convicted in a second trial held in Chicago on July 26, 1964 on one count of conspiracy and three counts of mail and wire fraud for improper use of the Teamsters' pension fund. That conviction resulted in a five year prison sentence.

He spent three years unsuccessfully appealing those sentences, but on March 7, 1967, he began serving a total of 13 years—eight for bribery and five years for fraud—at the Lewisburg Federal Penitentiary, in Pennsylvania, with Tony Pro.

When he entered prison, Frank Fitzsimmons was elected acting president of the Teamsters; he was a Hoffa loyalist. Hoffa was determined—perhaps obsessed—with running the Teamsters while in prison, through Fitzsimmons. But Fitzsimmons changed some of Hoffa's policies and distanced himself from Hoffa. While in prison, Hoffa resigned as president of the Teamsters, on June 19, 1974.

After serving less than five years in Lewisburg, Richard Nixon pardoned Hoffa; communing his sentence to time served. With one provision: Hoffa "could not engage in the direct or indirect management in any labor organization" until March, 1980.

Hoffa had become too toxic for the Teamsters; he was awarded a $1.75 million termination benefits from the Teamster's Union retirement funds; such a settlement had never been done before. The message was clear: *go, retire and don't come back.*

Hoffa went to court to invalidate Nixon's pardon restrictions, he argued that *he* had never agreed to the Nixon pardon non-union activities There was no *he side* to the pardon; Hoffa lost in court, after depositions in January, 1974; when it was decided that Nixon was within his rights to stipulate the non-union restrictions in the pardon, based on Hoffa's illegal activities when he had been a top Teamster official.

Hoffa continue to be obsessed with returning to the Teamsters as President, and reversing some of the procedures that Fitzsimmons had installed.

Hoffa turned to Tony Pro for help. Tony Pro was part of the

New York Genovese mob family. Hoffa also turned to Anthony Giacalone, of the Detroit mob family and his brother Vito.

The Giacalone brothers met with Hoffa three times at his lake home and apparently once elsewhere. They set themselves up as mediators between Hoffa and Tony Pro.

Hoffa apparently became increasingly agitated every time the Giacalone brothers arrived for a meet.

On July 30, 1975, Hoffa arranged to meet Tony Pro and Anthony Giacalone at the Machus Red Fox tavern outside Detroit, a place he had known and visited previously and presumably would feel safe there.

Several witnesses saw Hoffa near the Red Fox—using a pay phone, annoyed, or perhaps agitated, because Tony Giacalone was apparently late.

The FBI later estimated that Hoffa left the Red Fox area about 2:30 p.m. that day without a struggle, in the back of a maroon "Lincoln or Mercury," with three other people.

He was never seen alive again and no remains of his body were ever found. Ever.

> *... the clever use of garbage grinders and incinerators to make enemies disappear ...*

If nothing else, Frank Sheeran was a survivor; an independent contractor, a hitman for hire, for various mob families during those years, one of the very few non-Italians associated with American mob families. "The Irishman." Did that give him any sort of protection? He always had to know who he was working for, who his enemies were and how they could exact revenge for any perceived misdeeds.

The paperback version of Brandt's book is titled "The Irishman," as a tie-in to the film starring Robert De Niro, as Sheeran; Al Pacino as Hoffa and Joe Pesci as Russell Bufalino. Sheeran survived all the internecine warfare between mob families during those years—survived into old age.

This is the remarkable first paragraph—the *lede*—of the review of the film version, published in *The New Yorker*, Nov. 4, 2019 written by Anthony Lane:

"There Was Blood"
"The Irishman"

When you are old and grey and full of sleep, what will you talk about? Your grandchildren? The far-off scents and tastes of your own childhood? Your first love? Or that time when you walked into Umberto's Clam House and shot Crazy Joe, only you didn't whack him right, so he runs outta there, more like stumbles, and you follow the guy and finish him off on the sidewalk, you know, pop, pop, close the deal? The sorry fate of Joe is one of the many events recalled for us by Frank Sheeran (Robert De Niro), in "The Irishman," as he sits in a nursing home and summons up remembrance of kills past.

As Charles Brandt tells the story:

I Heard You Paint Houses *is a "whodunit," but it is not a novel. It is history based on one-to-one interviews with Frank Sheeran, most of which were tape-recorded. I conducted the first interview in 1991 at Sheeran's apartment, shortly after my partner and I were able to secure Sheeran's premature release from jail on medical grounds. Immediately after that 1991 session Sheeran had second thoughts about the interrogative nature of the interview process and terminated it. He had admitted far more than he was happy with. I told him to get back in touch with me if he changed his mind and was willing to submit to my questioning.*

Years passed. In 1999, Sheeran's daughter arranged to have a private audience, Brandt writes, for Sheeran with Monsignor Heldusor of St. Dorothy's Church in Philadelphia. The Monsignor granted Sheeran absolution for his sins so that he could be buried in a Catholic cemetery.

That absolution must have been a heavy lift; Sheeran had acknowledged that, over the years, he had been complicit in about 25 mob hits for various crime families.

After that, Sheeran contacted Brandt again and they began interview sessions, which lasted five years. Brandt states:

> *I spent countess hours just hanging around with the Irishman, meeting alleged mob figures, driving to Detroit to locate the scene of the Hoffa disappearance, driving to Baltimore to find the scene of two underworld deliveries made by Sheeran, meeting with Sheeran's lawyer, and meeting his family and friends, intimately getting to know the man behind the story. I spent countless hours on the phone and in person, prodding and picking away at the storehouse of material that formed the basis of this book.*

Brandt states that often criminals *want* to confess, even when statements are obvious lies or deceptions. (The Catholic church absolution, as example.) Sheeran read and approved the text as it was being written, then read and approved the entire manuscript when it was completed, Brandt states.

In the text, major sections of direct quotations by Sheeran are highlighted by over-sized beginning- and end-quotation marks in grey, a technique other writers and publishers might employ.

But what are the chances that one hundred percent of what he says is true? How much is self-serving—or deceptive—that Sheeran (and Brandt) state as true? Ans: slim to none (old joke—ans: slim to none and Slim's outta town.).

Critics of the book—and critics of Sheeran—include Bill Tonelli, "The Lies of 'The Irishman,'" *Slate* website August 7, 2019 and Jack Goldsmith, "Jimmy Hoffa and The Irishman: A True Crime Story?" *The New York Review of Books,* Sept. 26, 2019.

The denouement of the book—what happened to Jimmy Hoffa—according to Sheeran—is in Chapter 28, "To Paint a House," pages 248-258.

* * *

Frank Sheeran died December 14, 2003, at 83, surviving far longer than most of the mob family members from his earlier days.

As a military veteran, he was accorded gravesite military honors, with an American flag on his casket.

from I Heard You Paint Houses

I had seen *On The Waterfront* in the movies, and I thought I was at least as bad as that Marlon Brando. I said to Russ that I wanted to get into union work. We were at a bar in South Philly. He had arranged for a call from Jimmy Hoffa in Detroit and put me on the line with him. The first words Jimmy ever spoke to me were, "I heard you paint houses." The paint is the blood that supposedly gets on the walls or the floor when you shoot somebody I told Jimmy, "I do my own carpentry work, too." That refers to making coffins and means you get rid of the bodies yourself.

A Book of Great Worth
Dave Margoshes /2012

Enchanting memories of a world long gone ...

genre: fictionalized biography/ family history

Who could not be captivated and enthralled by this, the beginning of *A Book of Great Worth*:

"I did something stupid," the rabbi told my father.

It was 1925, New York City, a bar on the Lower East Side.

My father was a few years away from marriage, fatherhood, respectability, and so was prime to do stupid things himself; stay up late, associate with rough customers, drink too much, sing off-key—which really was the only way my father knew how to sing. But a rabbi doing a stupid thing? And not just any rabbi, but his good friend, Lev Bronstyn, who as more like a big brother to him than any of his own big brothers were.

"I'm not joking, Harry," Bronstyn said. "I mean really stupid." He took a sip of whisky. "It involves a woman."

"Ah," my father said.

"It's bad Harry," The rabbi said. Bronstyn had a long, often damp nose and prominent ears, which combined to make his head appear larger than normal. He shook it now. "Very bad."

Dave Margoshes grew up in New York city and in rural New Jersey. The memories, incidents, vignettes and stories in his book all came from his childhood—his parents, family, and extended family, some distant relatives from as far away as western Canada, where he would eventually live—and still lives. His father was a writer for Jewish/Yiddish newspapers, specializing in labor topics and issues.

Margoshes writes that his parents scrimped and saved and. once bought a piece of land outside Princeton, New Jersey, and built their dream home there. And later lost it during Hard Times. They then lived—for six months—in a converted chicken coop and. later moved into a place with no electricity and. a privy out back. Hard. Times. Very nearly Steinbeck's *Grapes of Wrath* hard times, on the east coast. He cried, at six, when the family moved back into the city.

He decided early that he would be a writer; as he later told the story ...

> *I became a writer early in the summer I was thirteen—actually, a couple of weeks before my thirteenth birthday.*
>
> *I remember clearly the precise moment. I had been writing before that, little sketches and simple stories, or pieces of series I'd abandon after few pages scribbled in my notebook, but mostly I had been thinking about writing.*
>
> *At this particular moment, I became an actual writer.*
>
> *I spent that weekend with my Father in Atlantic City.*

Margoshes went with his father, who was assigned to cover a national labor union convention in Atlantic City. Margoshes later thought it might have been his mother's idea; now known as "male bonding."

She gave him a ten dollar bill for the bus fare and spending money and some change for the subway.

He writes that it was really the first time he had been with so many strange adults—men his father knew; other reporters covering the convention. One, his father said, who had been a Communist and was then "a rabid anti-communist," one who had been a gangster but was then "a pretty decent chap," and a reporter, Victor Riesel, who had been blinded when acid was thrown in his face. Margoshes saw an attractive couple, twice at least, coming and going ... his father said "they had married the wrong people." and he—at thirteen—assumed they had an *assignation*—a word he had just learned.

He wrote much of this down in a notebook—

And the especially quiet moments—the last few words in the dark between father and son in twin beds in a hotel room.

> *Up until that point, I realized—not then but later—I had been attracted to writing because of the writing itself, the thrill of manipulating language—what at writers' conferences and university conferences and writing programs we refer to as craft, although I didn't have much of it at the time. But there are two other important parts to writing, parts I hadn't even been aware of, and I just stumbled onto them. I now had something very specific I wanted to write about and a vision of how I wanted to express it. Along with craft, I was now dimly conscious of art.*

Later Margoshes lived in Asbury Park; and his first real reporting job was with *The Asbury Park Press,* 1965-1966. During those days he never met Philip Roth, New Jersey native and noted novelist, but Margoshes said they rubbed elbows occasionally at writers' conferences and at the University of Iowa, later, where Roth was on the faculty. He also never met The Boss, Bruce Springsteen, but Margoshes knew some of the same bars in Asbury Park where Springsteen got his start. One of Springsteen's CDs (or albums—some of us still call them—albums) was titled "Greetings from Asbury Park, N. J."

Margoshes worked for daily newspapers in eight cities, including San Francisco, New York, Calgary and Vancouver, covering everything from politics to murder to cat shows.

He was also in the Writer's Workshop, the University of Iowa's program for graduate students, aspiring novelists and poets. He received a M.F.A. (Master's of Fine Arts) degree there. Margoshes was there when Kurt Vonnegut was on the faculty.

Hemingway served for less than one year as a reporter for the *Kansas City Star*, then moved to the *Toronto Star* as a reporter (from *star* to *star,* so to speak); he convinced the *Toronto Star* editors to let him be a European correspondent. But then in Europe, he transcended reportage—and began the novels that made him world-famous.

Get in, get smart, get out—was that originally Yiddish, or Pennsylvania Dutch—or perhaps just a universally-known adage?

Like Hemingway (and, of course, others) Margoshes had found his *true metier*; or conversely, he never lost the vision of the craft of writing he discovered when he was 13.

He has published 20-plus books of poetry, fiction and nonfiction, and is very highly regarded for his work.

Very highly regarded.

Margoshes moved to western Canada in the early 1970s and now lives outside Saskatoon.

His books now include (publishers cited are all Canadian companies):

Fiction

- *Wiseman's Wager*—novel—Coteau Books, 2014;
- *God Telling a Joke*—short stories—Oolichian Books, 2014;
- *A Book of Great Worth*—short stories—Coteau Books, 2012;
- *Bix's Trumpet and Other Stories*—short stories—NeWest Press, 2007;

- *Drowning Man*—novel—NeWest Press, 2003;
- *I'm Frankie Sterne*—novel—NeWest Press, 2000;
- *We Who Seek: A Love Story*—novella—Black Moss Press, 1999;
- *Fables of Creation*—short stories—Black Moss Press, 1998;
- *Long Distance Calls*—short stories—Coteau Books, 1996;
- *Nine Lives*—short stories—Thistledown Press, 1991;
- *Small Regrets*—short stories, Thistledown Press, 1986.

Poetry

- *A Calendar of Reckoning*—Coteau Books, 2018;
- *Dimensions of an Orchard*—Black Moss Press, 2010;
- *The Horse Knows the Way*—Buschek Books, 2009;
- *Purity of Absence*—Beach Holme Publishing, 2001;
- *Northwest Passage*—Oberon Press, 1990;
- *Walking at Brighton*—Thistledown Press, 1988.

His short stories or poetry have been in *40* anthologies or collections; his work was in *Best Canadian Stories* six times; three times in *Best Canadian Poetry* and *A Book of Great Worth* was named one of Amazon/Canada's Top Hundred Books for 2012.

A Book of Great Worth was published by the Canadian firm Coteau books, in Regina, Saskatchewan; it is not likely to be in any American bricks-and-mortar bookstores. It *is* on Amazon, USA; there are three endorsements *(blurbs* as they are called in publishing) on the back cover. All published blurbs are complimentary; these deserve to be cited for the tone of all three and the warmth the writers feel for Margoshes:

> *Exuberant, humorous and profoundly wise, Dave Margoshes' wonderfully conceived stories celebrate the hard-knuckled times of his father during the Twenties and*

Thirties in the Lower East Side of New York City. A Book of Great Worth *reflects Margoshes' deep understanding of a man's humanness and capacity to love as he strives to bring out the best in himself and others. This captivating invention is pleasure to read.*
   —Sandra Birdsell,
    author of Waiting for Joe

Ebullient with life, drama and character, these stories are compulsively readable and convincingly realistic yet suffused with an autumnal glow, the aura of time passing, the feeling we have for a loved one now gone whom we try to capture again and again in the imagination, in words—a really beautiful book.
   —Douglas Glover,
    author of Attack of the Copula Spiders

At once intimate and vast, these stories are rich with humor, history and great wisdom—especially regarding 'the intricate arrangements of the heart.' After reading this collection I was left with that lingering sense that the best writing always leaves me with—a strange mixture of sadness and deep satisfaction.
   —Johanna Skibsrud,
    author of The Sentimentalists

Reviewing the book in the Canadian publication *Quill and Quire*, March, 2010, Mark Sampson, a writer and reviewer in Toronto wrote:

It take some serious chops for an author to write a family memoir in which he or she is not the main character. It take even bigger chops to use the constituent parts of a family memoir to create a work of fiction—a collection of linked short stories, no less. Thankfully, Dave Margoshes is a writer possessed of chops in abundance and he pulls off these feats beautifully in his new book.

While labeled "fictions," A Book of Great Worth is essentially a collection of loving portraits of Margoshes' father (here named Harry Morgenstern) set in the 1920s, '30s and '40s. Morgenstern is a journalist who spent most of his career covering labour issues for New York's Yiddish newspaper The Day. The collection includes Margoshes' wonderful story, "The Wisdom of Solomon," a finalist for the 2009 Journey Prize; remarkably it's not even the best piece in the book. In nearly every tale, Margoshes reveals a moral conundrum that helped shape his father as a man and a writer, and these make for very compelling reading. From "The Farmhand," with all its tensions (sexual and otherwise), to the morality plays of "A False Mustache," "A Distant Relative," and "Music by Rodgers, Lyrics by Hart," Margoshes treats us to a wide array of virtuosic storytelling.

And, Sampson writes:

Margoshes spent many years crafting this collection—the earliest story dates back to the 1980s—but it's been worth the wait. Hopefully, A Book of Great Worth *will bring some much-deserved attention to this chronically underappreciated author. At the very least, he's done his father proud.*

At the end of the book, Margoshes writes:

As I continued to return to these stories, in between other writing projects, a few constants began to become clear to me. The most important was that, while the tone of the stores varies considerably, from sombre to comic, they're similar thematically in that they all show different glimpses of a fundamentally decent man in morally perplexing situations.

All the stories in this series walk that precarious tightrope between memoir and fiction. Of course, they're not true memoir—they're about my father, not me, though sometimes I appear briefly, as a child, listening to my father's tale. Sometimes I (the author) have myself (the character) ask a question or in some other way provide a foil for the character of my father. Mostly, though, the focus is on "my father," often in time periods before my birth.

The stories are written in a blend of first and third person—when the character of myself as a child is on stage, it's first person; but when the focus is on "my father" alone, it's third. This bumping together of forms and techniques inevitably raises a question or two in the minds of some readers; is this truth or fiction and how does the narrator know these things?

I worked hard, with the stories' structure and a sort of old-fashioned expository style, to make them feel like memoir—like truth—but, of course, most serious fiction writers do that all the time. We employ technique to garb our fabrications. I also worked hard to imbue these stories with a tension created by that unstated question of how the narrator came to know not just the stories, in their broad strokes, but the fine details.

Most importantly, I tried to honor my father. The best way to do that, I knew, was to get it right.

The ultimate evaluation of *A Book of Great Worth*:

The warmth of his nostalgia radiates from every page.

from A Book of Great Worth
"The Wisdom of Solomon"

There he was in Cleveland. My father liked to use this expression for his life in those days. "I was still chasing the donkey, trying to pin the tail on it." The donkey had led him away from New York and out west, where his intention was to see some of the world and, hopefully, write about it. But he'd gotten no further than Chicago, where he holed up in a cheap hotel room for several weeks and wrote, in longhand, the bulk of a novel, a fanciful tale of a sensitive boy growing up in the Lower East side that owed much to Joyce's Portrait of an Artist as a Young Man. *When his money ran out, he burned the manuscript—a surprisingly satisfying ritual—and he circled back to Cleveland, where he'd heard, from a poet fleeing the place, of a job on a Yiddish newspaper. His father and brother were both well-known journalists, and it had been important for him to make his own name, on his own, and he'd gone so far, once he got to Cleveland, as actually to change his name, to Morgenstern, which means morning star. Now, at last, he had his first real job on a newspaper, though it wasn't quite what he expected, and was beginning what he hoped would be a glorious career. If not glorious, than at least exciting, interesting. He saw himself as Don Quixote, the hero of the famous novel he had recently read, tilting at windmills—righting wrongs—not with a lance but a pen. First, though, he would have to learn to type.*

The Tattooist of Auschwitz
Heather Morris / 2018

*A question of accuracy:
the Holocaust, fictionalized*

genre: fictionalized history, biography

It was the darkest period in the twentieth-century, the Holocaust. The Shoah; *calamity* in Hebrew.

Between 1941 and the end of the Second World War in 1945, across German-occupied Europe, Nazi Germany and its collaborators systemically murdered some six million Jews, about two-thirds of Europe's Jewish population. The murders were carried out in pogroms and mass shootings; by a policy of extermination through labor in concentration campus; and in gas chambers and gas vans in German extermination camps, chiefly Auschwitz, Belzec, Chelmno, Majdanek, Sobibor and Treblinka, in occupied Poland.

It happened so quickly; Hitler came to power as Chancellor on January 30,1933; three months later was Dachau, March 22, 1933.

Although Nazi Germany focused on Europe's Jewish population for extermination, other groups were also targeted, including: Slavs, ethnic Poles, Soviet citizens and Soviet prisoners of war; the Roma (commonly called Gypsies); the "incurably sick," political and religious dissenters and gay men. Estimates of these groups exterminated may be as high as eleven million.

Jews were segregated into ghettos which culminated in the policy of extermination the Nazis called "The Final Solution to the Jewish Question." Senior Nazi officials discussed this at the Wannsee Conference in a Berlin suburb in January, 1942. As Nazi forces captured territories east of Germany, anti-Jewish measures were radicalized. Under the coordination of the SS with direction from the highest level of Nazi Party leadership, killings were committed within Germany itself, throughout occupied Europe and within territories controlled by Germany's allies. Paramilitary groups, the *Einsatzgruppen,* working with the German army and local collaborators, murdered about 1.3 million Jews in mass shootings and programs between 1941 and 1945. By mid-1942, victims were being deported from ghettoes across Europe in sealed freight cars to concentration camps where, if they survived the journey, they were worked to death or gassed. The killings continued until the end of the war; trainloads of prisoners enroute to the concentration camps were still given high priority late in the war, by the German *Reichsbahn,* even when the trains were badly needed elsewhere for the war effort. (The concentration /death camp trains only stopped during the very final days of the war when train crews simply abandoned their trains and fled, leaving prisoners still locked in the cattle cars.)

The Nazis invaded Slovakia; when they reached Krompachy, posters were hung in shop windows; the Nazis wanted one child, aged eighteen or older, for work duties. If a family did not give up a child, the entire family would be taken. The Slovakian government could not deny the Nazis anything.

Lale, born Ludwig Eisenberg, volunteered to go, to save his brother Max, Max's wife and two children and the rest of the family.

He was sent by cattle car to Auschwitz; reached there April 23, 1945, and got a tattoo: 32407. Lale was 25.

Gita, born Gisela Fuhrmannova, also from Slovokia, was transported to Auschwitz and arrived April 13, 194S. In the book, she was tattooed with the number 39402. She was 17 years old.

Lale is quickly exposed to all of the Nazi machinery of death; he is assigned to a building crew for the growing camp. At one point he watches as a truck pulls up to an old bus behind one of the buildings. Naked men are forced into the bus from the truck; some go willingly; others are hit by rifle butts. When the bus is completely full, he watches as a *Kapo,* the lowest-level Nazi guard, drops a cylinder down through a port in the roof. The bus shakes violently and screams are heard. He drops to his knees, retching. When all is quiet, the door is opened. "Dead man fall out like blocks of stone."

Later, he becomes ill and is eventually tossed onto a cart for the dead and dying. A stranger drags him off the cart and tends to him. A second man named Pepan, helps him. His recovery lasts seven or eight days. "What happened to me?" he asks. "Typhus," Pepan says, "you nearly died."

Pepan had an economics professor in France; the government didn't like what he had been teaching; he was sent to Auschwitz.

"I need an assistant," he said "do you want a job?" Pepan is a camp tattooist, a *Tätowierer,* in German.

Lale is reluctant; he can't do that to others—tattoo their numbers on their arms. Not that.

"If you don't, someone else will," Pepan said. "Work with me, but you must work quickly and efficiently and not make trouble with the SS."

Pepan introduces him one Oberscharfuhrer Houstek, who must approve. "What languages do you speak?"

"Slovak, German, Russian, Hungarian and a little Polish." "'Humph," Houstek said and walked away.

And with that approval, Lale became a *Tätowierer.*

The first day he sees an endless line of young women. The tattoo pen and ink and supplies are ready.

"I can't do this," he says.

"You can. You must."

Lale may have thought: do this or one of the Kapos will kill you ... with just one shot.

> *An arm is presented in front of him and with it, a piece of paper with a number on it. He tattoos the number into the arm. Then another arm and another number. And again, And again and again and again. He tries not to look up, into a face, into a person, into a soul. It becomes mechanical, one arm, a number, another arm, another number. He does not know names, nor faces.*

Eventually one of the arms presented to him was a young girl, who already has a tattoo. He gave her another. She was Gisela Fuhrmannova, later Gita Furman. Others he does not remember, perhaps he cannot force himself to remember faces. He does remember her; perhaps he cannot forget her.

They began to meet—furtively, quickly, a glance, a hello. All they could risk, one day, another day.

There was nothing remotely like a friendship in Auschwitz (or any of the other Nazi death camps); a person there one day might be gone the next day. Shot by a Kapo, disappeared into a truck or train, never to be seen again. Transferred to another camp. Dead of starvation, overwork, disease.

But, Lale and Gita kept seeing each other as they could—

Lale began to know some of the women who worked in a sorting area. Some called it "Canada," a serene, quiet land they know none would ever see. They searched through each incoming prisoner's possessions for diamonds, gold, gems, jewelry, currency.

Eventually they smuggled some of the diamonds and jewelry to Lale, who had also come to know a few construction workers who came into the camp every day from a nearby village. The brought in food; he gave them the diamonds and jewelry from Canada, a few at a time.

He encountered Josef Mengele, the angel of death, a chilling man. And Lale knew an adult male inmate who had been sterilized by Mengele. "The bastard," the man said.

Eventually, guards found some of the diamonds and jewelry he had hidden, waiting to trade for food from the outside construction workers.

"Give us names." They commanded. "Who gave all this to you?"

He didn't know any names. He never knew any names.

He was beaten. Savagely. "Give us names."

He was beaten again. And again and again. He never knew any names of any women in the Canada sorting area. He had no names to offer.

He was finally returned to his duties as the *Tätowierer*. He had given his captors no names. When he next saw Gita she asked what happened—"I was beaten," he said and nothing more and implied she shouldn't ask further.

In January, 1945, the whole atmosphere changed At Auschwitz and at adjacent Birkenau, where Lale was sometimes sent, for additional tattooing duties.

The local construction men stopped coming—Lale had no access to their food, even if he had risked giving them more diamonds and gems and jewelry from Canada. Trainloads of new prisoners slowed. Construction slowed.

Finally, most inmates were sent on a death march and on January 27, 1945, the camp was liberated by Soviet forces. Gita and several of her friends escaped from the death march and hid.

Lale and Gita escaped—without seeing each mother or promising to meet. He perhaps inadvertently took the wrong direction. He was soon captured by Soviet forces and taken to a "chalet," in a Russian camp, where he was given civilian clothes, a warm bed and meals. His job was to go into the nearest village and recruit local girls and woman for parties for the Russian officers, which apparently occurred every night. The lure for the women?—the same sort of diamonds, gems and jewelry that Lale had given the construction workers—that he had obtained from Canada. The women hatred the Russians—"pigs" they were called but apparently none of the women were mistreated and the "gifts" were godsends for them.

Lale escaped again and this time headed for Slovakia.

Walking, trudging, on and on.

He finally reached the border with Slovakia. An official meets him. He has no papers, no identification. He rolls up his sleeve and shows his tattoo. "I am Slovak," he says.

"Welcome home."

He reaches Bratislava and meets old family friends, who are astonished to see him. He tells them he must find Gita. They agree. He tried to buy a horse, a bicycle, a car. Everyone refuses. Finally he is able to buy a horse and cart, with some of the remaining gems he had hidden.

Gita is in Bratislava on a street whens he see a man standing up in a cart. It is him. She knows it.

She steps in front of the cart. The horse stops. He climbs down, unable to speak. He drops to his knees. She too, drops to her knees.

"Will you marry me?" he asks.

"Yes I will."

Only after Auschwitz, after all the death and the *Shoah* they had witnessed, only when their new life began—only then did she tell him her last name. To make herself complete again.

Lale changed his last name to Sokolov, the Russian last name of his married sister; better that than Eisenberg, in Soviet-controlled Slovakia. They were married in October, 1945 and he set up a company importing fabrics for sale. It became more and more successful. The Soviets united Slovakia with the Czech Republic.

In April 1948, he was reported to the Czech authorities for "exporting jewelry and valuables from Czechoslovakia." Two days later his business was nationalized and he was arrested—and sentenced to two years in prison.

They had escaped from Auschwitz; he had escaped from the Russians. They escaped again and were able to take a train to Vienna and from there to Paris. They found no work in Paris and decided to leave Europe entirely. They picked Australia, first deciding on Sydney, then they met a couple onboard the ship taking them to Australia; the couple raved about Melbourne, so Melbourne it was.

Again his business—and blessings flourished. She never expected to be able to have a child, but their son Gary was born in 1961, when she was 36 and Lale 44.

Gita died October 3, 2003.

After her death, Lale was pushed—and perhaps was determined—to tell their story. He and Heather Morris conducted long sessions two or three times week. It took three years for the complete story to unravel, in bits and pieces.

I don't have long, he once said, *I want to be with Gita.*

He died October 31, 2006.

* * *

Those who come to *The Tattooist of Auschwitz,* reading it solely as a love story, may be stunned. A Slovakian Jew, compelled to tattoo numbers on the arms of thousands of incoming prisoners, meets one woman in the line; she also Slovakian.

Amidst the carnage and the sheer terrors of Auschwitz, where any inmate could meet death at any time—being shot, death by starvation, disease, worked to death—the two fell in love, furtively, quietly, seemingly moment by moment when they could briefly evade their Nazi captors.

As a love story it is unforgettable, haunting ...

But ... but ... but ...

How much of this is true? How much contrived? How many errors of fact, of judgment?

In essence, how could errors of judgment, of historical fact, cloud the reception of this book?

In the book the key scene is when Lale tattoos the number on her arm—when they meet for the first time. The number 3 4 9 0 2.

But... interviews with Lale and Furman and their son Gary, in the 1990s indicate that scene never happened, as described.

And she said her actual tattoo number was 4 5 6 2.

A five digit tattoo number would have been impossible then too. A woman entering Auschwitz when she did would have had a four-digit number. Five digit numbers were only used later.

Other errors abound.

In the article "'The Tattooist of Auschwitz' and the History in Historical Fiction," in *The New York Times* Nov. 8, 2018, reporter Christine Kenneally writes "the book has seeming come out of nowhere to be translated into 17 languages, with (publication) rights sold in 43 countries. In the United States alone, there are a half million copies in print, and the book just hit No. 1 on The Times paperbacks fiction list."

The article "'The Tattooist of Auschwitz' attacked as inauthentic by camp memorial centre" by Alison Flood in *The Guardian*, Dec. 7, 2018, states there have been 400,000 copies sold in the United Kingdom alone.

Kenneally, in *The New York Times,* also quotes Heather Morris: "The book does not claim to be an academic historical piece of nonfiction, I'll leave that to the academics and historians ... it is Lali's story. I make mention of history and memory waiting together and straining to part, it must be accepted after 60 years this can happen but I am confident of Lali's telling of his story, only he could tell it and others may have a different understanding of that time but that is their understanding, I have written Laii's."

In Flood's article "'The Tattooist of Auschwitz' attacked as inauthentic by camp memorial centre," in *The Guardian*, 2018, she questions a scene in which Leli gets penicillin for Gita who had typhus: "...it would have been impossible for Sokolov to get penicillin for Furman ... this antibiotic became widely accessible only after the war." (And surely not in Nazi death campus *during* the war.)

It is worth reprinting *The Guardian* article in full:

Heather Morris's The Tattooist of Auschwitz, the story of how Slovakian Jew Lali Sokolov fell in love with a girl he was tattooing at the concentration camp, has been one of the year's bestselling novels. Its cover proclaims that it is "based on the powerful true story of love and survival"; inside, its publisher notes that "every reasonable attempt to verify the facts against available documentation has been made." But a detailed broadside from the Auschwitz Memorial has disputed this, claiming that "the book contains numerous errors and information inconsistent with the facts, as well as exaggerations, misinterpretations and understatements."

The report from Wanda Witek-Malicka of the Auschwitz Memorial Research Centre lays out concerns that the book's claims of factual authenticity will lead readers to treat it as "a source of knowledge and imagination about the reality of life" in the camp.

Morris has previously spoken of how Sokolov began to tell her his story at the age of 87, after the death of his wife Gita Furman. She initially wrote his story as a screenplay, then launched a Kickstarter to raise funds to self-publish it as a book, before finding a publisher. The novel has gone on to top charts around the world, with almost 400,000 copies sold in the UK alone.

"Ninety-five percent of it is as it happened; researched and confirmed," Morris told the Guardian earlier this year. "What has been fictionalized is where I've put Lale and Gita into events where really they weren't. They weren't together when the American planes flew over the camps, for example. Lale was on his own at that point I put him and Gita together for dramatic license."

At the back of the book, Morris thanks two researchers for "their brilliant investigative skills in researching 'facts' to ensure history and memory waltzed perfectly in step."

But according to the Auschwitz Memorial magazine, Memoria, numerous historical details of the camp are wrong. Witek-Malicka's fact-checking, which runs to more than seven pages, takes issue with a range of storylines, from the route taken to the camp ("the transport could not have travelled through Ostrava and Pszczyna ....(Morris) probably used the modern on-line search engine of railway connections," to Morris's account of the murder of prisoners in a bus being used as a gas chamber, which "does not find confirmation in any sources."

Pawel Sawicki, editor-in-chief of Memoria, said it was first prompted to look into the novel when it was asked to doublecheck the camp number of Gisela Fuhrmannova, Sokolov's wife, who also went by the name of Gita Furman.

"We were really surprised to find out that the number given in the book is not correct. It is a very basic but crucial detail in the story," Sawicki told the Guardian. "We have also had some information from our guides that visitors have been asking about the history of the tattooist. Some even received this book as a thank-you gift … So we became interested in the story itself and the further we got into the details, the more surprised we were to discover how (many) historical mistakes—small and big—about the reality of Auschwitz were there."

Because the book is presented as "based on a true story," and most readers "do not have enough knowledge to distinguish facts and fictions here," the Memorial decided to lay out the history behind the novel.

Witek-Malicka said it would have been impossible for Sokolov to get penicillin for Furman who was infected with typhus, in January, 1943; "This antibiotic became widely accessible only after the war." She also disputed a scene where Auschwitz physical Josef Mengele is shown sterilizing a man: "Dr. Mengele did not conduct sterilization experiments on men, but performed experiments on twins and dwarves."

While Morris's novel says two crematoriums were blown up during a revolt by Sonderkommando prisoners, Witek-Malika says only one was partially burned down, adding that scene where female prisoners deliver gunpowder to the prisoners by carrying it under their fingernails has no historical basis.

A major point of concern raised in the report "is the sexual relationship described in the book between the head of the camp SS-Oberstufuhrer Johann Schwarzhuber and the Jewish female prisoner Cilka." In practice, the report says, "the possibility of maintaining such a long relationship ... and according to the book, a semi-explicit relationship between a Jewish female prisoner and a high-ranking member of the SS hierarchy was non-existent."

The Auschwitz Memorial is not the first to flag concerns about the novel. An article in the New York Times in November pointed out that the number that Morris says was tattooed on Furman was 39402, but that Furrman herself testified that her number was 4562. Blogger Lisa Hill highlighted the penicillin error in June. Sokolov's son Gary told the New York Times that it bothered him that his father's name had been misspelled "Lale," rather than "Lali" in the novel.

The Auschwitz—Birkenau Memorial Museum concluded that the novel is "an impression about Auschwitz inspired by authentic events, almost without any value as a document."

"The nature of human memory, especially where the events recalled over 70 years ago, requires confrontation with other sources. From today's perspective, we can only regret that no specialist in the area of camp matters was invited to work on the book," the report ends. "Given the number of factual errors, therefore, this book cannot be recommended as a valuable title for persons who want to explore and understand the history of KL Auschwitz."

When approached by the Guardian, Morris declined further comment. She told the Australian, which first covered the report: "I have written a story of the Holocaust, not the story on the Holocaust. I have written Lale's story." *In November, she told the New York Times:* "The book does not claim to be an academic historical piece of nonfiction, I'll leave that to the academics and historians." *A spokesperson for her publisher told the Guardian on Friday;* "The Tattooist of Auschwitz is a novel based on the personal recollections and experiences of one man. It is not, and has never claimed to be, an official history. If it inspires people to engage with the terrible events of the Holocaust more deeply, then it will have achieved everything that Lale wished for."

But Sawicki took issue with Morris's response. "Can 'a story' be told without paying attention to the reality of the story? If this would be a complete fictional story, we could say that the author does not know much about the history of Auschwitz. This book, however, tells a story of a real person, his real tragic experiences, and this puts much more responsibility on a person who tells this story to the world," *he said,.* "The number of different errors in the book—not only in simple basic facts but also in the depiction of the reality of Auschwitz—can sometimes create more confusion than understanding. It turns a real story into an interpretation—very moving and emotional—that however blurs the authenticity of this true experience. We believe that the survivor's story deserved better."

from The Tattooist of Auschwitz

(Note: Baretski was a *Kapo*, the lowest-level Nazi guard. He apparently was a man-child; he had the personality and insights of a teenager. He had escorted Lale to a gas chamber—two of the dead bodies inside seemed to have the same tattoo. How did that happen? And why the Nazis would care at that point is a matter beyond reasoning ...)

They are led to a large steel door. In front of it is a guard.

"It's alright, all the gas is gone. We need to send them to the ovens, but we can't until you identify the correct numbers."

The guard opens the door for Lale and Baretski. Pulling himself up to his full height, Lale looks Baretski in the eye and sweeps his hand from left to right.

"After you."

Baretski bursts out laughing and slaps Lale on the back. "No. After you."

"No, after you," Lale repeats.

"I insist, Tätoweirer."

The SS officer opens the doors wide and they step into a cavernous room. Bodies, hundreds of naked bodies, fill the room.

They are piled up on each other, their limbs distorted. Dead eyes stare. Men, young and old; children at the bottom. Blood, vomit, urine and feces. The smell of death pervades the entire space.

Lale tries to hold his breath. His lungs burn. His legs threaten to give way beneath him. Behind him Baretski says, "Shit."

That one word from a sadist only deepens the well of inhumanity that Lale is drowning in.

"Over here." An officer indicates, and they follow him to one side of the room, where two male bodies are laid out together.

The officer starts talking to Baretski. For once, words fail him, and he indicates that Lale can understand German.

"They both have the same number. How can that be?" he asks.

Lale can only shake his head and shrug his shoulders.

How the hell do I know?

"Look at them. Which one is correct?" The officer snaps.

Lale leans down and takes hold of one of the arms. He is grateful for a reason to kneel and hopes it will stabilize him. He looks closely at the numbers tattooed on the arm he holds.

"The other?" He asks.

Roughly, the other man's arm is thrust at him. He looks closely at both numbers.

"See, here. This is not a three, it's an eight. Part of it is faded, but it's an eight."

The guard scribbles on each cold arm the correct number.

Without asking for permission, Late gets up and leaves the crematorium. Baretskl catches up with him outside, where he is doubled over and breathing deeply.

Baretski waits a moment or two.

"Are you all right?"

"No I'm not fucking all right. You bastards. How many of us must you kill?"

"You're upset. I can see that."

Baretski is just a kid, an uneducated kid. But Lale can't help wondering how he can feel nothing for the people they *have just seen, the agony of death inscribed on their faces and twisted bodies.*

"Come on, let's go," says Baretski.

Lale pulls himself up to walk beside him, through he cannot look at him.

"You know something, Tätowierer? I'll bet you're the only Jew who ever walked into an oven and then walked back out of it."

He laughs loudly, slaps Lale on the back and strides off ahead.

Epilogue

Your lists of books that have haunted you in the past may differ wildly from mine: here, in no real logical order, are some that may additionally remind you of your memories of classic books in your past:

Gulliver's Travels ... *Tom Jones* ... *Tristram Shandy* ... *Emma* ... *Frankenstein* ... *Jane Eyre* ... Dickens ... *Moby Dick* ... Lewis Carroll... Mark Twain, Tom Sawyer and Huck Finn ... any of Arthur Conan Doyle ... *The Red Badge of Courage* ... *Dracula* ... Conrad's *Heart of Darkness* ... D.H. Lawrence ... James Joyce ... F. Scott Fitzgerald ... Hemingway ... Faulkner ... Brave New World ... John Dos Passos ... Henry Miller (generally regarded as politically incorrect now) ... *All the King's Men* ... Saul Bellow ... Nabokov ... Jack Kerouac ... *To Kill a Mockingbird* (always popular I suspect because it is a perfect middle school morality novel) ... J.D. Salinger (his *Catcher in the Rye*, also a perfect book for 16-year-olds) ... *Catch 22*—Heller ... *In Cold Blood* ... Salman Rushdie ... *Schindler's List* ... *Dreams from My Father*, Obama and *Becoming*, Michelle Obama ... Tom Wolfe and the earlier Thomas Wolfe ... *Dispatches* and *The Things They Carried*, two timeless, classic war studies ... *Silent Spring*, Carson ... Samuel Beckett ... Thomas Paine ... Shakespeare ... the great Russian novels ... the Bible ... Maya Angelou ... Toni Morrison ... Margaret Atwood...

Whew!

If inspired to compile a sequel, *Schindler's List, In Cold Blood, Dreams from My Father* would surely be included, along with *Dispatch*es and *The Things They Carried* ...

Our e-mail address is: newcentbks@gmail.com. Feel free to suggest additional tiles and authors for a possible sequel.

About the Author ...

... a native of Ohio, Thomas Fensch began publishing books in 1970. He is now the author or editor of 40 previous books, including: *Steinbeck and Covici: The Story of a Friendship*, 1979, in print for 40-plus years and long considered a seminal work in John Steinbeck scholarship; *The Kennedy-Khrushchev Letters*, 2001; *The Man Who Changed His Skin: The Life and Work of John Howard Griffin*, the only full biography of Griffin, who wrote the American classic *Black Like Me*, 2011 and *Orwell in America*, 2018.

Almost all of his titles are available on Amazon and elsewhere.

Fensch has a doctorate in print communication from Syracuse University and lives outside Richmond, Virginia, with three 27-inch Apple desktop computers, a working library of 700-plus books and a posse of five dogs who follow him everywhere.